# TRINIDAD SWEET

# TRINIDAD SWEET

## THE PEOPLE, THEIR CULTURE, THEIR ISLAND

## Adrian Curtis Bird

*Cast Iron Gates to the Cathedral of the Immaculate
Conception, Independence Square, Port of Spain*

AN "ALL CLEAR" ENTERPRISE

# Dedication

To the people of Trinidad who make Trinidad sweet.

# Acknowledgements

Grateful appreciation is expressed to my longtime friend, Winston da Silva, for having vetted my text and uncovered several embarrassing errors. Also to my dear, sadly departed friend, John Newel Lewis, mentor and fellow-Rotarian, whose knowledge and advice proved valuable, particularly with regard to art and architecture. Thanks, too, are due to Melitta and her husband - for her encouragement when I was losing heart on the one hand - and his technical amendments on the other.

Were it not for the research by the reference library of UWI I would never have learned the facts about mauby.

My editorial advisor, Joann Carrington deserves full credit for having caused me to revise inelegant, exaggerated or misleading turns of phrase.

My dear friends, Boscoe and Sheila Holder contributed more than they will ever realise on many aspects of Trinidadiana.

Finally I could have never seen this tribute to Trinidad through to completion without the loyal support and patience during my surly periods, of my wife, Jennie, who even refreshed her typing skills to help me with some chapters. As the loyalest of Trinis she ensured that the picture I painted was a loving one of "Trinidad Sweet".

*Adrian Bird*
*Woodbrook, 1991*

# Table of Contents

*Formalities at Piarco*

# Preamble

"There's no point in going to Trinidad except for Carnival," said my travel agent. "That's usually in March. And the hotels are booked out a year ahead."

What sort of place was this? I asked myself. Nobody says you can only go to New Orleans or Rio for Carnival Why Trinidad?

"Aren't there any beaches?"

"Masses of them, and mostly empty I believe," he replied, "but if it's beaches you want try Barbados or Jamaica. No hotels on the beach in Trinidad."

"The girls look very attractive in these brochures," I persisted.

"It must be their Carnival costumes. I have a few clients who keep going back and are wild about the place. But we don't get many requests."

This backhanded recommendation brought me to Trinidad for the first time in 1961, before Trinidad and its sleepy sister island, Tobago, attained full independence from the United Kingdom.

I was bitterly disappointed.

Nobody had warned me that by arriving at the end of May I would see the end of the dry season. The lush jungle foliage was nowhere to be seen. The chain of steeply wooded hills stretching along the northern coast was brown and hazy from bush fires. I was too late for the spectacular natural Carnival put on by the yellow, mauve and pink poui trees, the coral orange immortelle and scarlet flamboyant. I was two weeks early to see this parched brown replaced by the normal mantle of vivid green.

It was quite a while before I could put my first impressions into perspective. I found that none of the highly reputed travel books presented a comprehensive picture of Trinidad. Only by first hand experience did one begin to understand why so few tourists choose Trinidad for a holiday compared to the other islands of the Caribbean.

Alec Waugh's *Hot Countries* of 1930 describes humorously the deficiencies of the only hotel then available. Patrick Leigh Fermor's *Travellers Tree* of the late 1940s describes a leprosarium on the remote island of Chacachacare; an interview with a leading calypsonian of the day and more complaints about Waugh's hotel, no doubt still serviced by the same staff.

David Frost's acid powers of criticism go to nought in his book on Trinidad. Each chapter is an article by an artist or intellectual grinding his particular hatchet. Aspirations and destinies abound, but no picture of Trinidad as an island let alone a country emerges. Perhaps the best feature of the book is its cover, picturing one of the loveliest Miss Trinidad's ever to compete in international beauty parades.

*Fodor's Guide* paints a heady picture of beaches, exotic sari-clad Orientals and teeming bazaars. They are all there if you look hard enough and have the ability to shut out all the mundane intruding elements. I do not blame a book which in covering the whole Caribbean focuses on what is unique in each island; but a misleading impression of Trinidad is created in the process.

Selden Rodman's book on the Caribbean (1968) makes an honest attempt at sounding the spirit of each island. The founder and only premier from 1956 - until his death in 1981, Dr. Eric Williams, is interviewed. More aspirations, but at least the mouldy Victorian setting and the swirl of electric fans were accurate. Those days have gone. The oil wealth swept aside most of the Victorian leftovers. Air conditioned Mercedes and squat multi-storied office buildings replaced them in the mid-70s. Rodman also interviewed and travelled on the island with the poet and playwright, Derek Walcott and his wife Margaret. The impressions described are accurate but sketchy.

Vidia Naipaul's novels paint a clear picture of how life used to be in the Indian communities, but it is "the Middle Passage" which derides with wicked accuracy the bourgeois deficiencies of the island Naipaul left behind him for the spires of Oxford. Trinidadians were offended that their famed son should mock their island. They knew the validity of his satire, and it hurt. The world who knew little of Trinidad smiled and passed on to the next island, having gained no picture of the country other than its small town colonial pretensions.

Only Robin Bryan's *Trinidad & Tobago Isles of the Immortelles* (1967) gives a good impression of life on the island. Mistakes are minor and the general personality and ambiance are well presented. For some reason (I suspect an affair of the heart) Bryan got trapped by the allure of Mayaro's beaches and left his job incomplete. Even that is a peculiarly Trinidadian failing for which he should be forgiven. Much has changed since his nostalgic days 20 years ago.

For this reason it was evident that a book was needed which could give the armchair traveller a more comprehensive idea of what Trinidad is like, and the jet-age visitor a better idea of what to expect and what highlights to seek out on his three day sojourn.

*Piarco Arrival*

## Chapter 1

━━━━━━ ▶•◉•◀ ━━━━━━

# Getting There is Not Half the Fun

Even returning Trinidadians dread the arrival at Piarco International Airport. It is not the actual landing which competent BWIA or other international pilots handle efficiently even in a torrential downpour. It is the down at heel appearance of the arrival areas, the surly attitude of customs and immigration officials and the delays. In Barbados, the last port of call forty minutes earlier, it was so different. The modern airport was clean and the staff seemed proud of their jobs and uniforms.

The flight is fine and the smiling hostesses, if they are West Indian, a delight to the eye and a promise of good things to come. Flying over the thickly-forested mountains of the Northern Range falling sharply into the sea above isolated beaches, confirms that Trinidad is not one more commercialised tourist factory. The Trinidadians on board chattered noisily the whole flight in their delicious singsong accent filled with picturesque and only half-understood words. Now they are quieter. If they have come from Miami or New York they are sure to be bringing huge suitcases crammed with electronic gadgets and other items purchased at a fraction of the home price. They wonder whether the customs officer will give them "horrors"; perhaps they will be in luck and find it is an old friend.

Pilots living in the Port of Spain area may let their wives know when to have dinner ready by taking a path over their house before making the approach to Piarco. This provides passengers with a good view of Port of Spain's suburbs strung out along the coast of the Gulf of Paria and into the steep-sided valleys of the Northern Range. Even before the aircraft has come to a standstill the knowing passengers will be ready for the dash into the terminal building. Clearly they have done this many times before. Long lines form quickly in the austere arrival hall no longer relieved by Carlisle Chang's intriguing mural. It was demolished to give access to the cargo room. Residents line up on the left side, visitors on the right.

The wait provides a good chance to study a cross section of Trinidadians. They are diverse in appearance but share two common features - their smart, even flamboyant attire and their vitality. The slacks of the men fit snugly on their trim hips, falling to perfection half an inch above the latest word in shoes clearly worn for the first time. Expensive monogrammed jerseys accentuate their muscled torsos. The ladies have a job to compete with their peacock males. Their jeans hug rounded buttocks lovingly. Their figures may not all be trim but even the opulent curves are in the right place. Dresses will be rare unless there is a current fashion for them. How is it that a little island at the bottom of the Caribbean is so style-conscious? The visitors are drab by comparison.

Dark skins predominate, but are they Negro? True African features are infrequent and a perceptive ear is likely to detect the accent of Grenada or St. Vincent where these are seen. The hair shows an African background, but where did that bony Spanish nose or those oriental eyes come from? There are many East Indians, slimmer as a rule because their diet has traditionally been less robust. But that fine-looking family taking their passports to the wicket, they could be

Indian or Negro. This must be the mixture of the two races known as "dougla". Pure white faces will be rare, Spanish and Portuguese complexions, rounded Chinese faces and the freckled skins and kinky reddish hair of the "reds" far more common.

All are talking animatedly in groups, black with white, brown with yellow. The family groups are themselves often mixed racially, but not that haughty African obviously proud of his wife, clad a little too conspicuously, in flowing white robes and a veil concealing all but her velvety brown forehead and her liquid black eyes. The Trinidadian feeling for personal theatre which reaches its peak at Carnival is evident in much of their everyday appearance.

Alone of all the Caribbean islands, slavery lasted less than fifty years in Trinidad. It is this which accounts for the unusual extent of ethnic mixes. The Europeans came first for the generous land grants, bringing slaves as labourers. Free West Indian blacks and native West Africans came of their own choice.

After emancipation the great majority of the freed slaves would not work on the plantation and a new source of cheap labour had to be found. Indentured labourers were brought in from China, Madeira and finally India. If this was not enough Christian Syrians also chose Trinidad as a haven from religious persecution under the Ottoman Turks. Small wonder, then, that there should be such an ethnic melange. "Here every creed and race finds an equal place" goes the National Anthem, and with such racial diversity it has special significance.

Trinidadians are justifiably proud of the example they set the world in ethnic integration, with only minor sectarian under-currents remaining. But although people from all over the world came to Trinidad in the past, it is not always so easy for the casual visitor.

His cross-examination at the immigration wicket could go something like this:

"What is the purpose of your visit?"

"To see the island and meet the people who I hear are very attractive."

"You don't have a visa!"

"No, I didn't need one for the other islands."

"From your country you are supposed to have a visa."

"But I'm only staying one week as a tourist."

"How do I know that? Many people say they are coming for a week and stay longer to get work."

"But look at my ticket. It's only valid until the 24th and my flight out is already confirmed."

Having made you feel like a refugee, he will in all probability magnanimously stamp you in for exactly the period of your stay. Hopefully this scenario will have been avoided by proper advice by the travel agent and airline on entry requirements into Trinidad. How is it that a people so friendly by nature can give such a hostile reception? Thousands of illegal immigrants swell the shanty town hillsides. When labourers were needed on building sites a lenient attitude was taken. Now that the tide has turned and locals are out of work it is different. Ever since Trinidad's Prime Minister Dr. Eric Williams told his people that he was not going to let Trinidad and Tobago become a nation of busboys, official attitude to tourism has been lukewarm.

It is not that Trinidad does not want visitors. It loves them to come and have a good time. Trinidadians all have relatives in Toronto and Brooklyn if not Birmingham and London. They travel abroad to visit them even when they are "brokes" from extravagances in other directions. When in their turn relatives come back to Trinidad, space will be found for them at home regardless of the inconvenience. Why then this negative reception by immigration officials toward overseas visitors who are patently not candidates as illegal immigrants? That same stern-faced immigration official will buy you a Carib beer if you "bounce him up" at Saturday's race meeting, put his arm around your shoulder and introduce you to his friends as if he has known you for years. That is his true character.

"Give a Trinidadian a costume and he will play he mas!" that can be the only answer. The role-playing bureaucrat in a uniform can be as infuriating in happy-go-lucky Trinidad as anywhere else.

Finding your luggage in the baggage lounge is the second ordeal. Whether by accident or design, airline flights inevitably arrive close together, compounding the mad scramble at the counters. Customs and immigration officials twiddle their thumbs for three hours until Pan Am, BWIA and BA land within minutes of each other, and all hell breaks loose. Returning Trinidadians will have been given a long list of items desired by friends and family. Sagging suitcases large enough for a corpse topple off the luggage rotunda. Luggage carts are jostled into position around the moving belt with as little regard for "first come first serve" as will be found on the roads. A friendly anarchy prevails and the worst thing you can do is lose your cool and "get vex".

Bags retrieved at last, shins banged a few times by rival luggage carts in the process - excused with friendly grins, and it is time for the customs examination ritual. Blessedly the green line system has survived its introduction. Unlike Heathrow there is nothing so trusting as a spot check. *Everyone* is stopped for it is accepted that Trinidadians, having a keen love of gambling and conceit in their own good fortune will, despite signs threatening everything short of life imprisonment, try their luck at having their luggage go through unexamined. Genuine tourists stand out like a sore thumb, fortunately, and they are likely to be waved on after the cursory opening of a bag.

The real melée is where the "heavy rollers" await their fate at the scarred and unpainted knee-high counters where customs officers indolently sort through concealed items, and sigh over the paperwork of more duty entry assessments. They do not have hearts of stone. They are only concerned in seeing a fair charge levied on those who deserve it, and, from the goods revealed, many do. Customs men have family and friends in the relatively small society of Trinidad's one million like everyone else. With an audible sigh of relief one can hear:

"Ent you Peggy Ali's brother-in-law? Oh, gorsh man, I glad it's you I meet." He does not have to say "Ease me up, nah man." It is written all over his face that he knows he will be dealt with generously.

Opened and unsearched items of baggage alike are affixed

with an adhesive fluorescent label. On leaving the customs area another official conscientiously cancels the label with the stroke of a large felt marker quite likely to leave an indelible souvenir on arrival in Trinidad on the suitcase itself. Around one last corner and Trinidad proper has been reached. Taxi drivers surge forward anxious for your trade. Crowds of relations, babbling eagerly as they lean on the barrier, await the fate of cousins and brothers arrived with goodness knows what exciting contraband from Miami or New York.

*Mayfair Villa, Longden Street*

## Chapter 2

———————•◉•———————

# Settling In

Some people cannot stand hot weather. They like to wear warm clothes and see their breath vaporise. The great majority like sunshine and the informality that goes with taking clothes off and dressing lightly. But even they want to avoid oppressive heat and sweat trickling down their backs. The first thing to be done on reaching Trinidad then, is to cast off excess clothing. Put that jacket and tie away unless you are paying official respects to high dignitaries in air conditioned offices. Put on sunglasses, or "shades" as they are known locally, to cut down the midday glare. Like the local residents, stay clear of the heat.

In metropolitan countries dawn is a time dreaded for its cheerless grey chill. Anyone civilised stays in bed if he can until the world has warmed itself up. But in the tropics dawn is one of the most delightful times. An early rise makes you feel great. In Trinidad it is cool and bright with dew still on the brilliant green foliage. The morning sky is as yet unblemished by clouds. Health enthusiasts will be out jogging around Port of Spain's central park, the Queen's Park Savannah, in shorts and vest. Stable boys will be exercising trim race-horses on the damp sand tracks. Early mass is well attended. Offices open at 8 a.m. an hour earlier than North America and Europe. By 6 a.m. the highways are already filled with cars dropping children at school before doubling back to the office. With even the lower middle classes owning cars, the roads are congested and an early start is essential to arrive on time.

How does a visitor to Trinidad share in the early morning joy if he cannot get a hotel breakfast before 7.30 a.m.? The only way is to go out before breakfast and come back invigorated with a heartier appetite and a smug feeling that you have got the jump on the rest of the world. Tennis is a delight at 7.00 a.m. but by 9.00 a.m. the sun is already baking the court. Later in the morning clouds formed by moisture rising from the forested hills and damp air blown westward from the Atlantic will provide welcome shady spells. Only mad dogs and Englishmen go out in the midday sun, sang Noel Coward. Stay in the shade, browse in air conditioned shops or cool off at the beach or a pool; but do not make yourself miserable sight-seeing in the heat of the day. The locals know better. Take the tip from them.

There are two options for visitors - staying at a hotel or with friends. In few places will it pay off as well as in Trinidad to avoid a hotel if you can, and get into the nitty gritty of Trinidadian life style. The reason for this is that Trinidadians follow a more lively way of life than not only other parts of the world, but the Caribbean itself. They are determined to make every day fun, not just the weekend. They may drink more than they should or deplete their store of energy from their jobs, but so what?

If you have made Trinidadian friends abroad they are very likely to have invited you to stay with them, and they mean it - just as they expect you to reciprocate. If you take them up on the invitation, do not expect any neatly reserved guest room. Families are too large and too fluid with relatives coming and going for that. Whatever rearrangements in bedding routine necessary to give you a bed to yourself will be done. Members of their family will be up before it is light so that everyone can have a shower. Trinidadians have strong traditions of cleanliness and not only bathe at least daily, but seemingly for hours at a time. Small wonder that the World Bank found it hard to accept that the daily average water consumption should be 140% greater than in Europe. This love of bathing is one reason why water distribution seems incapable of keeping pace with usage.

Eating arrangements will be informal. Rarely does a Trinidadian family sit around a table at the same time. Grace is said to oneself. Members of the family or friends passing by seem to eat when it suits them. There is always a pot on the stove. The food will not be piping hot, often barely tepid. Heat will be supplied in the pepper sauce. The cooking will be similar in many ways. Stewed meat, highly seasoned with overnight marination in herbs is a common backbone to a meal. But corn flakes, fried eggs, fruit juice and coffee is the daily start to the day for most. The children will more likely drink Milo, the older members of the family "green tea" as they call it - not to be confused with the genuine green tea of North Africa.

Just as meals are eaten indiscriminately at any hour, so it is not uncommon to find members of the family sleeping just as irregularly. One soon learns that Trinidadians are far from slaves to the clock. They are even proud of their lack of concern for punctuality, derisively called "Trinidad time". Invite someone for 6.30 p.m. and do not be surprised if he shows up without an apology at 7.15 p.m. If a party, known always as a "fete", is declared to start at 8.30 p.m. do not be surprised if the music is only being set up at that time, with the first guests arriving at 10.00 p.m. They make up for it, of course, by staying until 5 in the morning. There are too many intruding distractions to keep one's eye on the clock. The pleasures of life must not be rushed.

Punctuality on the job is consequently a running battle with the employer. Tolerance is expected for late arrival for the flimsiest reason. Far better arrive late than not at all. All too frequently the Trinidadian is struck down by sickness, real or imaginary. With such a warm and benevolent climate one might think colds and viruses few and far between. Far from it. A new virus sweeps into Trinidad every few months and each is inimitably christened with a timely and picturesque title. "Kung Fu" will be succeeded by "Jaws" and "Eleven Plus." Doctors offices will be filled by medical certificate seekers. Sniffles and sneezing are taken as signs of potential calamity. No point in taking a chance. Let me hit my bed before it gets worse.

Sometimes a more individual sickness will strike. A young man will complain, "Mah brain tired, man. I gotta cool mah head. Must be that dew I was in las' night." Or even more poignantly in the stress of the modern world, "Mah blood worn down thin. Ah know ah need a rest and a sun bat (bath)". White handkerchiefs are draped over the curly black pate of young men, knots neatly tied at each corner, like devout maidens going to the altar. But to them it is no joke. In the cool of evening the high humidity can indeed become condensed into moisture on a negroid scalp.

Iron tonics, vitamin supplements and a wide variety of concoctions cater to the fear of illness, lack of virility or manly vigour. "Get a head with a Guinness," "Mackeson puts you on Top!" "Malta gets you up!" The power of imagination plays a big role in a country where the echoes of the obeah drum are still heard in remote backyards. "Oh gawd, girl, mah foot paining me bad, bad, bad. Like that Tobago wahbine down the road been hexing me again. She jealous for so!"

*Hotels*

With typical carefree negligence, Trinidad has turned its back on the world tourist market. If tourists come at all they are expected to take the fifteen-minute flight across to the silver and azure beaches of Tobago. Whether this cavalier attitude can continue now that oil is in trouble, is open to question. There is still not a single tourist hotel on any of Trinidad's scores of idyllic beaches. There have been many plans, plenty of headlines and architect's models, but still no hotels suitable for consideration by a travel agent. Queen's Beach Hotel and Atlantis Beach Hotel have provided Trinidadians with discreet tranquillity on the endless beach of Mayaro's Atlantic coast but visitors from abroad rarely find their way to them. Carnival is different. Visitors from all over the world are bound to come to Trinidad for the greatest show on earth. As this takes place in its full splendour only in Port of Spain, that is where the hotels are found. Commercial activity has been adequate to keep the hotels happy with business visitors the rest of the year.

Dowager of the hotels is the Queen's Park Hotel overlooking the stables and grand stand of the Savannah. It is now barely in operation. The older and architecturally precious western wing built and designed by George Brown has been torn down and left in the final throes of demolition. The ugly central concrete block has been made more dreadful by a galvanised shed on the roof. A swimming pool has incongruously been added. It is as if the hotel belongs to two members of a family who cannot agree. Does one want to tear it down, and the other to modernise its existing state? Like an old family retainer, working only to accommodate those who have grown to depend on her, the Queen's Park lingers on. It would be cruel to make fun of her like former authors.

Across the far side of the Savannah is the hotel which usurped its place, the Trinidad Hilton. Hilton hotels are commonly the butt of tired jokes, but this one is rather special. It occupies a knoll giving it a magnificent view over the President's mansion, the Botanical Gardens and the forested hills rising behind them. Below is the Savannah laid out like a green or yellow carpet depending on the season. Downtown Port of Spain and the ships at anchor in "the stream" as the Gulf of Paria is known, provide a backdrop.

The hotel's site has an interesting history. It could well have been the President's residence. The colonial governors lived in town on the south side of Woodford Square. Colonel Fullarton wanted a country cottage and rented the 41-acre Belmont Hill for $100 a month. In the fire of 1808 the governor's townhouse was burned and Fullarton moved into Belmont Hill even though it was a modest wooden dwelling. Subsequent British governors were content with it on the rental basis. The steady northward expansion of Port of Spain made its position increasingly favourable. The only obstacle which prevented its purchase was a legal wrangle regarding

*Hilton Hotel from the Grand Savannah*

clean title. Because legal ownership was in doubt, the building became dilapidated. Young Governor Woodford did his best to acquire it without payment, claiming that it had reverted to the crown because title had been in dispute for twenty-nine years. He disregarded the fact that Governors had been paying rent to the putative owners for nine years. Spanish law required a 40-year title, and his claim backfired. The legal dispute dragged on from one court to the next. Woodford felt his chances were slim and looked elsewhere to build. Eventually Government had to buy the property, but Woodford had found more gracious grounds below the hill. Belmont Hill's prime location was by this stroke of chance left empty for 140 years as if waiting for the need for a Hilton Hotel.

Access to the Hotel is at the top level off Lady Young Road curling through the hills behind. The hotel rooms go down the hillside, floor by floor, with the first at the top and the eighth at the bottom. This gave it the name the "upside down Hilton." It is not this gimmick alone which gives the hotel its distinction. Unusual good taste was shown in its open-air design and use of tropical foliage. The main pool, shaped like the island of Trinidad has a miniature beside it in Tobago's cigar shape. The public rooms utilise tropical hues and themes to good advantage. General terraces give a sense of space. While the food in La Boucan may not be that terrific, there are two works of art that are. Geoffrey Holder's nostalgic mural of elegant creole ladies strolling in shaded woods, and Ken Morris' copper mural "Carnival", show the best that Trinidad artists can produce. The hotel belongs to the Government of Trinidad and Tobago and is leased to the Hilton International group on a mutually satisfactory management contract.

Competing with it for commercial travellers is the Holiday Inn. In dramatic contrast to the arboreal setting of the Hilton, the Holiday Inn is downtown across from the main post office in the busiest traffic congestion. A tall walled garden provides a certain measure of peace and quiet. The pool sports a bar with bar stools set into the pool so that guests can drink without leaving the water. Rooms overlook the Gulf of Paria with its foreshore of docks and the rusting galvanized roofs of warehouses. The hotel's pride is the revolving rooftop restaurant giving a fine panorama of the city's lights and those across the water of San Fernando and Point Fortin. Labour problems have plagued the hotel and in 1986 a group of businessmen acquired the hotel in the hope of improving matters.

Another downtown hotel is the more modest Errol Lau Hotel on upper Edward Street, but the area is to be walked through hurriedly at night. The Kapok has a pleasant setting just below Cotton Hill from which it has taken its name. It is the magnificent silk cotton tree's gossamer seeds that provide the kapok which fills pillows and life preservers. The Normandie Hotel was once famous for its French cuisine but its Normandie Village restaurant has "gone creole". It has changed hands more than once and has now been completely rebuilt in mod-Mexican style, including a delightful shopping arcade and art gallery. It lies a little way up St. Ann's Valley past the gardens below the Hilton. Further away from the centre of Port of Spain in the surrounding valleys can be found an assortment of other hotels.

Most noteworthy of these is Valley Vue Hotel idyllically set deep up St. Anns Valley, overhung by the forested hillside. This originated as Luciano's Restaurant and was later converted into a hotel which failed. It has been refurbished, has a discotheque and is popular for functions such as weddings. Valley View Hotel sits on a historic site. In early Spanish colonial days a Capuchin monastery had been there. All that remained later were the masonry foundations, which according to the Jardine family, who owned the property, made it the only remaining early colonial building in Trinidad, as all others of the period had been made of wood. The owner of the restaurant being built there, Luciano Marconi, was convinced the monks would have buried a golden treasure. The foundations were thoroughly destroyed in his fruitless search.

In Maraval we find the Tropical Hotel tucked away in Rookery Nook. It has survived many years of change around it and continues to offer air conditioned rooms to its coterie of guests. Bagshot House Hotel is still in operation with its vast shaded lawn in front to remind of its former glory. Further up Maraval Valley on Saddle Road is the Chaconia Inn popular and successful as ever. At times in the past it became almost a residential hotel occupied by succeeding teams of engineers and technicians working on expansion projects. It has reverted to a hotel for short term visitors who can enjoy its barbecued steaks and performances of a leading chanteuse. Near the end of Maraval Valley in posh Haleland Park is found Villa Maria Inn, a comfortable guest house looking out at the forested mountainsides. It is handy for those making trips to Maracas Bay, Las Cuevas and beyond.

Away from Port of Spain there is a scattering of other smaller hotels. The largest of these is Bel Air International Airport Hotel at Piarco with its fifty-six rooms. It is ideal for those overnighting to and from Tobago. Scarlet Ibis Hotel serves the University of the West Indies at St. Augustine, renting rooms on a long-term basis. The Asa Wright Nature Centre deep in the Blanchisseuse Valley maintains a picturesque old guest house for international birdwatchers.

On Gasparee Island to the west of Port of Spain, Fantasy Island Hotel has taken over from the former Gaspar Grande condominium project. On the road to Maracas hide Timberline's guest cottages in a striking setting poised above the sea in an abandoned cocoa estate. In the South the Royal Hotel is still open, but concentrates on its restaurant business. Visitors to the South are more likely to stay at Farrell House Hotel at Claxton Bay overlooking the Gulf of Paria and San Fernando Hill. TJ's Hotel in La Romain, San Fernando also offers tourist grade accommodation.

There are any number of other small "hotels" which are adequate only for an overnight stay or shorter. Most of these provide the accommodation for locals which every country has, not intending them for tourist use. All the hotels listed by the Tourist Board provide visitors to Trinidad with barely a thousand rooms. Guest houses add a few score more. Yet this has been enough for the demands of tourism except during the brief Carnival season. Now that there is a realisation that Trinidad should not rely on the enchantment of its sister island, Tobago, alone to develop the tourist potential, there are bound to be plans for bigger and better hotels.

*Trinidad Fete*

## Chapter 3

# *People of Trinidad*

Trinidadians are known throughout the Caribbean for their love of partying, drinking, dancing and generally having a good time. All it takes is two "Trinis" with a bottle and spoon for a party to start. There is always someone who plays the little four-stringed ukelele known as a "cuatro", and the rhythm section is complete with a nutmeg grater.

This does not mean the Trinidadians of African negro origin alone. It covers the spectrum of ethnic origins found in Trinidad - black, white, brown, yellow and especially the shades in between. This arguably constitutes the largest bloc, as there has been interracial blending from the earliest days. Not that certain groups have not resisted mixing with others. The Syrians in particular have been slowest to integrate and still (political strife permitting) send their sons to Lebanon to seek a bride from their home village of Christian background.

Ethnic mixture by itself is no recipe for a love of life and there is no obvious explanation how it has come about. Some will say the Mediterranean temperament of the Spanish and French, others the tribal rhythms of Africa, but there is no simple answer. Other countries like Surinam and Guyana have as great a diversity of ethnic origins, but little of the same tendency to "spree" at the drop of a hat. Carnival immediately springs to mind as typical of Trinidad mentality. How did an island that was part of the British Empire evolve this way? Certainly the British had little to do with it on the surface. Some history of the origins of the Trinidad populace is unavoidable at this stage.

The indigenous inhabitants of the island were the Caribs and the Arawaks, both of whom were effectively eradicated during the three hundred years of Spanish colonial rule. Those few remaining Caribs who had intermarried with Spaniards or negroes lived in the Arima area. Efforts to keep alive a tradition of the Caribs go back before Governor Woodford attended the annual King and Queen of the Caribs festivities from 1813 onwards. Such celebrations continue to this day in the Festival of Santa Rosa de Lima but the Carib ancestry is much diluted. Perhaps only in the indigenous architecture of the "ajoupa" huts does any pre-colonial trait remain. So much for the original inhabitants.

The Spanish colonists remained an impoverished band from 1531 to 1783, struggling to make ends meet with only a handful of slaves to help them. Then came a sophisticated French planter from the island of Grenada 80 miles to the north, Roume St. Laurent, who saw that the island's considerable potential could be realised if a massive influx of settlers were enticed by generous land grants. So strongly did he feel that he went to Madrid and persuaded the King of Spain to this effect. The Royal Cedula of Colonialisation of 1783 was the result. This attracted in particular French plantation owners from Grenada and Martinique, which had recently fallen into British hands. There was such a good response to this invitation to Catholic non-Spaniards that in short order the French out-numbered the Spanish two to one. Six years later, as if following them, the British in turn captured Trinidad in an almost bloodless invasion, so few Spanish troops were there to defend the island. Ironically Martinique was ceded back to France shortly afterwards where it remains to this day. The French colonists, many of loyalist sympathy could not move back, and decided to throw in their lot with the local Spanish under the alien rule of the British, possibly in the hope that one day Trinidad would form part of the French empire. With uncommon good sense, Governor Thomas Picton, seeing the British outnumbered five to one decided to continue the administration under the existing Spanish laws. The strange tapestry of interwoven cultures was on its way.

Considering its fairly congenial climate and fertile land, it is interesting that Trinidad, unlike its sister island Tobago, should have been overlooked in the three-sided chess game that took place throughout the Caribbean between France, Spain and England in the 16th, 17th and 18th centuries. Trinidad was ideally placed to prey on the galleons of the Spanish Main. It was mainly to pre-empt the French from gaining such a strategic advantage that it finally attracted Admiral Abercrombie's attention.

Like the Caribs and Arawaks before them, little remains from the Spanish colonial times apart from the many place names. There is nothing standing of the original Spanish capital of San Jose de Oruña, St. Joseph. Only foundations remain of a Spanish convent in St. Ann's Valley behind Port of Spain, as they do of the cannon batteries at Cocorite and Gasparee island. It was the 19th Century influx of Spanish from the neighbouring mainland of Venezuela only seven miles away at its nearest point, that gave Trinidad its pockets of Spanish language in villages of the Northern Range, and the invigorating Christmas music of "parang". This word is a creole corruption of "paranda" found still in Venezuela and the Canary Islands from whence it originated. Spanish country dances, cockfighting and perhaps stickfighting were also absorbed as part of Trinidad's culture at the same period. By and large Spanish impact on present-day culture in Trinidad is minimal in relation to nearly three hundred years of Spanish colonial rule. There are some families such as the Farfans and Salazars who may be able to trace Spanish colonial origins, although the Farfans now use a French pronunciation of their name.

*The Creoles*

It was the French planters therefore, who were to dominate society and the economy from 1783 onwards. To a surprising extent they still do. They resented the Protestant British government and throughout Trinidad's colonial history there was continuing animosity between the British Protestant and French Catholic factions. Family ties with France and Corsica, from which a number of today's leading families came, were sustained by schooling their children in Paris and keeping up the French language in the home.

French patois was the lingua franca of the countryside, and is still deeply woven into vernacular speech. Disregarding the veneer of British officialdom at the top, the French "creolocracy" set up their own snobberies and social values through which they led and dominated indigenous society. The few Spanish and Venezuelans, the Portuguese and Irish fell under the leadership of the French. Many maintain that despite being a small minority today, "society" is still ruled by their elitist attitudes.

If one wonders how this could have happened in a basically black community, it is as well to remember that the French creoles represented effective opposition to London's Whitehall. If any one group were to lead Trinidad toward self-government it would be the Catholic European creoles.

Englishmen and Scots came in their numbers during the 19th Century, buying estates and establishing import and export companies. More of them were in sugar than in cocoa which the French planters largely had to themselves. Until the collapse of cocoa prices in the 1920s, cocoa estates prospered. The ornately decorated wooden estate mansions were the scene of lavish balls. By all accounts the creole plantocracy lived in a style reminiscent of the Ante Bellum South.

Family networks grew stronger and more pervasive over the years among the French creoles. They regarded Trinidad as "their" country. This contrasted with the British who always seemed to be yearning for "home" and were more likely to be absentee landlords.

Andrew Cipriani, of Corsican descent, established himself as the working man's friend. When he became mayor of Por† of Spain it was from his leadership that concepts of self rule blossomed. The fact that he was white was no barrier to his national popularity.

At the end of the Second World War fortunes were made by the businessmen from war surplus abandoned at give-away prices by the American forces. The moneyed class further consolidated its position by the boom in land prices that took place when Port of Spain was chosen to be the capital of the new West Indies Federation.

When the negro academic, Dr. Eric Williams, ousted the Portuguese Bertie Gomes as Premier, the French creoles must have discussed the implications late into the night. What effect would this turn of events have on their control? Dr. Williams was obliged to accept that the business sector was outside his direct control. He depended on it to keep the economy in motion. Though he might revile the creolocracy in his political diatribes, he essentially left them alone. The creolocracy in return kept out of politics, knowing that Eric Williams saw on which side the nation's bread was buttered. When the oil bonanza fell into his lap, it would be a different story.

During the 1970 uprising the French creoles did not panic and flee the country, expecting a bloodbath. They set up vigilante committees, used banned CB radios and generally looked after their own. Their attitude was "This is our country. We shall still be here after the last black face has emigrated to Brooklyn". This commitment to the nation of which they consider themselves the aristocratic elite, provides a valuable backbone to the national morale. They firmly believe the black majority, known for its lack of commercial expertise will never be able to run the country properly. Let them have their political power provided they do not make too much of a mess of the economy.

## The Africans

To run a sugar estate profitably, cheap intensive labour was needed in the form of slaves. The Martinique and Grenada planters were obliged to bring their slaves with them. No new slaves could be acquired in Trinidad as the African slave trade was already ending by that time. Besides the French planters, many freed blacks from the United States and other parts of the Caribbean had little compunction about owning slaves of their own. Historians indicate that there were more black owners of slaves in Trinidad at the time of Emancipation than white, though the average slaveholding by blacks was small. This is not too surprising when one realises that 70% of the total non-slave population was made up of "free coloured," 5,275 out of a total of 7,538. Emancipation of the 17,439 slaves came in 1834, just 51 years after the Royal Cedula had started the land grants.

After an abortive experiment with an apprenticeship system, the freed slaves soon drifted away from the estates to set up their own small holdings in the virgin bush. This short 51-year period of slavery in Trinidad no doubt explains why there is much less slave-consciousness in Trinidad than other parts of the Caribbean, despite efforts of calypsonians and politicians to make audiences think otherwise. Beside this, the treatment of slaves in Trinidad, while rarely good, was arguably the best in the Caribbean because of their shortage and the stringent penalties for the mistreatment of slaves under Spanish law. Without the Africans to work the estates, estate owners had to bring in cheap labour in the form of indentured workers on 5-year work contracts. From this need arose the unusual variety of ethnic origins which make up Trinidad today.

### The Chinese

The Chinese were the first ethnic group used to meet the need for cheap labour. A trial batch of 147 was brought from Penang, Malaya as early as 1806, a full generation before the emancipation of slaves in 1834. The Slave Trade from Africa terminated in 1807 only ten years after the British captured Trinidad. Half of the Penang Chinese were wiped out by illness before their contract was completed, and subsequent batches after emancipation proved ill-suited to the rigours of estate labour. Shopkeeping was more their line. But having failed as a source of estate labour, the flow of Chinese into Trinidad did not stop. While never as great as other ethnic groups, wives and relatives were brought in from the Hong Kong and Canton area all the time up to independence in

1962.

Official census figures of 1970 put the number of Chinese in Trinidad at only 1%, and after the social upheaval of 1970 a great many decamped to Canada and the U.S. reducing the proportion to 1/2%. Yet the Chinese, like the Syrians, play an important part in Trinidad life and are much more in evidence than their numbers might suggest. Both in Port of Spain and San Fernando there are many stores, groceries and particularly restaurants run by Chinese. In fact Chinese restaurants predominate. It is the practice to make the midday meal the largest for the day, contrary to what might be best suited to the hot climate. As there are few restaurants other than Chinese, this means that the bulk of white collar and shopworkers have Chinese food for their main meal. Mountains of rice, noodles and bean sprouts are consumed with curried beef and shrimp.

Traditionally the surburban and village groceries were run by "the Chinee man" who, ever-smiling in the face of deprecatory remarks, worked long hours and ended up sending all his children away to university to become doctors and dentists. Not all Chinese took as long to rise in social position.

The Lee Lum family, for one, had so well established themselves in the 19th Century that it was with Randolph Rust that the first oil exploration took place in the south of the island. This same family issued their own coinage for use in country parlours - now collectors' items.

The Lee Lums and other Chinese families were pillars of the prestigious All Saints Anglican Church on Queen's Park West from the early days.

More than ten per cent of the more than 400 medical practitioners are Chinese, and a similarly high proportion is found in other professions. It is almost a surprise when one of the top three scholastic honours is not won by a Chinese Trinidadian. The first Governor General after Independence in 1962, Sir Solomon Hochoy, was a Chinese born in Jamaica who had lived in Trinidad since the age of three. He rose to the top of the civil service and was well loved and respected by the community for his dry wit and placid efficiency.

Trinidad's Chinese came from the Canton area of South

China, and from the two backgrounds so well described in James Michener's *Hawaii*, the Haka and the Punti Associations for each group still flourish on Charlotte Street, Port of Spain, and close ties are kept with relatives in Hong Kong. Despite this the Trinidad Chinese integrated well into their adopted island. Grandchildren may still be able to understand their grandparents' language, but it is rare for them to be able to speak it. They intermarried more readily into other ethnic groups and produced many of the most exotically glamorous results.

*The Portuguese*

Madeira was next considered a suitable source of indentured labour as its European peasantry was used to subtropical agriculture. Trinidad was slow in tapping the source, only bringing in a thousand Portuguese from Madeira and the Azores. British Guiana moved more quickly and brought over 20,000 Portuguese into their territory. The first that landed in Trinidad were Kalleyite Presbyterians seeking religious refuge. Those that followed were Catholics. Neither group could adjust to the harsh sun and water-sodden fields of the sugar estates during the rainy season. They did better in the shade of the tall immortelles pruning the cocoa trees. They also prospered as market gardeners and as small shopkeepers.

Although never enjoying the power of the French creoles, the Portuguese community did well for themselves and played a significant role in blurring the lines between the black and white sections of the community. Today by far the richest man in Trinidad is of Madeiran descent, and has continued to support the peasantry of his home village in Madeira, besides being a discreet philanthropist in his adopted island. Over the years many Portuguese drifted into Trinidad from British Guiana. There were no immigration barriers to such a move between two British colonies. Today it seems as though most of the Portuguese Trinidadians have Guyanese roots.

*The Indians*

The final wave of immigrants started in the 1840s and proved by far the most successful. These were the indentured

Indians, 90% of whom came from the Ganges Valley through Calcutta. Trinidad's humid climate was not strange to them. Officialdom did not anticipate that they would wish to remain in Trinidad after serving out their five years, but this became increasingly common. Up to 1885, 70,000 Indians had been brought to Trinidad and a large proportion opted to remain and make a new life in the New World. Indentured Indians continued to arrive to the end of the 19th Century, only terminating in 1917 when the laws were changed. 24,425 Indians were accounted for in the census of 1871, representing a quarter of the total population.

The indenture system has been much maligned and criticised as close to slavery. Freed negroes used to ridicule Indians because unlike them, their servitude was voluntary. However for those who left India for Trinidad, it was the means of breaking out of generations of repetitive poverty into a new and better life. Within the five years of their indentureship more could be saved than in a lifetime in India. So thrifty were the Indians that they were felt to contribute nothing to the growth of the community through normal spending.

Unlike the Portuguese and Chinese they kept to themselves and did not for a long time intermarry or even cohabit with native stock - by then already getting well mixed up. Eventually a new section of the population came into being, the "douglas", half Indian, half negro. How large a proportion of today's population are a mixture of these two backgrounds would be very hard to determine as the lines of definition would be so blurred, but it is substantial.

No two authorities would be likely to agree where to draw the lines between the permutations of racial mixture, so intermingled have the people of Trinidad become. "Trinidad whites" are distinct from "white Trinidadians" and "red" is more likely to be a derogatory term than a definition of the mix where 'cafe au lait' skin colour gives way to blotched freckles and kinky reddish hair.

Coming from a background of rigid caste barriers, the Indians were already well mixed up with their fellow passengers on the long sea voyage by way of religion as well as caste by the time they arrived, weakened by sea-sickness and the uncomfortable conditions. The great majority were Hindu, only 15% being Muslim, who were themselves divided into Sunnis and Shiites. The Hindus built little backyard temples with pyramidal roofs and whitewashed walls muralled with the Hindu pantheon of Hanuman the monkey God, Ganesh the elephant God with Lakshmi and Lord Krishna. Muslim mosques raised more elegant pointed domes in which their community could worship. Missionaries made earnest efforts to win these groups over to their respective Christian denominations. The Canadian presbyterian missions had notable success in this regard in the South.

After a hundred years the Indian community today is well on the road to becoming properly integrated into the mainstream of Trinidadian life, but it is only in the last twenty years that most of the barriers have fallen. Indian films were shown in Hindi without English subtitles until the 1960s. Today there are even more Indian films, but they are now dubbed in English or subtitled.

To generalise one can say that the Indian community is still essentially rural. Bound exclusively to agriculture they are not, having developed into the full spectrum of business from transport to manufacturing. With eight years of unprecedented oil boom prosperity, a great many made fortunes. They were prepared to work hard and not fritter away the proceeds. Their thrifty temperament paid off as did their compulsion to acquire land and hang on to it come what may.

With the social unrest along racial lines in 1970, many of the estate owners of British background were sure they saw the coming of a Guyana-style decline. They were glad to sell off their land at $500 to $700 an acre. By 1974 land values had doubled, and by 1977 doubled again. By 1980 they stood at four times what they had 18 years before. This dizzy spiral continued to 1982 at which time the oil prices levelled off and Trinidad realised that the fantasy of ever-increasing prices had ended.

Even before the days of oil prosperity, one often heard of taxi drivers apparently owning only a tapia hut and the taxi (jointly with the hire purchase company) putting a large number of sons through university. There are plenty of lawyers, doctors and other professionals of negro origin, but they are outweighed numerically by the Indian professionals.

Government is far and away the largest land-owner, exaggerated firstly by the purchase of the sugar estates and latterly by the acquisition of Texaco's holdings. Private land has been steadily moving into the hands of the Indians. While the Syrians might have recognised real estate as the big money game, they concentrated on the commercial area of Port of Spain and its better residential suburbs. Only occasionally did they speculate on agricultural land for which there was a sporting chance of obtaining residential planning approval. Such permission would jack up the price from $5,000 an acre to $5 a square foot, equivalent to over $200,000 even after allowing for development costs.

Even though Indians and Negroes stand even in numbers, each reflecting 41% according to the 1980 census*, the Indians accepted for thirty years a declining political role and concentrated on economic advancement and the acquisition of land. After the death of Hindu sugar union leader, Bhadase Maraj and DLP head, Dr. Rudranath Capildeo, the DLP faded out, and the rural Hindus had only the relatively ineffectual leadership of lawyer unionist, Basdeo Panday in the south. Meantime the spoils of political tenure went to the PNM factions. The PNM relied on firm support from the mainly Negro urban unions, but maintained a good posture of multiracialism by having two (moslem) Indians as senior ministers, together with Chinese and even a Syrian.

It was in the municipal elections of 1984 that signs of the PNM's forthcoming demise first appeared. When the PNM was finally routed by the National Alliance for Reconstruction in the general election of December 1986, it did not have the racial overtones of the Indians arising at last against Negro domination that one might have feared. Instead it was a swing of people of all ethnic groups away from a PNM which

*Previous estimates did not allow for the important question of the estimated 300,000 "small island" illegal immigrants who evaded the census; but this factor did not affect the outcome of the 1986 general election.

gave every sign of being worn out in governing, to the alternative which happened to include the traditional rural Hindu opposition, sitting on the sidelines for twenty years.

*The Syrians*

Mention has been made earlier that the Syrians have been slowest in lowering their ethnic social barriers. They were the last group to be added to Trinidad's potpourri, if one excepts the handful of Jews at the time of the Second World War.

The first Syrian family came from what is now Lebanon in 1913. They were Maronite Christians seeking refuge from the Muslim victimisation of the Ottoman Empire. The requirement for emigration was 100 gold sovereigns, no mean sum in those days. Those leaving had been farmers of olive groves and vineyards giving a respectable income. Syria was in the French "sphere of influence" so Marseilles was the entrepot through which Syrians made their way to the New World whose pavements were reputedly made of gold. "America" covered the continent from Argentina to Canada, no special distinction being made of the U.S.A.

Martinique was the port of call from Marseilles, being a French island. It was there the first couple with their nine-year-old son landed, expecting to find a cousin to help them settle in. After asking around they learnt he had sought greener pastures in Trinidad. They followed him there only to learn he had moved on again to Demerara.

Weary with travel, the couple decided to try on their own in Trinidad, and looked around for a suitable occupation. They saw Jewish peddlars carrying bundles of cloth in back packs to the remote country areas and said, "For several thousand years the Syrians have been able to trade as well as the Jews - we shall copy them." As soon as finances permitted, the rest of the couple's children were sent across, together with cousins and acquaintances from the Maronite villages.

Numerically the Syrians do not merit a percentage point in the census but they came to dominate the cloth and dry goods trade. In the boom years of the 1970s they led the way in commercial real estate entrepreneurship and bound themselves irrevocably to Trinidad's economic and political fortunes. Speaking their gutteral Arabic on the galleries of their Woodbrook and St. Clair homes, the men play dominoes and cards while discussing the fortunes of Beirut. Intermarriage with non-Syrians is fiercely resisted.

There were stories in 1962 of a Syrian girl having a love-affair with a non-Syrian Trinidadian and getting pregnant. At the time of her labour she was packed off to Tobago; both she and her baby were reputedly strangled and never heard of again. Two eldest sons of leading Syrian families successfully ignored the threats of disinheritance to marry Venezuelan brides, but it has been very gradually that the community's barriers have been breached. Even while Beirut was in the process of demolition through civil strife in the early 1980s, Trinidad Syrians were still being sent to find their brides in the home villages of their forbears.

That child of nine was dean of the Syrian community until he died in 1986 so it is not surprising that the prejudices of this highly successful group should survive. In time no doubt, they will yield to the erosion of social intercourse at the teenage level.

*The People of Trinidad*

These then are the ingredients of Trinidad's racial mélange. As many Indians as negroes who together with their mixture, the dougla, make up 85% of the population. Another 10% are sufficiently mixed with European or Chinese as to be recognisably something other than negro or Indian. The remaining 5% are clearly Chinese, Syrian or European. Some who might be considered coloured in North America or Europe are considered white in their darker tropical setting. But even this 5%, the Syrians excepted, is likely to have some darker antecedents.

The negroes have been steadily supplemented for the past thirty years by an influx from the "small islands." Not least is Trinidad's sister island of Tobago from which many leading civil servants have emerged. Grenadian and Vincentian families have entered illegally on schooners both to Port of Spain and the south. Not without justification does St. Lucia-born playwright and poet, Derek Walcott state "every Trinidadian black family admits with bemusement that it has small-island origins..."

Token attempts to restrict this infiltration were made during the years of prosperity when extra artisans were needed for the building boom. The Indians muttered that it was a conspiracy by the negro politicians to prevent being outnumbered by Indians in the polls, and there may be some truth to the charge. Faced by a toppling economy George Chambers' government took sterner measures to prevent the steady flow, actually shipping some back. So many have relations already established in Trinidad that effective measures are not easy. New shanties emerge overnight on squatted land. Grenada and St. Vincent are backward agricultural islands and the bright lights and job opportunities of Trinidad have an inevitable appeal. It is said that there are more Grenadians in Point Fortin than in Grenada, but this is an exaggeration.

There are still Hindu and Moslem schools in predominantly Indian areas but all are government assisted financially and must follow the dictates of the Ministry of Education. There has been an extensive school construction programme aided by the World Bank which provided government primary and secondary schools to the burgeoning population. The result is that there is a good racial mixture in the bulk of schools.

"Eleven plus" exams still determine which students go through to the more select secondary schools. No statistics are available to see if any one ethnic group loses out on the chance of education at the handful of top schools. By any country's standards the mixture reflects the full spectrum of backgrounds.

Similarly in job opportunity there are few areas where racial selection stands out. Government took steps with the commercial banks to promote suitable action. The banks were told bluntly that their staff did not reflect the ethnic makeup of the community, and asked why was this? The more conciliatory banks bent over backwards to obey. Other banks were less eager to employ negroes arbitrarily and still showed a high percentage of Chinese faces behind their counters. In the Civil Service this bias appeared to be offset by the number of negro faces, but by no means to the exclusion of Indians. To an outside observer it would seem as if there is a very fair apportionment of jobs. If all elements of racial selection have not been eradicated, it would be hard to find another country which has come so close. This is not to say ethnic bias is gone. But it has been reduced to an exemplary degree and promotes the high level of racial harmony of which Trinidad is justifiably proud.

*Racial Harmony*

Brazil usually gets credit for being the most advanced country with regard to racial harmony, and among the largest countries this is possibly true. They are a long way from being devoid of racial prejudice whatever impression the abandon of Rio's Carnival may give to the casual observer.

After the advanced and long-standing degree of racial integration in Trinidad, one is surprised to see how few of the smartly dressed businessmen carrying briefcases on the streets of Sao Paolo, Rio, Belo Horizante or Brasilia are black. Conversely, one cannot fail to notice that black men and women hold the great majority of lower jobs as cleaners and labourers. Only the occasional swarthy Portuguese face is seen among the menial occupations.

One might assume this is only a reflection of history and the educational process; but a manager of a Canadian bank who had worked in Jamaica and married a charming and attractive Jamaican of medium brown complexion and African antecedents was incensed to learn of the constant snubbing and biased treatment meted out to his wife by black and white shop assistants alike. In a supermarket she would be ignored by the cashiers if there were any Europeans in line. This is not an isolated case. Similar occurrences were reportedly widespread in Brazil according to those whose sensitivities to racial interaction have become sharpened by living in the West Indies.

With two thirds of its free population being black even

in the days of slavery, and a very short period before the slaves were freed, it is not surprising that a black middle class should have given Trinidad a head start in racial matters over any other country with a black majority.

This may seem contradicted by the elitist attitude of the white creoles, or by the coloured who have an outspoken pride and preference for a 'clear skin' - a fairer complexion. The French creole elite families made strenuous efforts to keep their blood "unsullied" by exotic strains, but most white creole families have dark antecedents without going back very far. The permutations of a small society where many have enjoyed comparable economic standing for so long makes it impossible otherwise. Black and not-so-black plantation owners and merchants have sent their sons to Oxford or Cambridge and their daughters to Catholic finishing school in Kent for several generations.

Black doctors and lawyers have been eminent from the start. They aspired to the exclusive confines of the steward's enclosure of the Turf Club where they would rub jacketed shoulders with the paler elite of their small society. They acquired all the social attitudes of their whiter colleagues and became part of the creolocracy in their hearts if not in their minds, and were envied as such by those of lesser station in life, black, white or "red".

The Port of Spain schools played an important role in this social integration. Queen's Royal College, an Anglican establishment in its endearingly ugly turn-of-the-century edifice on the Grand Savannah, led the way, followed by the Holy Ghost Fathers at St. Mary's College. All races rubbed shoulders in uniformed rows in the classroom and battled rival schools on the playing field.

Indians were left out of this integration process until much later because they lived in the country areas and kept to an Indian way of life and religion. In San Fernando where Indians had become merchants and jewellers, the process was quicker among those who had adopted Christianity. A new caste system was formed based on social standing. This was less defined than the rigid one left behind in India. Parents of means had strict ideas as to who their children should marry, and more often than not their wishes prevailed. Theirs was not the *laissez faire* nonchalance of Carnival. A hierarchy became established within the various elements of the Indian community which has largely remained intact even today.

The extent to which Indian sects have kept to themselves is typically illustrated by the following. A Muslim girl of 24 who worked as a bank clerk in Port of Spain, threw a birthday party at her home. Seeking her house in El Socorro which fronted onto a small grassed savannah where cricket was played, a banking friend went to a house and asked for the Mohammed residence.

"Mohammed? That must be over on that side. We don't know which house. You will have to ask over there - we are Hindu." So much for the intimacy of village life.

A Hindu family in Marabella had made no attempts to marry off their petite and very pretty eldest daughter so that she would stay with the family and care for her parents. She worked as a book-keeping clerk and fell in love with a negro co-worker. Their marriage was attended by none of her family who have effectively dis-owned her. This in 1983.

These are extremes of non-integration and are marked exceptions to the mainstream of racial harmony. Go to any of the numerous weekend "fetes" and see all shades in musical abandon. The girls and erstwhile girls will be displaying their shapely figures in the tightest of blue jeans. A good number will be winding their pelvises in exaggerated sexuality. The males will be dressed in well-tailored slacks and the latest in fashionable shirts. The love of being smartly turned out is apparent, and new "threads" are customarily bought for each major fete.

The music will be "hot" - the latest off the hit parades mixed with local calypso tunes of the current season. The dancing is subtle and skilled. Any "foreigner" will stand out like a sore thumb bobbing away out of rhythm while his curvacious partner tries to keep him at arm's length and hopes he will eventually catch the beat with her. The tempo of calypso appears obvious. (It is the delayed action of the feet so that the body is slightly ahead of the music which non-Trinidadians find tricky. Despite the lithe movement through the body, the head scarcely moves.)

Fetes take place throughout the year. There used to be a respite from calypso after Carnival for the duration of Lent out of deference to the church. The calypsonians complained that their music was local and it was biased to curtail only local music. The radio stations now play calypsoes throughout Lent. Previously the church permitted stations one break from this abstinence on St. Joseph's Day. This has gone by the boards and fetes are held every Saturday.

It is when the new calypsoes are presented in the "tents" early in the New Year that the biggest season of pre-Carnival fetes gets under way. Because Carnival moves with Easter this season may be as short as five weeks or as long as ten.

Visitors taken to a pre-Carnival fete can be excused for suspecting it is one long orgy. How can such glamorous couples dance so energetically and suggestively, drink and smile so much for so long? The majority of the crowd will be of dark complexion, true mixed up "Trinis"-African-Chinese-Portuguese-Scottish? It's hard to tell which, varying to pure African, pure Chinese, pure European, pure Indian, even pure Syrian now that the younger generation is breaking away.

Sometimes several girls will come as a group, "make up a lime" in the local parlance. Most, but very possibly, not all, will leave in the same group depending on whom they encountered. More often a couple or two will make a date in the normal way and meet up with a larger group of their friends. An unoccupied long metal table will be commandeered, bottles of scotch, rum and mixers will be purchased from the bar with bowls of ice to serve their needs for the night. Other friends will drop by to chat, have a drink and dance a "set" with one of the girls. The dance area is likely to be a tarmac tennis court or parking area at a club's premises. The crowd will be intense, and those who object to close body contact from all sides while dancing may find it claustrophobic. Young bloods will go to any lengths to avoid paying the prices of admission or the need for an invitation, "storming" by making holes in fences and climbing the walls. But it is rare despite the presence of such elements for the atmosphere to be anything but pure abandoned joy.

Fetes such as these, used to have a brass band and a steel band alternating the music. The expense of steel bands and their fickle behaviour as to when and how long they should play has caused DJs to take their place. Truckloads of speakers will be set up around the dance area to create such a volume that not only is conversation impossible, but the sound shakes you to your core. Trinidadians like loud sound in their cinemas and all around them. They sleep peacefully through the barking and howling of dogs that drive a visitor to distraction.

It is the brassbands which the crowds love most. The bandleader will sense the climax at the end of a set of tunes. He will abandon the melody and build up a crescendo of repetition until all but the most weary or lack-lustre are bouncing with arms raised, screaming with an orgasmic fervour until the music finally lets them sink back to reality. Hence the name "jump-up" for such dances.

*On Stage*

## Chapter 4

━━━━━━━━━ ◗•◉•◖ ━━━━━━━━━

# *The Phenomenon That Is Carnival*

What temporary insanity possesses thousands to dance in the streets for eight solid hours in the broiling sun, and then do the same again the following day? It is the unique form of madness known as "Carnival Fever" that sweeps Trinidad every year.

Only by playing masquerade in a carnival band can one appreciate the pulsating obsession that provides such endurance. The throb of the music keeps you shuffling along interminably. It is only when the music stops that your feet begin to burn from the baking asphalt. A quick gulp from the flask of rum passed hurriedly from mouth to mouth, a new calypso tune strikes up from the brass band on the truck accompanying you, and you are off again until darkness falls. Eventually the revellers make their weary way home for a plate of pelau and a welcome bed if they can find one - so many friends will have come to stay.

Carnival bands are produced in the larger towns of Trinidad and Tobago, each of which would be considered a spectacular show in any other part of the world. It is in Port of Spain that the major bands compete for the coveted Band of the Year prize. More people will rather come from San Fernando to play in a Port of Spain band than play in their home town. For this reason Port of Spain is far and away the major spectacle for visitors, and the Carnival that one really thinks of. The spirit is equally fervent in all the smaller versions, however.

By gazetted ordinance the police have closed off the streets to vehicular traffic in the area which will be paraded by bands. This stretches from Independence Square in the business area up to the Grand Stand on the Queen's Park Savannah, built originally for horse racing, but used for other major spectacles. Other restrictions as to the path the bands can take are set down by the National Carnival Commission (NCC) which succeeded the Carnival Development Committee (CDC) in an effort to have a smooth flow of masqueraders pass in front of the judges and the thousands of visitors from all over the world. Many maintain that the effect of the CDC and NCC has been to commercialise and stifle the true spirit and spontaneity of Carnival. The prizes they offer are still small  in relation to the expense of producing a band, and there is no obligation to cross the judging stage at the Savannah. But that is where the television cameras are capturing the pelvic gyrations, mammary undulations and unrivalled uninhibitedness which the masqueraders want the world and their neighbours to see. Without the organization provided by the NCC, Carnival would almost certainly degenerate into sprawling confusion.

A lot has been written about "every man is a king for two days" before he returns to his humdrum life. Very few masqueraders play "big mas"; the great majority are happier in a tunic, a pair of leotards and a halter top (if female) than a bulky costume. Some big bands have stopped putting out a king or queen, so costly is the costume to produce and such a nuisance on the road. Fortunately the kings and queens are still there for us to admire, and Carnival is richer for the memories such great masqueraders as Peter Samuel have given in inspired costumes and with inspired performances requiring great strength and theatrical musicality.

In a large band there are some one to three thousand revellers. They are divided into fifteen to twenty sections, the infantry, as it were, of the army, and then, most resplendent of all, the king and queen of the band. There are many smaller bands, and in them the cameraderie is stronger. Every band must be registered in advance with the NCC and the police. A banner must be borne aloft in front of each band displaying its name, theme and registration number.

This Parade of Bands is only the culmination of a complex mosaic of factors that converge for the final magic of Carnival Monday and Tuesday, the latter better known abroad as Mardi Gras - Huge Tuesday. Planning a band starts even before the costumes of the current year have been carelessly discarded into trash cans or the gutter. The band's designer will sketch out costumes of the main sections as soon as the theme has been decided and agreed with the leader of the band. The NCC has established categories within which to judge bands such as historical, fantasy, military, etc. but each band leader picks a theme which he feels will be the best vehicle for his next display. There have been such memorable bands as *The Grandeur of Rome, The Court of Catherine the Great, The Flagwavers of Siena, The Snow Kingdom, Somewhere in New Guinea, Land of the Kabuki* and *Paradise Lost* and as many other varied subjects as the most fertile imagination can conjure up.

Orders for the materials to be used must be sent out months in advance to the supply houses of the world. So many ostrich plumes were used in *Somewhere in New Guinea* that one could only imagine every African ostrich denuded. Such mass purchasing places the bandleader in a serious position financially. It is only from the eventual popularity (or otherwise) of his band, and the payment for costumes by those who will masquerade in the band that he will hopefully recoup his massive expenses. No government agency subsidises or underwrites his risk. There are cash prizes for winning bands, but although increased in recent years, they are still so small they would pay for less than one major costume out of hundreds.

Often the house of the bandleader will be the "camp" for operations. Bedrooms become storerooms for piles of material and the family is lucky if they can find a place to sleep. The garden will most likely be roofed over with a temporary shelter of canvas or galvanised iron sheeting. Benches and tables are set up for the workers headed by professional assistants like the wirebenders on whose expertise so much of the finery of Carnival costumes depend. Each skilled artisan will command a team of volunteers who will come by after work. In the office, an artist's rendition will display each costume and its cost. Professional tailors, seamstresses and even shoe makers will take up residence in the camp yard measuring each masquerader for his and her costume individually.

Week after week the work goes on, and gradually each costume emerges like a butterfly from a chrysalis into the resplendent mass of colour and artistry the designer intended. The boots or slippers must be comfortable enough to wear all day on the hard, hot road yet strong enough to take two days of abrasion shuffling to the music. The body costume must be comfortable and cool. The head piece properly padded with foam and fitted so as not to be swept off by the masqueraders's gyrations or in the swirling, dusty breezes that always accompany Carnival. The standard with its aluminum staff must be strong enough to stand up to two days' hard usage. Canny masqueraders will add pockets to their costumes for flasks of rum, some money and car keys. No mask is worn on the face despite the name "masquerader". Masks are forbidden to avoid the chance of underhand violence.

A stranger will wonder if there is any membership qualification to join a band. Can anyone join any band? The big bands will welcome foreign visitors into their throng even though they will stick out like sore thumbs mimicking the natives' prance to the music when they cross the stage. This is especially true of the bands tourists frequent like those of Stephen Lee Heung, Wayne Berkeley, Peter Minshall and Edmond Hart. Others such as Mavericks are strictly limited to 500 persons to preserve mobility on the road and a more intimate spirit of camaraderie. Many other bands, big and small, will be from neighbourhoods where an outsider will feel ill at ease. The choice is usually made by where your group of friends are playing. You may not be in the same section, but on the road where most of the two days is spent, there is no objection to breaking section, and chipping along with your friends in the band or even by-standers, keen on joining in the fun of the band for a block or two.

"Hug up any woman in the band," the calypsonian may tell you, but it is unlikely to be that carefree. Trinidadians fete so much that they have a wide circle of acquaintances. A visitor may see a masquerader flask in hand sway into a crowd and emerge with a luscious girl under his arm, to shuffle together down the procession of the band. Almost certainly he will have known her before, if only slightly. This is not to say that complete strangers will not hit it off together during Carnival as they do throughout the world on such occasions; it is merely to caution the common belief that you are entitled according to the rules of Carnival, to pick out any girl that strikes your fancy to have her dancing at your side in the band, your arms around each other's waist. Husbands may defy the strictures of their wives, get drunk with their cronies or "frien' up" a chick they have had their eye on; wives, more rarely, will incur the jealous wrath of husbands by playing in a band where they can, and sometimes will, get up to as much mischief as their husbands. Hopefully all will be forgiven when Carnival is over, but inevitably it is a season when many liaisons cannot stand the strain of such abandon, and irreparable breaches are created. Even the tolerant Trinidad cannot be immune to the fires of jealousy which the permissive ambiance of Carnival creates.

Strangers to Trinidad are often confused by the "playing in a band" they hear on all sides, thinking some musical instrument is involved. Each masquerader has to play his costume according to its varied character. Similarly strangers will expect every Carnival band to have a steelband with it. All the major bands have one or more brass bands piled into trucks, amplifiers pounding out the sound so that all masqueraders will have the blare of brass to keep them going.

Only calypso tunes will be played, some for over half an hour on end so that the tune is indelibly engraved into your brain.

The steelbands will be on the road too, but not to accompany a masquerade band. They will have chosen their own theme and be wearing their own, less splendid, costumes. They too will be playing only calypso. As each band passes in front of the judges, masquerade band and steelband, the tune they are playing at the time will be noted. At the end of festivities the judges will announce which calypso tune won Road March, one of the most highly sought prizes for the calypsonian. The Road March is an interesting amalgam of the tune's popularity to the band leader who chooses it, and the masqueraders who dance to it. There may be a handful of equally popular tunes when Carnival starts. Hour after hour on the road the musicians will pick up the sense of which tune is infusing most spirit into the revellers, and will reflect it back by playing it more frequently. The calypso that makes Road March must have something catchy about it to survive the repetition. The calypsonian who brought out the tune may never have made the semi-finals of the calypso contest; but if his tune strikes the fancy of the bands, his fame and fortune are made. One calypsonian, Lord Kitchener, is laughed at for his verbal presentations, but has an uncanny sense of what will be popular and effective with the steel bands and the brass bands. He is rightly called the Road March King.

## Calypso and Steelband

Nobody can appreciate what calypsoes mean to Trinidad without living there a while. A visitor will often assume calypsoes are mainly for the tourists, a form of ertzatz culture lacking all freshness and spontaneity. As he steps from his taxi at the Botanical Gardens, an apparent calypsonian will latch onto him to play his tune. The words, will on the face of it, have been made up on the spot for they will have something topical about the tourist, his manner of dress, the fact that he has two ladies with him, that he is bald, or what not. While these kerbside troubadours exercise ingenuity in applying their trade, it is a far cry from the annual crop of calypsoes. They have developed formulae to the two or three tunes they play to meet the slightly varying circumstances.

It is the opening of the calypso "tents" in the first week of the new year that starts the magic of the new Carnival Season even though Carnival is still many weeks away. No longer under canvas, but now in union meeting halls and public buildings, the four main groups of calypsonians present their programme of tunes to an avidly waiting public. Each group will have twenty to thirty calypsonians in its stable. Some will be comic, others highly serious on the themes of injustice to the black man, many scandalous, a few so dirty as to be nauseating. By the time the programme starts at 9 o'clock you will already be getting numb in your metal chair. This will soon be forgotten as the action picks up, led by the "emcee", often a calypsonian in his own right, but also a teller of witty and rude stories. At 11.30 p.m. you are glad for the chance to stretch your now dead legs and jostle to the caged bar for liquid refreshments. By the time the show has finished you will be weary. Many tunes will have bored you, others fired you up, so that you are certain they will be road march. Provided you are a local, you will have laughed yourself sore. If a visitor, you will have been at a loss to catch what was said and what it meant, so quick is the repartée and foreign the local parlance.

From these calypsoes will emerge the dozen or so which have fresh and appealing tunes. Every calypso will be new so far as the words are concerned, but few calypsonians are gifted enough to be able to produce new tunes every year. To the keen ear of the audience, echoes of a previous year's tune will often be spotted. The new tunes will be captured on tape and taken back to the pan yards and brass bands where they will be worked on hour after hour until each band has developed its own rendition for the weekend Carnival fetes. Even after the initial crop of tunes, others will emerge when a calypsonian finds one song is a failure and abandons it for another. Very few calypsonians can manage more than one or two tunes a season, and only a few are hits. The radio stations cooperate by playing the new calypsoes throughout the day.

The arrangements done by a steelband are far more complex than those of a brass band. No music is written down and the arranger has to hear all ten sections of his steel pans in his head before any practice can begin. Night after night from eight to eleven o'clock, hundreds of youngsters will congregate at their pan yard, memorising the pattern of notes for their pans. These are so complex for the tune chosen for the Panorama competition, that it must be unique in musical experience for the youth of a society, often unemployed, who might otherwise be roaming the streets in delinquent gangs, to be absorbed in mastering their music. There are well over a hundred steel bands spread throughout the country. The largest will have 100 "beaters" in the full Panorama side which competes on the Grand Savannah stage in front of the judges. Before the numbers grew too large, all bands throughout the country met in Port of Spain for the Panorama preliminaries, which lasted from morning to after midnight. Spectators would jump up on the stage to jump with the band they fancied, delaying its progress across the stage. Such anarchy was wonderful for the participants, but hell for the judges.

For a greater degree of order, the bands are now divided into regional groupings playing on different days. The dozen or so bands receiving the highest points go forward to the national semi-finals, and the top eight from that go to the finals. Special care and top quality equipment is required to record steelband music well. It can best be appreciated outdoors in the tropical night. Only then can the magnificent resonance and bell-like purity of sound that the pans now achieve be fully appreciated. Each band has its own musical characteristic and style. Only a trained ear can hear these facets, but every Trinidadian ear is now well trained. The full "road side" will probably learn only a handful of tunes besides the Panorama tune to which they will have devoted so much time. However, the more skilled pan beaters who comprise the "stage side" of twelve to fifteen panmen will have acquired a full repertoire to be able to perform as a dance band.

This same stage side will compete in the biennial Steelband Festival held later in the year which has nothing to do with Carnival, at which they will play classical music, professionally arranged and conducted by a qualified musician. While this demonstrates the heights to which pan music can aspire, to many it is removed from its natural idiom of Carnival and the road.

## The Pre-Carnival Season

With the new season's crop of calypsoes mastered, the brass bands are ready for the weekend pre-Carnival fetes. These were traditionally held at sports clubs in the open air, as the chance of rain is slight at that time of the year. Before all the oil boom dollars were flowing there would be only one fete a weekend. As the crowds grew larger for the fetes, so they proliferated, until today there will be four or five Port of Spain fetes each weekend prior to Carnival. A tradition at these fetes is the Old Mas' competition at which the Old Mas' bands will parade in front of the judges and the audience arranged around the central tennis court.

There is nothing fancy or splendid about Old Mas'. This is the crude burlesque centering on bawdy themes. Each band will have its title displayed on a crudely lettered banner, under which its thirty or forty participants will pass, each holding up a placard, preferably mis-spelt and punning the title of its character. The title may mean nothing until the masquerader plays out his role. Some are very clever, many obscene, but all are taken in good humour even by the little old ladies who always seem to be the ones in the front row. After four or five bands have performed, all to the music of calypso tunes, prizes awarded to the best, the masqueraders remove their rough costumes for more normal party wear, and join the rest of the crowd in the dancing and drinking that will carry on until four in the morning. The neighbours will get very little sleep that night, but it's all for a good cause. It is by this means that the sports clubs raise funds to meet the bulk of their expenses for the coming year.

With each weekend, Carnival draws closer and the general excitement reaches fever pitch. For those who do not appreciate the rowdy, brash and alcoholic celebrations there are more genteel aspects of Carnival which may for them be the high point. High on this list used to be the Carnival Queen Show arranged by the Jaycees. Errol Hill points out in his study of Carnival that the Carnival Queen was one of the original elements of Carnival celebrations.

This show fell away during the racially volatile period after 1970. After a hiatus of several years, the more conservative South reintroduced the Queen Show with great success, and emboldened by this, the North was happy to resume the popular spectacle. They were not the displays of fair-skinned beauty of the pre-1970 era. Many beauty pageants, a Miss Universe and a Miss World had washed away such colonial cobwebs. The contestants were now predominantly dark, displaying elegant, locally designed gowns and exotic hairstyling with regal poise. To link the contest with Carnival there was no bathing suit parade. Instead specially inspired and hugely elaborate queenly Carnival costumes were created. The judges were exhorted not to judge beauty so much as the best characterization of the spirit of Carnival. In the glamour of the event with each sponsored queen handed out by her tuxedoed escort, nobody really cared for the rules as much as for their favourites. Loyalties ran high and loud. The evening was one of beauty, style and glamour. For the vast throng this spectacle was the zenith of their Carnival, devoid though it was of steel bands and calypso. They could retire to the comfort of their television sets to watch the rest of the national spectacle at a sedate distance. But, alas, the Carnival Queen Show is now a thing of the past.

For some years there was another fine show during the Carnival season, the Buy Local Competition. This was inspired by Government as a means of attracting attention to the widening range of locally manufactured goods. Initially a success, the quality of the shows deteriorated and with it popular interest. Once gone, this experimental addition to an already full Carnival menu was not missed.

Equally popular with the more sedate are the Kiddies' Carnival shows put on at several venues for fund raising purposes on pre-Carnival weekend afternoons. Individual costumes in varying age groups are the main appeal. Talented ladies sew sequins and velvet into costumes more exquisitely made than those of the big masquerade bands. Toddlers of three, show their costumes off proudly, and many of them have already mastered the calypso rhythm to sway and stomp like professionals. The older children are expert and will very likely be playing with their parents in a band on Carnival Tuesday. To build up the spectacle of Kiddies Carnival, the upper middle class schools in Port of Spain have been bringing out bands to supplement the individuals. All the brilliance and expertise of the Carnival tradition is there, and were it not for the way that the big bands dwarf these school children's efforts, they would be worthy of international acclaim.

Government has in recent years actively promoted participation in Carnival by children as a means of inculcating an awareness of Trinidad's unique cultural tradition. Schools throughout the country are encouraged to put out bands, and many do. They congregate in Woodford Square in the heart of Port of Spain, and parade up Frederick Street through the crowds, mainly of relations, lining the pavement to the Grand Stand at the Savannah. Music is supplied all along the route by "dee jays" with recorded music blaring out from loudspeakers specially installed for the occasion. A great deal of creative work goes into these efforts by the schools, and the children are genuinely enthusiastic about playing mas' just like the grown ups. The quality of the costumes is inevitably much lower than that of Kiddies Carnival where parental pride and purse has not been spared.

### Dimanche Gras

Despite the dominant French cultural influence in Trinidad, the phrase "Mardi Gras" is not used in Trinidad in the same way it is in New Orleans. "Carnival Monday" and "Carnival Tuesday" is the way the big days are referred to. But the prelude to it is Dimanche Gras, Grease Sunday. This is a stage presentation televised and aired on radio to the nation at the usual concourse, the Grand Stand. It is always a long and unwieldy show. The eight finalist calypsonians each sing their two contributions. On the huge wooden stage with audiences in front and behind in the North Stand the calypsonian is a long way from the familiar intimacy of his "tent" with his musicans at his elbow. He or she (there are several high quality female calypsonians including one former

Road March titlist) will have the handful of chorus accompa-
nists bobbing and swaying as they sing their falsetto over in
one corner of the stage. The unfamiliar and demanding
setting overcomes all but the most assured calypsonian, who
strides from side to side of the stage, whipping his microphone
cord along with him.

After the calypsonians used to come the finals of Panorama
where the vastness of the stage is needed. The steel pans used
to resound under the tin roof of the stands, but the anvil-like
note of the break drum sounds clearly above it all to give the
beaters their timing. Small wonder the hearing of panmen is
irreparably harmed by the weeks of overpowering noise. The
results were not announced until a few days later, which was
just as well as loyalties run fiercely for favoured bands. Dance
routines will be interspersed through the proceedings, and a
comedian or two. Some times an effort is made to string the
night's entertainment together with a story line. So often
have these efforts failed that discretion dictates against
further attempts. The kings and queens of the bands will be
paraded again to an audience that may have seen them twice
before. In previous evenings of entertainment the kings and
queens of the masquerade bands will have competed first for
the semi finals then for the finals. Even before their bands
have made their first entry onto the streets the winning king
and queen will have been chosen.

Unlike the floats of New Orleans and Nice, Trinidad
Carnival like Rio de Janeiro, is a festival of movement of the
body. It follows that the costumes must have a minimum of
engineering devices to assist them so that the masquerader's
ability to play his costume are retained. Through the 60s and
70s the king and queen costumes got bigger and more unwieldy.
Kings would come staggering on stage dragging a mountain
of colourful feathers on a framework of aluminium and cane
that could weigh 200 lbs. Wheels would be secreted at the
edges to help support the weight. Only with great effort could
the king, lost inside his costume, make the giant framework
shudder to the time of the music.

The queens, too, carried a lot of weight both in their
costumes and on their strong bodies. Often they are out in

front of the costume like a pony pulling a trap. Designers knew that any small costume, appearing by itself on the vast flood-lit stage as distinct from being in the company of the band of which it was supposed to be part, would be lost unless there was an impact in size and colour. Quite correctly, the judges set rules for mobility marking down or banning costumes which did not meet the standard which retained the true spirit of Carnival. Despite this the queens are not the leggy beauties of the Carnival Queen Show put on by the Jaycees, but robust troupers capable of carrying a 40 lb costume on stage and dancing with it in apparent happy abandon.

The irony of this development is more readily appreciated when the band makes its first entry before the public on Carnival Monday. Rather than risk the massive king and queen costumes getting broken or dirty en route many will be left in the safety of the mas camp. At best the costumes will appear in less than full fancy. For Carnival Tuesday, the grand finals, when the crowds are biggest and the judges' decision will be determined, the king and queen costumes will be brought out, but often with another occupant to carry it along the road until the judging stands are reached. There are now four official judging stands - the Grand Stand and Independence Square being the main judging points. Only when the king and queen are about to cross the stage in front of the judges do they exchange places with their porter and don their full regalia. Judged, as the kings and queens are at Dimanche Gras out of the context of their band, the best queen or king may come from a mediocre band, but this is unlikely. While some bands have dropped out of competing seriously in the king and queen category, and some have even stopped having them in their band at all, it's true to say that without these major characters to add the highlights to a passing band, the overall spectacle would be greatly reduced. The combined genius of Peter Minshall's design with the theatri-cal portrayal by Peter Samuel of "the Serpent" in *Paradise Lost* or "Midnight Robber" in *Danse Macabre* provided memories to be carried to the grave.

## "Jouvay" and the Parade of Bands

Dimanche Gras ends with the crowning of the calypso monarch, the King of Calypso for that year and the King and Queen of Carnival. But Carnival has not yet begun. It is now after one o'clock, and most of the crowd drift off to parties which will last until the first tinges of dawn mark the sky at 4.00 a.m. The day is about to break - Jour Ouvert, shortened over the years to "jouvay". Throughout the streets people are scurrying to the panyard or overnight resting spot of the steelband they have chosen to follow through the streets to the Independence Square stage. It is there the mayor of Port of Spain will officially open proceedings by crowning two persons who have played no other part in the preliminaries, King and Queen of Carnival. Who they are does not really matter. They are not seen or heard from again.

Although it is still dark there is an air of suppressed excitement in all the tee-shirted and blue-jeaned groups of friends congregating with the steelbands. There is a pervading air of goodwill, even though many are exhausted from the long night's festivities. If there is drunkenness it is not reflected in churlish behaviour. Girls and women are unlikely to receive attempts to pick them up unless they actively encourage it. Nothing must spoil "we mas". Considering the circumstances it is a miracle of good behaviour. The carriages for the pans are giant playpens of metal tubing, roofed over to shield the beaters from the broiling sun and the night's dew which can easily cause a head cold in the panmen's kinky locks. The supporters will assist by "pushing pan", shoving the carriages out of the drains needed to carry off the wet season's downpours. Many will wear the tee shirt of the band, or have their hand stamped in violet to show that they are regular supporters who have paid a small band fee. Other fans will not be excluded, but lack the sense of belonging.

From all areas, Belmont, Woodbrook, behind the bridge on Picadilly Street, the steelbands will be converging simultaneously towards the downtown stage on Independence Square. Inevitably there is a traffic jam and the band's pace is slowed to an intermittent crawl, but the pan music never falters. The sun is now up and throats are getting dry.

Vendors of oranges on the pavements do a thriving trade. The bands each go through their repertoire of the season's tunes. Very likely one will get the sense that one tune is emerging for the Road March prize, but it is still too early to say. Until recently brass bands did not enter J'ouvert, but they will hold the balance for the judges' decision.

Besides the steel bands and some brass bands will be the Old mas Bands of Red Indians, pirates, devils, tramps, skeletons or what-have-you. These are not the middle class bands that toured the pre-carnival dances. They will improvise their music with biscuit tins and whistles. The large stand of spectators in the front of the Salvatori Building will watch them with amusement as they perform their antics. The earlier steelbands will also pass. Many however find that time has run out on them and they will have no chance of getting across the stage before J'ouvert officially ceases at 10 o'clock. Their weary followers will be anxious to have a bath and two or three hours sleep before they don their costume for the Parade of Bands.

Largely because of J'ouvert, many masqueraders opt not to play in their masquerade bands on both Monday and Tuesday. Monday's bands will appear with less than half of their numbers, and many will leave behind the less convenient or fragile portions of their costume. There are tourists whose schedules ill-advisedly have them leaving Trinidad on Monday night. They will see the bands on Monday and be well impressed with the spectacle, never to know how Tuesday's bands would have excelled.

Playing mas' on Carnival Monday is in no way undermined by the low turnout. The roads are less crowded, the bands can move more rapidly to the Grand Stand and Independence Square, and the less encumbering costumes are easier to wear. That night after the band has returned to its camp, the revellers, many still in their costumes, will go to an evening fete. The biggest of these is the one at the Country Club which is limited to overseas visitors willing to pay for entry and to the 5,000 or so members who may frequent the club at no other time during the year.

The following morning, Carnival Tuesday, will see the full

turnout of the band, resplendent in head piece, standard, gauntlets, and face make-up with spangles which help ward off the hot sun. Legs will ache from the previous day's exertions, but once the brass band strikes up and the masqueraders get into sections, fatigue fades away and with a new-found vigour the band sets off for the final day's dancing through the streets. There are crowds deep on the pavements, looking out for their friends and family, cameras at the ready. Rum flasks will be out early. On Tuesday the bands set off no later than 10 o'clock in the hope of getting to the Savannah before there is a total impasse. Only the bands that leave from a nearby venue will be lucky enough to get across the Grand Stand stage before midday. The rest will reach a standstill on Charlotte Street, Memorial Park or Keate Street. The masqueraders will get bored, and sit on the curb, eating sandwiches hidden in a pocket of their tunic. "DJ" music will take the place of the brass bands on the trucks. Standards will be stored on the music trucks until, perhaps after a stagnation of three or four hours, the band moves forward again, and the magic words sweep back through the band "We are next on stage!"

Back on their feet, exhaustion forgotten, the masqueraders gather their costumes together and get into sections, aided by the marshalls of the band who see to it that the harmony of colour is not spoiled by mavericks from other sections or even by-standers who have found their way into the band. The approach to the Grand Stand stage is along the grass of the race course, dry and dusty from the thousands of boots that have already passed across it. There are bleachers on both sides where families will have rigged up sheets as shade from the sun. The music trucks will go ahead to pass behind the vast raised wooden stage and remain there while the sections pass so that each will have the full benefit of the music to prance and sway to the calypso rhythm to best advantage. The thousands of visitors in the stands on each side will appreciate not only the splendour of the costumes, but the frenzied spirit of the masqueraders. Every reveller is there to be seen having an ecstatic time by his family watching on television, and no one would let whatever exhaustion he or she may have felt a short time before be seen while on stage. Each section seems determined to prolong its time on stage as long as possible, going back and forth, while the band's marshalls urge the section forward to make room for the next and prevent the impact of the band as a whole from being lost.

Coming off the stage is an anticlimax. You have spent your last reserves of energy jumping and descend into the cloud of dust of the race track. Snowcone vendors and sweet drink carts do a brisk business. Boyfriends and girlfriends from different sections meet up again and make their way off the Savannah along one of the prescribed routes set by the NCC to reduce congestion on the streets, something they are unable to achieve going into the Savannah. The band will stop on Victoria Avenue or Kew Place for the masqueraders to rest. Many will beg the garden hose from a resident to cool themselves off. Then the music strikes up again, and although the masqueraders never thought they could manage it, they are up again for the chipping dance down to the stage at Independence Square. It is likely to be growing dusk when the band proceeds back to the suburb from which it emerged that morning. Costumes will gradually be getting more sparse as the masqueraders discard inconvenient portions, giving them to eager children pleading from the pavement, or throwing them into an empty lot.

All that now remains is Last Lap. Some will remain or rejoin their band at its camp after a quick meal at a friend's home; others will go to join their friends at the Country Club, Chinese Association or some other popular venue. They will continue their revels, dancing in pairs or groups until, almost with relief, the stroke of midnight comes and with a sigh heard throughout the nation, Carnival is over.

*Hosay drummers and Tadjah*

## Chapter 5

————————•‣•◉•‣•————————

# *Festivals of Light and Colour*

Reference has already been made to the multiplicity of ethnic backgrounds found in Trinidad. There are the Hindu and Moslem East Indians, the Chinese, the dominant French Creoles and the Negros who had little of the slave background of the other Caribbean islands and retained more of their African customs.

We have seen how in a rural community Hindus on one side of a village green may be deliberately unaware of the Moslems living adjacent to them. We have seen, too, how the Moslems, reflecting less than 15% of the East Indian community follow the two Islamic paths of Sunni and Shiite teaching, with the Sunnis being in the great majority. Even the Sunnis are often riven with dissension between rival factions for reasons more of personality clash than religious difference.

How best can one describe the religious scene of Trinidad, when ethnic and religious groups are so interwoven? A quar-

ter of the East Indians are now Christian due in large part to
the efforts in the South of the Canadian Presbyterian missionaries. Yet Hinduism is still the second largest religious
group with 25% of the population after the Catholics' 34%.

Asiatic purists of Hinduism are inclined to sneer at the
Trinidad version of the Hindu religion as diluted and mean-
ingless. As Shiva Naipaul makes clear in *North of South* any
Hindu Trinidadian is beyond redemption in the caste structure by virtue of having "crossed the black water" to Trinidad
in the first place. The many little Hindu "mandirs", gaily
decorated with scenes of Krishna, Ganesh and Parvati are
tended by pundits who have had little access to the mainstream of Hindu belief. Yet in many ways Hindu traditions
continue unchanged. Red and white flags on long  bamboos
flutter outside Hindu homes across the countryside to honour
Satyanarayan and Hanuman. A bank clerk may without
warning appear shaven-headed at work to ignore the jibes of
his fellow workers. He is a Singh, a member of a Sikh family
for whom such periodic rituals are prescribed.

One may go to buy milk from a local dairy to find the
teenage daughter of the house kneeling, dressed in white,
with a pundit at the foot of a mango tree in the front yard
where a small shrine has been made of white pebbles forming
a square on the earth. Flower petals carpet the little square.
A brass lota half-filled with water and two flickering deyas
stand on the petals. The pundit takes the girl through the
prayers of her "puja". The family is not in attendance, but go
about their business handing over bottles of fresh milk in
washed rum bottles corked with a twist of paper. This is the
equivalent of a confirmation rite into the girl's religion, a
private yet very public affair so different from the formalised
church settings to which Christians are accustomed.

During the days of indentured labourers and until the
last generation, the weddings of Hindus were termed "bamboo" or "bush weddings" and were not recognised by law until
the Marriage Officers' Ordinance as late as 1946. Now all the
pundits and others legally empowered in their various sects
to perform marriages are published in the official gazette.

Carnival is nominally a religious festival but has lost all

its religious aspects, having evolved into a magnificent spectacle involving months of preparation. The greatest Hindu festival, Divali (pronounced De-walli) has lost none of its religious significance and is a magnificent spectacle of a more subdued kind. This is the Festival of Light. The Hindu population set out on the edges of upper storey balconies or in intricate designs in front gardens, the little clay deyas filled with coconut oil. Deyas burn brightly as votive lamps to celebrate the conquest of the forces of light over those of darkness, commemorating the safe return of Rama, his wife Sita and brother, Lakshman after slaughtering the dark demon king, Raman. (Other sources more simply say Divali honours Lakshmi). Most spectacular of all are the out-door displays on village savannahs where bamboo is split into halves and pegged into a complex but graceful fantasy of curves. One of the most splendid can be seen at the edge of the road to the airport just beyond the Old Southern Main Road. The little deyas are carefully balanced into the central hollow of the split bamboo so that when lighted on the evening of Divali, a fairyland of gentle lights welcomes the world. This may be a Hindu religious festival but every Trinidadian delights in the evening of flickering lights that cover the land.

One can compare it in the Christian faith to the night of All Saints for the Anglicans and one night later to All Souls for the Catholics. The cemeteries throughout Trinidad are lit with candles on the graves of the departed. Although these are multi-faith cemeteries, few Hindus will have graves there. They opt instead for cremation. There are two sites where this can be done; the banks of the Caroni River by the arterial road to the South and at Mosquito Creek beyond San Fernando, where proper parking facilities have recently been completed. Great pyres of logs are set ablaze while relatives and friends stand by in respect. Even a Christian wishing to be cremated had to use one of these two sites until the 1980s. The Catholic power elite were successful in blocking a crematorium for Port of Spain until the leader of the country, Dr. Eric Williams chose cremation in place of burial in 1981. Hasty arrangements were made for a portable crematorium to be flown in for the ceremony at the old sea plane base at Chaguaramas.

Shortly after, a crematorium was built next to the Long Circular shopping mall, but its active use was delayed for some time after. Cemeteries in Trinidad are as mixed and democratic in their content as most Trinidadian families. Catholics, Jews, Anglican, Moslems and Baptists lie side by side in family graves. To wander between them is a lesson in the ethnic and religious kaleidoscope that is Trinidad.

The other Hindu festival that is celebrated throughout the island outside of Port of Spain is the Spring Festival, Phagwa. The original religious aspects may still be there, but to a non-Hindu observer it seems mainly, like Carnival for the Christians, an excuse for the Indian community to forget their inhibitions and kickup their heels in singing, dancing, drumming, drinking and general abandon, albeit without the sexual overtones asssociated with Carnival. Stages are prepared on village cricket grounds for the singing competitions in which the sporting of Rama and Sita are commemorated. The exotic music is blared out over the countryside roads. The boys sing, wave and scatter a red dye called "abir" over those they pass. It is a noisy, joyous event that unites the Hindu community briefly, and makes the whole of Trinidad aware of the Hindu presence.

The Moslem community is far more restrained. About 90% of them are the main-stream Sunnis who fast during the month of Ramadan and attend the mosque for prayers as required in the Holy Koran. The end of Ramadan, which is determined on the lunar calendar and is accordingly at a different time each year, is marked by Eid ul Fitr, a national holiday just as the Hindu Divali is, in deference to these two religious groups. Although the Moslems had a clearer church hierarchy, they, like the Hindus, suffered problems over the validity of their marriages. It was not until the 1930s that Moslem marriages were recognised by law.

Curiously it is the minority Shiite sect of the Moslems who account for the one Moslem festival that is in the Trinidad tradition of shortlived splendour and extravagance. This is the ten day festival of "Hosein", or "Hosay" pronounced "who say" to mark the martyrdom in 680AD of the prophet Mohammed's grandson, Hosein, in the struggle for the caliphate of

Arabia. Determined, like Ramadan, on the lunar calendar "Hosay" is at a different time each year according to when the twelfth moon of the Moslem year is sighted and the month of Muharram commences.

Queen Victoria gave her formal consent in 1863 for the local observance of "Hosay" and it has been celebrated ever since - not without occasional trouble. Worst was 1884 when the East Indians of Naparima were undeterred by a police proclamation that their procession should not pass through the streets of San Fernando. When the unruly crowd got out of hand, the Riot Act was read. In the ensuing scuffle, twelve people were killed. Today "Hosay" never deteriorates into bad behaviour. Despite the congested crowds, a sense of 'bonhomie' prevails, just as it does on J'ouvert Morning at Carnival time.

Work is done in the backyards of the traditional makers of the twelve-foot high replicas of the tomb in which Hosein was buried, known as "tadjahs." Each is an original ornate masterpiece of tinsel and coloured paper over a wooden frame surmounted by the familiar onion-shaped domes of an Islamic temple. It requires six or eight men to drag the tadjahs slowly along the street through the festival crowd. In former years crescent moons weighing 160 pounds were worn as a headdress five feet high. Blue crescents were for Hosein's brother, Hassan, who, as caliph was poisoned, and red for Hosein who tried unsuccessfully to take his place.

In St. James, the tadjahs only make their appearance on the last two days of the festival. Those responsible for the course of the tadjah make no attempt to decorate themselves with costumed finery. All is concentrated on the tadjah. Four or five such tadjahs make their appearance, each accompanied by its band of tassa drummers. The tadjahs spread out a hundred yards apart so that the whole length of the Western Main Road through St. James to the Cocorite Flyover is filled with celebrants. The tassa drummers beat their clay or wooden drums with their hands or curiously bent wooden sticks, creating unique rhythms unlike those heard in the non-Indian communities of Trinidad. The goatskin of the heavy clay drums must be tight to produce the right tone. Little fires of woodshavings are lit in the gutter as the procession edges along. The tassa drummer squats on his hunkers and holds the skin to the heat of the flames. When it is tight he leaps up to rejoin his fellow drummers. The older men will have large cylindrical wooden drums draped horizontally across the belly. The beat of the drums is accompanied by the chant of devout women behind each tadjah hour after hour into the night.

It is at night that "Hosay" is best seen. Throngs of chatting carefree youngsters, predominantly male, mill about unconcerned with any religious aspect of the procession. Flames from the brief,gutterside fires cast orange shadows on the varicoloured brilliance of the tadjah. The tassa drums never cease, one rhythm followed by another, tired drummers being replaced by others equally skilled. At the end of it all comes anticlimax. The glorious tadjahs are ceremoniously dumped off the bridge into the Maraval River. In other areas where "Hosay" is celebrated they may be cast into the sea or another river. This seeming waste of hundreds of hours of devoted artistry is in fact the spiritual consummation of the religious observance, a sacrifice of the holy tadjah. In return for this sacrifice it is hoped that prayers for recovery from sickness or adversity will be answered.

To the casual spectator unaware of the religious significance, the tadjah lies broken and forlorn on the river bed until the next rain storm sweeps it out to sea. But there is always next year when equally brilliant examples of traditional craftsmanship will be displayed to the admiring crowds.

The crowds that follow these tadjahs are far too large to be the Shiite moslems to whom it has religious meaning. For a hundred years Hindus have joined in, and these days there will be many representatives of the Trinidad potpourri. Only the most devout orthodox Sunni Moslems will steer clear. In the same way Christians and Hindus alike will be invited to Moslem marriages and funerals. At the mosque there will be the customary removal of shoes and the division into separate groups of men and women. Similarly non-Moslem men will be invited to join in the prayer ceremony to bless the opening of a "halal" chicken and chips outlet. Translations into English from the Koran will be provided so that all present can participate.

The "Black Muslims" who achieved worldwide attention with Abu Bakr's attempted coup in 1990 are a more recent off-shoot of the Islamic faith. They have not yet been accepted into the mainstream of the religion. The membership is not exclusively negro; there are Indian "Black Muslims" as well.

At all social events, a visitor to Trinidad cannot help but be impressed at the mingling of coloured skins and ethnic origins. In the same way, there are few indications of barriers between widely varying religions. While it is true that conservative Hindu families may still disown a daughter who marries a negro co-worker and that marriages are strongly preferred between the same religion and racial group, inter-marriage is no longer unusual. The East Indian community was late in integrating into the Trinidad mainstream, but from the Second World War on, marriages with negroes were not rare as can be seen from the number of douglas now in the community.

So far as the Christian community is concerned, which comprises nearly 70% of the nation, each denomination is ethnically intermingled. Apart from those of British origin, the Anglican church has had a pre-dominance of negroes. The Chinese are divided between the Anglicans and the Catholics. Predictably the Catholic church has a complete cross-section from the haughty French creoles to humbler folk of the darkest hue. Both the Anglican and Catholic churches have an increasing number of East Indians in their congregation. But it must be observed that the Hindu community actively resisted conversion to Christianity. Up to 1921, after missionaries had worked for a generation, only 10% of the Hindus had abandoned their faith. Today 24% of the East Indians are Christians of one denomination or another.

The Irish brogue heard even today from Catholic pulpits is being replaced at last with local colour. The present Anglican bishop is a dougla mix of negro and Indian (and has a Japanese wife). The Catholic archibishop comes from a well-known family of predominantly French antecedents, yet one can see at a glance that other racial origins run in his veins.

The Presbyterians got off to a flying start with the Kalleyite

Madeirans, and this was later reinforced by the efforts of the Canadian missionaries in the South and the extensive presence of Scots planters and traders. The Methodists are also well established and enjoy a reputation for liberal enlightenment on controversial areas such as family planning.

From early days the Baptists had a strong foothold in Trinidad. The loyalist negro soldiers who fought in the American war of 1812 for the British against their former American slave owners, were rewarded with grants of land in the villages around Princes Town which still bear the names of the military companies from which they had come. Possibly more than any other Christian denomination, the Baptists vary in their religious pursuits from a fairly conservative church service to the extremes of religious fervour and frenzy.

The Shouter or Spiritual Baptists can often be seen in public places commanding attention to their rites. At Dhein's Bay on the coastal road to Point Cumana, a group of Baptists, predominantly women, will often be seen up to their knees in the sea, their heads wrapped in white turbans, while their pastor, holding a long gilded crook, clad in an impressive gown will be deeper in the waves. The upper section of a cross, embedded in the sand, shows above the waves. Aided by an assistant, he will dunk the faithful into the waves for spiritual regeneration. In the heart of Port of Spain's Independence Square a similar group will hold a service, sounding bells, singing and reading from the scriptures. They will also go to lonely magical grottos like Blue Basin and Maracas Falls to light candles on the rocks and commune with the ancient spirits said to be there.

From all accounts this is tame compared to the scenes within their church at which it is common for members of the congregation to "catch the spirit" passing into a religious trance of shouting, writhing, leaping and frothing. In this approach to Christianity they are similar to other Pentecostal churches who look to the teachings of the Bible which says that spiritual knowledge is to be gained through the "speaking of tongues," the trance-induced state of mind which is central to their worship.

To those who see this manner of religion as too extreme, it

is tempting to ascribe it to the racial background of its negro exponents and say that it is a leftover of the pre-Christian activities on the African continent. Certainly there is a wealth of evidence in such well-documented cases as the Rada community of Belmont, that pure African religion, unadulterated by Christian interference was prevalent in Trinidad during the 19th Century, gradually becoming absorbed in various forms, into the religious fabric.

Which brings us to Shango and Obeah, as voodoo is called in Trinidad. The line between the Christian spiritual cults and those emanating from Africa with only a veneer of Christianity, is a fine one. It is a subject which has been well documented in fascinating studies. After independence in 1962, there was a predictable swing by the African-origin community against European values in favour of what they saw as "African roots." In the process, the progress towards a truly Trinidadian culture was sadly lost. Musically this trend came out in pseudo-African drumming and dance that was more likely to have its origins in Hollywood than Dahomey. In religion there was a new interest in African tribal religion and greater respect for the remnants of African religion that has been kept alive in Shango ritual. The steady influx of Tobagonians, Grenadians and Vincentians also played a role.

Tobago is well known to Trinidadians to be much more a home for obeah. Tobago women are feared for the spells they are reputed to cast on rivals and on their menfolk. With many Tobagonians filtering over the years into Trinidad society, their beliefs and practices have been absorbed with them. In remote country areas like Toco, such beliefs may have been indigenous, but it seems to be mainly through Tobagonians that a healthy respect for obeah remains to this day in Trinidad society. The fact that there were also East Indian obeah men and women did nothing to reduce its influence. Mention is made in another section that in 1978 a young girl was excused from murder of an old lady who she was convinced was a soucouyant. Below the superficial crust of everyday life is a hidden world of spells and fears that is hard to conceive.

Panties or bras are stolen from backyard laundry lines on which to place hexes by rival lovers. It is not uncommon for a person, male or female, young or old, to fall mysteriously ill: When a physician can find no answer, a secret meeting will be made with an obeah woman. Often this woman will accept no payment, but will instruct that certain herbs and medicines be obtained from a pharmacy. A bush bath may be prescribed. Or she may go into a trance and speak through a series of voices. These voices are usually the same four or five persons who seem to lurk near the surface of the subconscious nether world. The voices, competing with one another to be heard, will hopefully indicate the course of action that should be taken. At other times it is the old lady's bush bath which will serve as a remedy. When she wakes she will be unaware of the voices that have spoken through her, although she is aware they are at her call.

Were it not for the reappearance of these same voices through different sources it would be simple to poo-poo the whole business as superstitious nonsense. As it is, even the well-educated reserve a cautious respect for this area of knowledge as yet imperfectly explored. While obeah is primarily African in background, it has pervaded all those who live in rural areas, Indian, Chinese and European. Not many people get directly involved in it, but it would be hard to find a Trinidadian who has not had some indirect experience through a relative or friend.

It is not from the occult or to Afro-Caribbean identity that most Christian denominations are losing their members. As in many parts of the world, it is the energetic singlemindedness of the Mormons, the Seventh Day Adventists and the like that has made the greatest inroads. In the 1980 Census, "Other" denominations (which include Baptists) jumped from 11.1% in 1970 to 16.6% in 1980, the only religious category to make gains. That knock on the door on Sunday morning when you are feeling a little guilty about skipping church and are considering a rum punch picnic at Maracas, will probably be from a pair of Jehovah's Witnesses whose limpet tenacity would credit an Avon salesperson. New churches spring up regularly as the zeal of these churches is reflected in the increase of converts.

One is likely to see two other religions represented by their flambouyantly garbed priest in downtown Port of Spain. The Maronite Syrians fled Lebanon to escape the persecution to which they were being subjected in what was later to become Lebanon at the hands of the Moslem Ottaman Turks. The Syrians have remained conservative in most aspects of their culture including religion, and their bearded priest topped with a hat like that of the Greek orthodox, used to be seen striding from one Syrian shop to another. Inevitably, however, the fathers at St. Mary's College and Fatima College have made inroads even into the Syrian community and a considerable number of Syrians are now devout Catholics. The other flamboyant priest seen more often in the lanes of Belmont will be the archbishop of the Abyssinian church, resplendent in his purple robes garnished with gilt embroidery, ornate mitre on his head and golden crook in his hand useful to ward off stray dogs.

Despite the militancy of the newer sects and the occult undercurrents beneath the surface, it is not surprising that Trinidadians generally tend to be open-minded and less dogmatic about the spiritual side of their existence than people who live in a homogenous society. It is a reflection, certainly, of the pluralistic background of religions in which every Trinidadian finds himself. When black, white, brown and yellow members of the same church are sharing the communion chalice, how can racial bigotry flourish?

*Midday shower on Frederick Street*

# Chapter 6

•◉•

## *Two Seasons*

Lying within sight of the mainland of the South American continent 12 degrees North of the equator, one might assume Trinidad to have an equatorial climate. While the rainy season is clearly marked it is nothing like a monsoon, and the dry season is interspersed with showers. The saving grace in the urban areas of the East West Corridor is the range of wooded hills, the Northern Range, which rise sharply behind. Cool air currents slide down from these hills to cool off the midday high from its normal 86 degrees farenheit (30 degrees Celsius) to a pleasant 73 degrees (23 degrees Celsius) before dawn. A few days a year it will reach the low 90s. In the valleys of the Northern Range it can get down into the 60s which seems so cool that blankets are needed.

One reason it gets no hotter is the cloud coverage of 50%. There are few cloudless days. By midday big billowy clouds will puff up to provide intermittent shade. In the rainy months from June to December those clouds will grow blacker, and a torrential downpour for 20 minutes can be expected during the lunch hour. Office workers have a ready excuse for being late back to work. An umbrella would be little use in such heavy rain. A plastic raincoat would have you dripping wet from the inside in no time, so intense is the humidity. A cold from such a drenching would provide a doctor's certificate for a week's sick leave.

One of the sights of Port of Spain is to stand under one of the many overhanging balconies of ornate 19th Century cast iron on lower Frederick Street during such a downpour. The deep gutters fill with rushing water as the drains contend with the refuse tearing down to the waterfront. Cigarette packages and fruit juice cartons are whisked down the street. Each block is an island surrounded by a 12" deep moat at the kerb. Some try to vault these moats for the higher street centre. High-heeled shoes are removed, skirts lifted and leaps performed. Such heroics often end in mishap. Many a comely young lady has landed on her rear in such circumstances to a barrage of "picong" from bystanders, most of it lewd, much of it crude.

As suddenly as the shower began it stops. The sun will come out like a searchlight and there will be an oppressive humidity. The streets will steam as the heat of the tarmac evaporates the rain. The drains swallow up the detritus of the gutters from all the way to the Savannah. Bystanders will return late to their offices having enjoyed the entertainment of a good "lime". By 4.30 p.m. even the clay tennis courts will have dried off enough for play.

In the middle of the wet season come two or three weeks of dry weather. This is called "petit careme." Usually in September, but sometimes early October, these sunny days provide a welcome change. The hills are at their greenest, the gardens lush with four months' rapid growth.

By Christmas the rainy days start to dwindle, and one wonders if the dry season has arrived. By New Year there are still occasional heavy shows, but the days are windy and the ground soon gets baked dry. Dust swirls along the streets with the usual paper rubbish. It is now that the trees fringing the Savannah and covering the hills behind start their symphony of brilliance. First come the pink and purple poui. Overnight they exchange their leaves for thick blossoms crowding every branch. Within a week the ground below will be carpetted with the fallen blossoms as the new leaves take their place.

Next come the most glorious of all, the yellow poui, an incredible daffodil yellow from the lowest branches to the tip, and not a leaf to compete with the show. Usually each yellow poui will explode into show one at a time. Only above the Botanical Gardens on the ridge of Poui Hill are the poui dense enough to be assured of many trees trumpeting their brazen glory at the same time. Such natural magnificence has to be seen to be believed, like the scarlet of the ibis in the Caroni Swamp. Legend has it that the poui must bloom three times before the arrival of the rainy season. This is yet to be clearly established. The venerable Field Naturalist Club has given its members the task of keeping tabs on the blossoming dates of individual poui. Some will bloom more than once, but few if any, the three times of legend. It is the overnight transformation which provides the drama. That tall, common or garden tree on the corner, never before noticed, suddenly drops its canopy of green to display its daffodil brilliance, just as suddenly reverting to green foliage. In much the same way the Carnival revellers transform themselves for two days in equal splendour.

Poui is only one of many families of flowering trees that don their masquerade each dry season. Outside Port of Spain at the head of Maraval Valley on the way to Maracas, one can see the mighty immortelles towering over the cocoa that they shade with their crown of brilliant coral-orange flowers. The various flowering cassia, yellow, pink, strawberry - can be seen in all Port of Spain suburbs. The brilliant mauve of petrea dances in the dry wind for a few days before reverting to its greyish olive green. The front gardens of older homes that could afford the luxury of the space needed, display the vivid flambouyant whose greedy roots let nothing grow beneath the scarletty orange canopy of flowers.

Frangipani trees look artificial with their scaly angular limbs, but the delicately shaded blossoms from palest yellow to the red-eyed centres are like jewels on the leafless branches.

Menacing 5" striped caterpillars with waving stingers from their tails must be carefully avoided when picking a frangipani flower. Bougainvillea hedges sprouting long spiny branches waving in the wind are at their best in the dry season, their common magenta and purple bracts varying to the rarer white, pink and apricot hybrids. The shorter daylight hours at Christmas trigger off the poinsettia to wear its leaves a velvety scarlet. White poinsettia has the poetic name of snow-on-the-mountain in Jamaica; when the bushes are in dense clusters on a Trinidad hillside they live up to their Jamaican name. Seedlings sprout readily under the bushes, but die in the dryness unless moved into a damper setting.

One after the other the masquerade of flowering trees and shrubs marches through the months from January to May. Gertrude Carmichael's calendar of flowering trees and shrubs lists sixty-four species for special months supplemented by a further thirty-three that bloom throughout the year. Flowers do not prosper as there are voracious parasol ants waiting to slice off the blooms and carry them off to their underground nest to keep the fungus growing on which their young grubs depend. Determined gardeners have to place water-filled anti-formicals around the base of young plants to provide a barrier against crawling insects, but there are still the flying ones to contend with.

Though such insects consume gerbera, zinnia, roses and chrysanthemums it comes as a shock to North American visitors to find that there are no mosquito screens on the windows and doors apart from the oil camp bungalows of the South where such American habits prevailed. In the U.S. the flying insect population proliferates to such an extent in the summer that life without screens would be unbearable (apart from the cities where life is unbearable for the insects). One could justifiably assume that the insect life in Trinidad would be much greater. Possibly their natural enemies are more effective. There are mosquitoes in many areas but the standard solution is to burn a "cock-set", a green coil of incense impregnated with repellant. Cockroaches may come flying into the house to be splattered by a sandal. A dozen moths will flutter round the security lights watched hungrily by the pretty green leaf insect and the ugly "wood slave" lizard which will make a meal of them by morning. Why are there no more? One does not question how nature has been so kind. In an island with so many natural blessings one very soon takes it for granted.

With the winds of the dry season coming more from the north than the usual east, the waves at the beaches on the north coast build up in size. Maracas Beach is fourteen miles from Port of Spain reached along a precipitous and spectacular coastal road along the jungled side of the mountains, and it is by far the most popular. The closer beaches on the Carenage have rather muddy sand and water brackish from the fresh water of the Orinoco River, and often floating with rubbish carried along the coast from Port of Spain. Without a breeze, the sea at Maracas can be as clear and as tranquil as the St. James coast of Barbados. With the northerly, the rolling swells come surging into the deep bay. Lifeguards are busy putting up red flags to mark where an undertow has developed. The breakers are exhilarating to ride by board or with the body all the way up to the beach. Sometimes they build up as a sharp wall that cannot be ridden but must be hurriedly dived through before tons of water crash down and knock the wind out of you. In the rainy season such big waves are rare. More likely the rain showers will calm down the waves. The sea water is so pleasantly warm that the rain feels cold. When a shower sweeps across the bay, as many people will dash into the sea as those who shelter under the eaves of the vendor's huts where smells of bake and shark rise from the charcoal grills - "coalpots", on which they are being cooked. After several days of heavy rains the streams leading into the bay can give the water a brownish cast and it is so unsalty as to be nearly drinkable.

Even in the worst of the rainy season there are crowds at Maracas Beach on a Sunday. During the week it is invariably sparsely occupied. That is the time to walk down the long curving beach to the fishing village at the western end and buy fresh king fish and carite from the fishermen. Despite any downpours the sun will soon return to dry out wet bathing towels, and the temperature will always be in the warm 80s.

To those who live in Port of Spain, going to Maracas holds delightful uncertainty. The weather may be broiling hot in the city, with storm showers on the beach, or vice versa. The waves may be negligible or so intimidating that if you are experienced enough to swim out beyond the breakers, it may be ten minutes before there is a lull in the twelve foot swells to let you beat a hasty retreat to shore. Whatever the weather, the spectacular coastal mountain scenery is worth the drive.

Moonlight picnics at Maracas around a big bonfire to keep the sand flies away and several cuatro players bringing back half-forgotten calypsoes, are an unforgettable experience. Unfortunately the prosperity of the 70s had an unfortunate spinoff of an increase in crime. Back in the bad old days before the oil bonanza, a couple could have a romantic sojourn on the sand unmolested. As in most parts of the world, those days have gone and it is sensible to take no chances of muggers and rapists being around. Should one chance to be at Maracas during a moonless night when the tiny organisms which create phosphorescence are in the water it will be an enchanting sight. The breakers light up as they crash and each tiny bead of water is lit like a pearl.

By the end of May there are occasional rainy days to show that the long dry spell is over. Reservoirs will be low and there will have been a curfew on the watering of lawns. With June the rainy season has arrived. Heavy black clouds pile up during the morning for the midday downpour. There will be several days when the rain will pour without end, as if the heavens have opened after their long rest. The rain comes down so heavily that two inches can fall in an hour. Culverts and drains have become clogged with rubbish and as a result there will be flooding in the valleys where the flow-off is impeded. The Caroni River will overflow its banks and the Indians living in houses raised on wooden or concrete stilts against such flooding will be seen ferrying themselves onto higher land in the flat bottom boats they keep handy.

Within a week the burnt brown of the Northern Range has been transformed into a lush green. The hardy poui seedlings survive the bush fires and put on their delicate green leaves. Lawns that were dusty and bare spring to life and need cutting once a week. The air is cleaned of haze that has hung over the island from the bush fires, and the clarity makes San Fernando Hill, the Montserrat hills and Mount Tamana visible again from Port of Spain's foothills.

Guttering is bent with the weight of water gushing down the galvanised roofs. The plots of the market gardeners are flooded - and price of vegetables skyrockets. From June until the end of August there will be bright hot periods but it will be rare to have a day without at least one torrential shower. One forgets how a few weeks ago the country was parched and everybody complaining about the long dry season. So the year progresses with its two seasons, wet and dry, hot all the time.

*Kiskadee*

# Chapter 7

# *So Many Birds*

Throughout the year you are likely to be awakened each morning by a discordant symphony of birdsong. This may sound like an exaggeration in a country already noisy with barking dogs and hooting traffic; but the refreshing racket made by the birds is remarkable. Trinidad is renowned for its wide variety of species which number approximately 400. (Two dozen are so rarely sighted that their presence is uncertain). In his book on the birds of Trinidad and Tobago, Paul Herklots was able to identify one hundred separate species in his first month on the island, which gives some idea how readily they are seen.

It is likely to be the noisy kiskadee which attracts your attention first. He is a raucous little fellow the size of a starling. His yellow throat and white face striped with a bandit mask of black. Very aggressive about his territory, he is always quarrelling with other invading kiskadees. His name is a corruption of *"qu'est ce qu'il dit?"* which accurately reproduces his strident song.

A much smaller bird but with similar markings of a black mask across his white and yellow front is the sucrier, known more commonly as "siquier" or bananaquit. Both names imply correctly his love of sweet fruit. Hotel guests will initially be amused by the boldness with which they land on the breakfast table on one's balcony to rob sugar from the bowl. In a short time their greedy fearlessness loses its novelty.

Equally keen on sweet fruit, but more selective, is the blue tanager, often called the soursop bird from that predeliction. It takes continual vigilance to pick the horny ripening fruit from the tree before it has been pecked into by a family of these attractive blue-feathered birds.

Visitors are most likely to be fascinated by Trinidad's humming birds. Not for nothing was the island called "Iere", the land of the humming birds by the Amerindians. Only because Jamaica had already pre-empted it for its national crest was Trinidad forced to adopt the resplendent scarlet ibis. (The sister island of Tobago is represented by the cocrico, the noisiest of birds which has been compared to a grouse having hysterics).

Contrary to expectation the hummingbird is not shy, and with fifteen different kinds on the island, they are commonly seen hovering at hedges of hibiscus, sipping the nectar from the vivid blooms. Best of all they favour the long hanging pink flowers of the bottle brush tree, which looks so much like a weeping willow apart from its tasselled flowers. Humming-birds can occasionally be seen at rest on a branch. Small wonder their iridescent plumage of blackish green was used for intricate ritual costumes by the Amerindians before the Spanish conquest.

Less likely to appeal to visitors are the menacing turkey vultures or "corbeaux" as they are always known locally in deference to the dominant French background. Great flocks of them hop obscenely among the debris of the rubbish dump on the Beetham Highway known as the "Labasse." They are equally repulsive at the western corner of Maracas Bay where they gorge on the offal of cleaned fish. Hopping from one scrap to the next, half-extending their five-foot wings for balance as they do so, one forgets the invaluable sanitation service they provide. That bloated carcass of a dog by the edge of the highway is unlikely to be collected by a sanitation truck before the corbeaux have stripped it bare. In fact they were imported by the Spanish to do the scavenging and a substantial fine was imposed on anyone doing them harm.

With such a bird constantly in evidence it was unfortunate that the largest bank on the island should have as its symbol a black spread eagle. Small wonder the local populace would make allusion to the menacing sign complete with red claws and beak as "the corbeau," fitting the common attitude to the predatory nature of banks generally.

Less menacing in appearance is the brown dove whose wobbling walk along pavements and grassy slopes is almost as common as its cousin the European pigeon. Glossy black starlings are equally as prevalent in Trinidad as they are on English lawns.

This cannot be said of the common Amazon parrot, but after stringent gun ownership laws were imposed, their dwindling numbers have reversed. Every evening a flock of twelve is a regular sight returning to lofty Imperial palms around the tennis courts of Tranquility Square with their characteristic panicky flopping flight and raucous screech. Discordant though their voices may be, one cannot forgive the irascible British colonial who tired of being woken at dawn each morning by a flock starting on its daily rounds. He took his shotgun and wiped them out to the horrified anger of his bird-loving compatriots.

Equally distinctive in flight, but a picture of grace by comparison is the yellowtail. His long tail sticks out behind his black body like a surfboard on which he coasts from the high branches of one tree to the next.

Observant visitors will spot what look like coconut shells suspended high in the tops of poui and casuarina trees from a hammock of woven vines two or three feet long. These are the remarkable nests of the showy golden yellow orioles known locally as caciques, the title of Amerindian chieftains. It is fascinating to watch these yellow and black birds laboriously bring strands of grass and weave them into a master-piece of structural engineering that can withstand the strong-est of the dry season winds.

Another unusual sight at the edge of the grassy roadside is the diminutive glossy grossquit. He sits on the road or on a plume of grass in his unmistakable glossy blue black plum-age. You doubt your eyesight when he jumps vertically into the air eighteen or twenty four inches, landing in the exact spot he started from. He gives his song as he jumps as if the song itself propelled him into the air.

Less often seen but easily recognised on a quiet path through the hills, is the toucan, likely to be sitting on a high dead branch. His comically large beak seems out of place with his severe black body, unlike the showy macaws. These can be readily admired in the tall aviary overlooking the main road around the Savannah as one passes the zoo.

Less showy than the macaws but compensating with fine songs are the "picoplat" and the "chickichong." These little birds, with a wide variety of others, are prized as cage birds for the stream of joyous sounds that they produce. It is birds such as these on which large bets are placed in Tunapuna on Sundays to see which songster will outdo his rival within a given time.

The scarlet ibis used to be seen in the Port of Spain zoo, but without the brilliant scarlet plumage of his wild brethren of the Caroni Swamp who can find the little pink crabs which give them their brilliance. We see in another chapter what a pleasing excursion it is to visit the Caroni Bird Sanctuary at sunset only ten minutes from Port of Spain.

No excursion is required to see flocks of snowy white cattle egret on the Grand Savannah. Like many Trinidadians, the cattle egret is an immigrant from Africa, albeit a voluntary and recent one. It is only in the last fifteen years that they have established themselves in new surroundings so readily, and are now a picturesque addition to the local scene.

Separate mention is also made of the World Wildlife Centre at the late Asa Wright's estate house deep in the lush Arima Valley which attracts bird lovers from all over the world. Less well known is the bird sanctuary on the refinery camp at Pointe-a-Pierre. Needing lakes to operate the refinery, one lake was utilised for an impressive collection of water fowl. In the past, visits could be made to the sanctuary by prior arrangement with Texaco's public relations department. Now that Government has acquired Texaco's assets, including the wildlife, it is possible that the public will have readier access to the little known preserve.

There is one bird that only those walking in the deep woods of the northern range will hear, but not see. This is the anvil bird. In the still of the forested trail the metallic sound of a hammer beaten on an anvil rings out. The peculiar acoustics of his call give it a ventriloquial effect which makes it impossible to tell from which direction the sound came. Great patience while hiding still in the undergrowth with sandflies savouring your blood would be required to see this mysterious bird. He is not much to look at anyway, to judge by his portrait in bird books. He is better left a bird of mystery.

Ornithologists know of Trinidad's rewarding store of birds and go there just for that purpose, but even the casual visitor will be impressed with the number of birds seen and heard. Only during the two dusty windswept days of Carnival do the birds fade into obscurity as the local populace dons its competing finery.

*Picong at the Crease*

# Chapter 8

# *More than Calypso Cricket*

To the sporting world, the West Indies is synonymous with the brightest in cricket. Their adventurous batting style, often referred to as "calypso cricket", seems a reflection of the relaxed, almost abandoned mood which creates calypso music. As the birthplace and chief exponent of calypso, Trinidad cannot claim equivalent pre-eminence on the Caribbean cricketing scene, although they have always contributed a fair share of the test sides.

Learie Constantine is undoubtedly the finest all-rounder that Trinidad ever produced and is considered the only man who would win a place on a team of the all-time greats on the basis of his fielding alone. He was born to pure negro middle class parents into the cricketing aristocracy. His father was the first West Indian to make a century at Lords on the maiden tour of 1900. Uncles on both sides of his family nurtured his natural talent. Despite a curtailed education, Learie's popularity as a world class cricketer caused him to be chosen as the first chairman of the General Council of Eric Williams' victorious PNM. He stood successfully as a member for Tunapuna, served as Minister of Works, and was subsequently made High Commissioner to the United Kingdom. After withdrawing from politics, he stayed in England where he qualified as a barrister late in life. He was one of the first members of the three-man British Race Relations Board, became a Governor of the BBC, Rector of St. Andrews University and finally the first negro member of the House of Lords as Lord Constantine of Nelson (Duchy of Lancaster, not of the Five Islands). Perhaps he, more than any other black man, proved to the English and the white world that colour of skin had nothing to do with excellence in gentlemen's sport or nobility of spirit.

The patrician Jeffrey Stollmeyer was a more expected product of European creole moneyed privilege. His grandfather had built "Killarney", the northernmost of the Magnificent Seven residences on the Savannah usually called "Stollmeyer's Castle." It was Jeffrey's uncle who inherited it, leaving him to be brought up in the idyllic Santa Cruz Valley on the family cocoa estates he was later to manage. Jeffrey and his brother, Victor, who became a leading solicitor, made their test debut together as teenagers in the final test before the 1939-1945 World War. Although Victor did well with an innings of 96 he was not selected again, possibly because he had run out his captain in the course of making his score. Jeffrey however became the elegant opening batsman of the post-war team in 32 test matches, and led it as captain for fourteen test matches from 1953 to 1955. His graceful drives and leg glides were universally admired. Jeffrey was a sufficiently well-rounded athelete to have represented Trinidad at soccer from 1943 to 1946.

His contemporary, the stalwart Gerry Gomez represented the West Indies in twenty-nine matches before becoming director of a leading sports goods firm, and a hard worker in a wide number of other sporting associations. Andy Ganteaume, from one of the oldest French creole families was less lucky as a test cricketer. He made 112 runs in his maiden test inning, substituting as opening test batsman for Jeffrey

Stollmeyer who was ill. His century took four and three quarter hours which apparently did not reflect the lively approach expected of a calypso cricketer as he was not picked again. His solitary innings leaves him with the highest test average by any West Indies batsman.

From an entirely different background was little Sonny Ramadhin, the first East Indian cricketer to be selected from his rural village for the West Indies squad. He and the equally modest Valentine from Jamaica mesmerised British and Australian batsmen with endless bouts of superb spin bowling. Ramadhin played on forty-three test sides.

The only Trinidadian to exceed this figure was Dereck Murray who kept wicket for the West Indies team for forty-nine test matches starting in 1963, setting many records in the process. Bernard Julien, an attractive all-rounder, figured in twenty-four test sides but later disgraced his colleagues by accepting a lucrative contract to play in South Africa, thereby debarring himself from further Caribbean cricket.

Other Trinidadian test names familiar in the cricketing world are Raffick Jumadeen and Inshan Ali. The Queens Park Oval was represented by Larry Gomes, Charlie Davis, Joey Carew and Willie Rodriguez. Today it is little Gus Logie, Ian Bishop and Brian Lara who represent Trinidad on the West Indies team.

Trinidad has not produced a never-ending supply of fast bowlers like Barbados, and this seems to reflect the differing social geography of the island. Cricket in Port of Spain is centred around the Queen's Park Oval where club, regional and test matches are played, and a handful of other sporting social clubs whose membership is certain to reflect the whole cross-section of ethnic variety.

Out in the countryside every village has its cricket pitch, and the local community is likely to be predominantly Indian. As a result Trinidad produces from such grass roots origins the skilled spin bowlers. Barbados and the Leeward Islands in contrast, where the population is 90% negro, has cricketers of a physique able to excel in the pace attack.

The alternative venue for test or Shell Shield regional

matches to the Port of Spain Oval, is Guaracara Park on the former Texaco refinery at Pointe-a-Pierre. It does not compare in its capacity nor beauty to the Oval whose massive samaan trees are backed by the splendour of the hills rising behind them. It is in the members' stand of the Queens Park Oval that the full flavour of Trinidad "picong" can be appreciated in its full zest. Very possibly the witticisms and criticisms from among the audience will provide more entertainment than the field of play.

The Oval has a large membership and even when sports are not being played, the bar along the back of the members' stand will be thick with members each evening. They have a well-deserved reputation for being staunch "groggists" which must contribute to the ready flow of "ole' talk."

Very often there will be soccer matches to watch on the field below. The cricket pitch gives way to soccer during the long rainy season. Until the construction of the Jean Pierre Sports Complex not far away on the other side of Woodbrook, the Oval was the only soccer pitch which could hold a large crowd.

In recent years soccer has attracted an even more enthusiastic following than cricket, a phenomenon which will probably come as a surprise to those outside the West Indies. Starting with a high level of inter-collegiate competition, the national youth team and senior national squad arouse great interest in playing the other national teams of the Caribbean circuit from Surinam to Guatemala. An increasing number of Trinidadian stars are winning contracts to U.K., much as cricket stars have joined the county teams in the U.K. While cricket is still very popular and Trinidad emerged victors in the 1984/85 Shell Shield Championship, the fact that less prestigious schools like Belmont Secondary can produce a winning soccer team creates strong popular appeal with the mass of sports enthusiasts. Unlike cricket where patient discipline is required, a soccer star can rely on his natural talent and a strong pair of legs.

The twenty eight cricket pitches on the Grand Savannah during the dry season are transformed into a dozen soccer pitches when the rains come. There is even room for two rugger pitches with a third available behind the President's mansion at La Fantasie Gardens. Rugger is likely to attract those who have played it while studying abroad. For that reason it is not a sport with mass appeal like soccer. Trinidad does well against its old rival, Guyana, in the Macgregor Cup. Martinique and Barbados also field national rugger teams to keep alive national rivalries in the Caribbean. Both soccer and rugger have the advantage over cricket that a match can be played after work from 4.30 to 6.00 before it gets dark, as the rainy season is during the summer months. Requiring a longer time span and without the long evenings of a British summer, cricket matches are restricted to weekends.

Field hockey is another wet season sport that is enthusiastically played in the Port of Spain area by both men and women   players. The St. James Barracks ground is used exclusively for hockey, while that at La Fantasie Gardens is shared with rugger. Whether or not a male bystander enjoys field hockey for its own merits, he will be hard put to walk away from the lithe rounded hips and buttocks clad in the briefest of snug shorts worn by the girls.

Blessed with a warm climate the year round, there is no winter lay off. Only at Carnival time does interest in sporting activity abate. Even during the height of the rainy season, lawn tennis is likely to be played on the venerable clay courts of Tranquillity Square Lawn Tennis Club, founded 1884. Rain may stop play on the lightning fast hard courts adjacent to the members' stand at the Oval. Tennis is no longer restricted to private members' clubs. Public courts in Port of Spain and San Fernando facilitate widespread participation, and tennis is now taught in public schools. If Trinidad and Tobago has not done as well in recent years as it did formerly in the Brandon Trophy championship between countries of the English-speaking Caribbean, it is more due to an increase in the standard of other areas than any slackening of interest in Trinidad and Tobago whence many boys and girls win tennis scholarships to colleges in the United States.

Tennis has happily lost any elitist image it once had, but this cannot be said of squash. The limited number of courts (air conditioned except for those at Pointe-a-Pierre) limits play to a small coterie in the upper incomes.

With ready access to beaches, one expects Trinidad to be an

island of swimmers. Swimming never flourished as a competitive sport because there were few pools of suitable length. Apart from the annual Port of Spain cross harbour swim, organised swimming was ignored until suitable pools were built in the 70s and 80s. The latent talent of youngsters who were likely to spend every weekend in the water has been developed with respectable success in international swim meets.

Hasely Crawford achieved Trinidad and Tobago's greatest international acclaim when he won the 100-metre sprint at the Montreal Olympics of 1976. Silver medals had been won in the 440 yards by Wendell Mottley, later to become a minister in George Chambers' government and by the nation's 4 by 440 relay team. There has been a steady flow of secondary school athletes to the colleges of North America on athletic scholarship. The biennial Southern Games at Texaco's Guaracara Park and the Tesoro Games, sponsored by that oil company, have maintained a high standard for so small a nation, attracting top-flight American contestants besides Trinidadians abroad on scholarship.

Also attracting contestants from overseas is the sport of cycling. Italians, Venezuelans, British and French commonly compete in the main road race events and in the Arima velodrome. The heat of midday can make one forget how cool the dawn is. It is then the cyclists are training on the Hochoy Highway or down on the quiet roads of the former U.S. Navy base at Chaguaramas. Trinidad produced from creole European stock, a Pan American Games gold medallist in Roger Gibbon. For many years he was referred to as the Golden Boy of cycling; today his endeavours are as a corporate executive, and it is Gene Samuel who stars at cycling.

Golf is a sport where one would correctly expect those of mainly European origin to predominate. It is the youngsters whose parents enjoyed membership of St. Andrews Club in Port of Spain and the oil camp courses of Pointe-a-Pierre and Point Fortin that bloomed into the nation's top golfers in later years and represented their country in the Caribbean Hoerman Cup. Former caddies, turned professional are now giving them a run for their money in national contests after the U.S. Navy Base course at Chaguaramas was opened to the public.

Sailing is another sport which requires a high income base

to provide the best in equipment. There was a small sailing club at Point-a-Pierre, but with the prosperity of the 1980s, class boats and larger cruisers grew in number at the Trinidad Yachting Association. During the windy dry season Mirror dinghies, International 14s, Flying Dutchmen and Lasers flit around a course between the Five Islands and the mainland. Cruisers go further afield to the Venezuelan oil rigs for an overnight race. Traditional highlight of the racing season is the President's Cup when all classes of boats compete over the same course and Lasers will very likely win in light breezes. The Easter Race for cruisers is customarily across the 80 miles of open sea to Grenada. During the years of political uncertainty in Grenada, Tobago was used as an alternative objective, but unsuccessfully as one has to beat all the way against the strong current.

It is to Tobago that the powerful motorboats race on their annual Great Race. If the waters of the north coast are choppy as they often are, the race is more likely to be one of endurance than speed. All too often the boats which have excelled in calm waters in the Gulf of Paria, break down on the Tobago course. Media coverage of the event is thorough, down to scenes of rum punch and bikini revelry on the beach at Store Bay when the race is over. Small wonder that Tobagonians dread this annual invasion of their customary solitude, so different a people are they in every way.

Among the more sedentary sports, Bert Manhin single-handedly kept the Trinidad flag flying in international pistol competitions. Bridge has its following, as does chess among the serious-minded. More popular along these lines are draughts played with ebullient gusto by taxi drivers waiting for a fare, and "all fours", the populist equivalent among card games. To a bystander unfamiliar with all fours, the noisy bravado as the cards are slapped down, and the (legitimate) signalling between partners make a colourful spectacle. Of all card games it comes closest to being a spectator sport.

In one sport in particular Trinidad and Tobago stands equal with the world's best. Not surprisingly this implies a sport that not many countries play. Because of its British heritage, the girl's sport of netball is well entrenched in public schools. With superb muscular physiques, tall negro girls are at no disadvantage playing against teams from England, Australia and New Zealand. It was largely because they were hosts to the International Netball Championship in 1982 that the sport complex was built at Mucurapo Lands. The complex was then named after Jean Pierre who led the national team to a shared world championship.

With the Jean Pierre Complex, Trinidad has a facility in which all sports and contests can be held. Apart from mass functions like soul and pop concerts, steelband competitions and the like, other sporting spectacles like boxing can be staged. Boxing enjoyed a sudden surge of interest when Claude Noel won the WBA world championship, albeit for only a brief period. If he had held his title longer he might have had a BWIA plane christened after him like Hasely Crawford, and Penny Commissiong, Miss Universe 1977. As it was, a stretch of highway in his native Tobago bears his name instead.

Small wonder that Trinidadians should be a nation of sportsmen and women who take full advantage of a warm climate the year round and generous facilities. We have seen what a wide range of sports are available to them, and the result can be seen in their curvaceous figures on all the beaches and at social events. By many a nation's standard, the intake of alcohol will seem high by the average Trini (if there is such a person) but their "joie de vivre" and energetic pursuit of pleasure, sporting and social, gives them a spirited anima-tion in which alcohol plays little part. Even those who prefer their sports by proxy, have the widely popular sport of horse racing available to them.

There is one criticism often levied at Trinidadians in sport, in art and nearly every field. They are accused of relying too much on their God-given talents and failing to apply themselves with prolonged application to any discipline. "Life too short for that, man!" And so with carefree ease, they excuse their failure where more was expected of them, and look for a handy scapegoat.

*Swizzling Callaloo*

# Chapter 9

# *Callaloo Cuisine*

The multiplicity of ethnic backgrounds of Trinidad lead one to expect the food of the island to show unusual diversity in its preparation. While this has not resulted in a gourmet spread of internationally renowned delicacies, cuisine in Trinidad has a number of highlights and unusual variety.

Before the days of refrigerated cargo ships, meat was imported pickled in barrels or salted. Wild game shot locally was a delicacy, but one that also required long hours of stewing and heavy seasoning. Even though the word "barbecue" is one of the few (with "hammock") which the Caribbean has given to the English language, this form of cooking was not a traditional one in homes. If it is now popular, it is from the post-war American cultural influence. The buccaneers got their name from cooking on a "boucan", an open hearth where game was roasted or dried on a spit. Grilled meat is rare in Trinidad homes compared to stewed meat cooked in the heavy metal stew-pot.

So too did the lack of fresh or frozen vegetables in the days of schooners cause the West Indian diet generally to veer to the easily stored but starchy "ground provision." The root crops - dasheen, cassava, tannia, eddoes, diminutive "topi tamboo", sweet potatoes, yams (different in the West Indies from sweet potatoes) are supplemented with starchy plantain (to all appearances an oversize unripe banana) and green "figs" as bananas are mysteriously called. There are also breadfruit and chataigne,which is known elsewhere in the Caribbean as "bread nut." We all know that Captain Bligh of *Mutiny on the Bounty* fame brought breadfruit to the Caribbean as a cheap food for plantation slaves. It is similarly supposed that the other starchy vegetables became ingrained as a part of the negro diet because it was cheap. Now that Irish potatoes are readily imported more cheaply than any local ground provisions can be marketed, they have also become entrenched as part of the Trinidad diet. Popular though rice remains, Trinidadians apart from the East Indians eat as much or more potatoes than rice.

If these starches are not enough, macaroni pie is commonly served on the same platter with rice and three other starchy vegetables. Small wonder that dieticians deplore the low intake of green vegetables and roughage, while doctors contend with widespread digestive problems. Slavery is long gone and many who would be hard put to find a slave ancestor have stubbornly adopted this starchy diet.

The one green vegetable a Trinidadian will get enough of is the leafy section of dasheen. This is the main component of "callaloo," one of Trinidad's culinary stars. It is a dark green soup to which ochroes and a variety of other ingredients will be added, depending on the individual family recipe. Garlic, of course, will be there, just as it is in almost every dish. Some callaloo will sport crab claws and coconut for flavour, others ham bone or pig's tail. Every household has its own variations and what is available is used. Callaloo is so thick as to be almost a stew and can be served on a flat plate on rice. Because it can be made with so many different ingredients the word "callaloo" is used to describe people of diverse ethnic origins.

"She part Chinee, part Indian, with a Portugee mother -

a real callaloo."

Non-starchy vegetables are there for the asking. Huge succulent pumpkin is boiled with ground provisions. The spiky christophene needs a stuffing of cheese to give its marrow-like flesh some flavour. Tomatoes, cucumbers and "sweet peppers" will be served with water cress and a leaf of lettuce as a "salade." But it is mainly the vegetarian Hindu section of the community which buys spinach called "bhaji," salad beans, bitter wrinkled squash called "caraili" and a variety of other esoteric greens. Ochroes, melongene (as eggplant is called) are widely used in the concoction of stews and casseroles, as is the turnip-like white radish which can equally be used like its smaller red namesake in mixed salads. Korean sailors off the deep-sea trawlers take basket loads of these white radish back to their vessels. Another vegetable of oriental origin popular with all groups of the community is "pakchoi", the elongated Chinese cabbage with pearly white stems. Good quality cabbage is now grown by Trinidad's market gardeners. Local carrots are also grown but are a long way from the elegant long-legged beauties still imported from Canada to supplement local production.

Because the meat is stewed for long hours, a high grade beef or veal grained with fat, is not used. Lower grade hard lean cuts are preferred which would be tough unless cooked to near disintegration. Fresh local beef is available in the market, the slaughter supervised by a Muslim imam to certify the meat as "halal" (killed in the manner prescribed in Islamic law) for the faithful. Hanging techniques are rudimentary and as a result local beef is not yet aged to best advantage.

Pork is excellent in Trinidad, much of it coming from the sister island of Tobago. A blood sausage called "black pudding" is made from hog's blood and onions, highly seasoned. This is a popular meal, particularly when served in a fresh hops bread. The fortunes of pig farmers have varied widely in the past as we see elsewhere. Profits have depended on the subsidy of imported feed grain and the fixed price for the end product. Volume of production oscillates crazily from near dearth, creating black market premiums, to overproduction when new farmers or backyard raisers jump on the bandwagon to benefit from high prices.

The same has been true of the poultry industry. Chicken was traditionally a festive treat, reserved for Sunday with the callaloo. Local production became so efficient, and with subsidies all along the path of production from feed, to growing, to processing, profits were assured. Chicken became the cheapest meat available making possible the boom in chicken-and-chips parlours. To reduce the subsidies to the poultry industry became a highly sensitive political issue in the 1980s, by which time the nation had grown accustomed to seeing chicken often on the plate.

No such safeguards applied to fish. Fishermen raised prices to whatever the market would bear. The commonly eaten carite and kingfish tripled in price during the oil boom, as did all the other choice fish - cavalli, grouper, red fish and even shark. This last is very tasty at any time but especially so in the wee hours of the morning when fried and served in a piping hot "bake," or better still on Sunday morning at Maracas Beach. Shrimp, too, used to be available at modest prices except for the choice oversize ones. The shrimp industry became an important export earner to Trinidad until the Venezuelan authorities got difficult with the Cedros fishermen for poaching in their waters. International trawler fleets stripped the brackish coastal waters clean off the Guyana and Brazil coast.

We speak later of the delectable tree-oysters served around the Savannah. No chip-chip from the beaches of Mayaro find their way to Port of Spain. Only those who sieve the diminutive shellfish from the wet sand and make stew at their beach house will savour them. Mussels abound at the mouth of the Nariva River, but it was an Italian restauranteur who first took the initiative in the 1960s to serve them. Blue crab has always been popular because of the contribution they make to callaloo. Equally succulent when curried, they are sold at the roadside trussed in bundles. Popular, too, is the meat of the giant turtles which come each year to lay their eggs on Trinidad's northern and eastern beaches. Conservation groups patrol to prevent their slaughter by hunters too ignorant to let them lay their eggs first. That turtle meat is no longer available from the bloody counters of Beetham Market, can be taken as a sign that the turtles may be saved from extinction.

Hardly a fish in appearance, the esteemed cascadura holds a special place in the folk lore of Trinidad. Taste this ugly little fish once and you will return to lay your bones in Trinidad, we are told. Yet it is not easy for a visitor to put this fable to the test. Cascadura is not a restaurant dish. It is served at private homes by those who have access to a supply. Some keep the scaly lizard-like fish in drums of water outside the kitchen door until they are ready for the pot, probably in a spicy curry. These fresh-water fish have the ability to survive through the dry season under the caked mud until the rains return. They are troublesome to eat. Bones and scales must be sucked individually to get the meagre flesh. A knife and fork have no place here.

Just as beef used to reach Trinidad salted, so did fish. Salt-fish has a strong flavour and this has caused it to remain a part of Trinidad diet, even though imported frozen fish was available in supermarkets to supplement local catches. Salt-fish pie is almost as common as macaroni pie. Other tasty dishes like "buljol," a stew of salt fish with tomatoes and onions and "accra" which combines a fried floury batter with shredded saltfish keep alive a taste for the tangy fish. It is not due to the predominance of Catholics that fish plays so large a part in local dishes. Along with all the Latin American colonies, Trinidad was excluded by papal decree from Friday fish days. The conquistadores had to keep their strength up with meat so as to be able to impose Christianity on the New World's reluctant pagans.

Spanish colonial dishes still form an important part of the menus of local meals. "Sanscoche" is the gallicised version of what is the Caribbean version of Spanish "sancocho," a stew of salt beef, ground provisions, ochroes and other local vegetables. The little fried meat pies, "arepas," can be found in identical form in Venezuela, as can "pastelles" served mainly during the Christmas season. These cornmeal pancakes are folded around highly seasoned ground meats, olives, capers and raisins. They are then individually wrapped in a banana leaf and tied with fine twine until they are boiled piping hot for serving. With so much work involved, it is small wonder that most households nowadays buy them ready-made from a professional caterer.

Many Trinidadians are convinced that "pelau", their favourite food at fetes, is a local invention little known elsewhere. It is, of course, only a local version of the same dish as the Persian or Turkish pilaff known throughout most of the Mediterranean and corrupted in Spain to "paella." Rice and pigeon peas are stewed up with meats and much seasoning to make a tasty dish whether served hot, or more commonly, tepid from the deep pan to the succession of hungry feters.

Pepper sauce is added to pelau as it is to most Trinidad dishes to give the already highly seasoned food a lightning bolt of searing flavour. Those unaccustomed to its heat are likely to cough and choke on even the tiny dab added to food. Hardened palates require a generous dollop to get the same effect. In such cases it is questionable whether the flavour of the food can still be discerned. Pepper sauce is common to the British West Indies but in other islands a more temperate version is usually served. Should you go to market in sandals and crush one of the little yellow peppers underfoot, the juice will raise blisters on your foot. Rubber gloves are worn while making pepper sauce, and woe betide should even a tiny portion go in your eye. The home-made brands are invariably the hottest, but even the many commercial versions must be treated with respect. Also popular as a party dish, particularly for Sunday morning rum punch parties, is "souse," pig's trotters or head are marinated overnight in lime juice, onions, cucumber and peppers, hot and sweet. The flavour is delicious but the chewing a gristly matter.

From the earliest days corn meal played a part in many dishes when the colonists found that corn grew readily. Coocoo is a starchy pudding of corn meal and ochroes; dumplings made of corn meal, cassava or wheat flour are added to many dishes. (If it were not for the very active sporting and social lives, all these starches would give Trinidadians an ungainly corpulence).

It is from the Indian community that the more exotic side of culinary fare emanates. Many dishes have been absorbed into the national cuisine; others are found only on festive occasions like marriages in Indian homes where original traditions have been retained. "Roti" is a local form of the Indian chapati, a pancake of wheat flour cooked on the flat iron "towah" placed over a charcoal-burning "coalpot" or gas burner. A flat wooden spatula pats it flat and flips it to cook on the reverse. Deftly folded with curried potato, beef, chicken goat, liver or shrimp inside, this forms a common meal from roadside and parlour vendors to all Trinidadians. The best version of it is "dhalpuri" roti where seasoned ground split peas are sandwiched between the thin layers of dough. Watching roti being made and cooked fresh plays a big part in enjoying it.

There are other forms of roti such as "paratha" more popularly called "bust up shirt." Instead of a neat round pancake, paratha is shredded into a jumble and taken from the serving bowl in fingers onto one's plate to sop up all the succulent gravies.

The same split peas used in dhalpuri are used to make "dhal", a thick soup usually served over rice. Little fried dumplings called "phoulari" are made from ground split peas as are "barral," "bara" and "sahina." In the latter the split peas are sandwiched between layers of spinach leaves and fried a golden brown. A variety of this made with melongene, as eggplant is known, is called "birgane."

One of the most popular snacks is "doubles" comprised of two bara (thin fried bakes) sandwiching two spoonfuls of ground channa with pepper sauce or chutney for flavouring. According to research by the TV programme "Gayelle", an Indian vendor used to sell them on Independence Square in the 1950s. People used to ask for "two bara with channa" but shortened this to "doubles" for convenience. They are now popularly being called "channaburgers".

One popular food which will not melt in the mouth is "channa." Whole or split chickpeas are roasted with pepper sauce making an appetiser so crunchy that one fears for one's teeth.

Curries are enjoyed by the whole community, Indians and non-Indians alike, even though the Indians make them a speciality. Curried goat and curried mango are favourites beside the more common curried beef, lamb or shrimp. With pepper sauce inflaming so many dishes one would expect to find curries fiery hot. In fact it is only by choice that this is so; the curry is only moderately hot but pepper sauce is often added.

With all the starchy vegetables and dumplings, boiled and fried it is still a pleasure to sink one's teeth through the brittle crust of a large bread roll called a "hops bread" into the feather-light interior. These rolls are made from specially imported high gluten flour. Good hops make a bakery's reputation. Queues form to buy a quart of hops, piping hot from the ovens. Hops appear to be one of the few culinary specialties in which the French played a part. With such a strong French cultural influence otherwise, it is strange that food in Trinidad is distant from French cuisine. The Spanish love of onions and tomatoes on food even of a delicate flavour is there with a vengeance.

We have observed elsewhere that many of the restaurants are run by Chinese to the extent that Chinese food is national in acceptance. Trinidadians have their main meal at lunchtime and they are more than likely to "eat Chinese." Little Chinese food is prepared at home in consequence. That would be too much of a good thing. Another minority group, the Syrians, have their own groceries where pine nuts and other special ingredients can be found. They stuff the grape leaves from front yard vines with minced lamb, but keeping to themselves so much, have contributed nothing to the mainstream of Trinidad cooking, apart, perhaps from "gyros" which are Middle Eastern in origin but came to Trinidad from North American fast food outlets after they had proved popular there.

One imagines the tropics to be filled with a profusion of succulent and varied fruits. The variety readily available is not as great as in temperate climes. The orange and grapefruit are supplemented by the little "portugal," an easily peeled tangerine. Pineapples are grown, but are small in size. The water of coconuts is widely drunk for its beneficial effect on the kidneys and grated coconut is an ingredient in many dishes. Bananas come in a wide variety from the large "gros michel" to the tiny and succulent "siquier" (originally "sucrier" like the fruit-loving bird). Pawpaw grows locally with difficulty on account of blight, but imported pawpaw from other islands is always available. Watermelons have no trouble in growing in the Nariva swamp area. In season they are piled along the roadside where vendors will try and persuade you that theirs are the sweetest.

Mangoes are the highlight of Trinidad fruit. They come in scores of varieties from the bulbous "Graham" with thick, firm peach-like flesh to the fibrous little hog mango. Folk songs and calypsoes recite lists of mango types - "rose" best for chutney, "calabash" to fill you, "vert," "starch," "cutlass," "long", "doodoo" all have their followers. But the universal favourite is the "julie" when it is in season.

Other fruit can be bought less readily. The rough-skinned sapodilla has a caramel brown flesh to match its flavour and three glossy black seeds. Guava has the strongest bouquet of any fruit. It grows wild on the hillsides and must be picked when turning from green to yellow before the birds or insects reach it. It is best served as a stew or jam, a delicious nectar or made into the popular guava "cheese." Strangely distorted and bulbous fruit with spikes will provide a refreshingly different punch or ice cream. This is the soursop so beloved by the blue tanager that he is known as the soursop bird. Pommerac trees bear profusely; relatives with a tree are glad to give away sackfuls of the bright red fruit with sweet flesh as white as cotton wool. The blossoms of this tall tree forms a carpet of strawberry pink beneath its branches. Sugar apples flourish on the islands of the Bocas. The fruit is a cluster of sugary seed pods, greyish green on the surface, but white inside.

Other fruit such as the pommecythere (pronounced "pommsittay"), star apple, cashew, nutmeg, caimet, chenette, balata, tonka, piwa, governor plum, sweet sop, Barbados cherry, gri gri, grou grou boef are rarely for sale and are found chiefly on the tables of those who have a tree in their garden. The cashew and nutmeg are prized for their nuts, as was the tonka until it was banned for use as a food flavouring.

A queen among fruit, but served as a vegetable or salad is the avocado. The most prized variety is the elongated Pollock. To those in Europe who cut into a force-ripened avocado of waxy consistency and little flavour, the succulence of a tree-ripened fruit cannot be imagined. It is so tender that it can be spread on bread like butter, and was indeed known to the French colonists as "faux beurre."

The local cuisine of Trinidad would not be complete without mention of its distinctive beverages. Ginger beer is home-brewed by most households from the readily grown knobby tuber for Christmas. Sorrel is also available only at Christmastime. The bright red blossoms from this low bush are stripped from their central pod to be steeped in boiling water with clove and cinnamon before being drained and sweetened. The result is a glorious ruby nectar of unique flavour. Less likely to appeal at first taste is mauby, a bitter almost medicinal drink, infused from the bark of *colubrina aborescens*. This tree does not grow in Trinidad, but its bark has long been imported from islands to the north by the "marchands", vendors plying the islands on schooners. Once the taste is acquired nothing quenches the thirst more effectively. Ponche creme is another Christmas libation, a potent rum eggnog made with condensed milk.

The whole Caribbean is renowned for its rum, but the excellent rums of Trinidad are less known than those of Jamaica and Barbados, which are better marketed abroad. To most Trinidadians a beer is a "Carib" based by Danish brewers on "Tuborg", although Heineken, Guinness and Stag are well brewed locally and have their following. Only recently have the brewers of Carib been able to outpace local demand to find a footing on the international market. Trinidad "wine" is made artfully from grapefruit, bananas, pumpkin and rice to provide a cheap access to temporary euphoria. "Charlie's Red" was long the workingman's chaser for a neat overproof rum.

Here then is the gamut of local food, fruit and drink in all its variety. A visitor will be fortunate to sample a fraction of what has been described. Seasonal availability will account for part of this, but also the failure of hotel restaurants to provide more than a few token local dishes like callaloo and fried plantain. Fast-food convenience makes it hard everywhere to keep alive the old time-consuming culinary traditions that live on in fewer and fewer private homes. Tasty creole dishes like cowheel soup were always to be found in unprepossessing eating places on Henry and Park Streets in Port of Spain, but they would be discovered by only the most enterprising visitors. The diverse clientele of the Breakfast Shed on South Quay swear that it is the culinary Mecca of Trinidad, but prefer to let it remain little recognised as such.

Petrodollar prosperity gave Trinidadians a taste for the juicy steaks of Miami. Tenderloin and rib-eye steaks filled the freezer cabinets of supermarkets. Now that those days of extravagance are past, there has been an upsurge of fashionable creole restaurants. "Le Cocrico" was one of the first to offer superb cuisine of this type, but it did not survive. Over a hundred restaurants are listed in the Yellow Pages. At the risk of unfairly omitting some equally deserving names, the following restaurants come to mind in Port of Spain: Back Yard, Cafe Savannah, Cascadoo, Chateau Creole, Cocoa House, Lagniappe, Monsoon, Rafters, Shay Shay Tien, Singho and Veni Mange. In San Fernando, Soong's Great Wall and Horace's could never be omitted from a shortlist of the best. Despite the wide variety of restaurants available, there are still those who would maintain that when it comes to eating, the diverse side-walk snacks are hard to beat.

*"The University of Woodford Square"*

# Chapter 10

──────●•◉•●──────

# A Word on Politics

With such a complex background of ethnic origins and religions, Trinidad's politics could be expected to be equally splintered into factions. Fortunately this is not the case. Trinidad would seem the least likely place for a one-party system, but this is what in effect evolved. A political stability has resulted which has given confidence to foreign investors.

*Background*

In 1956 the racially mixed government of Albert Gomes, too long associated with the colonial masters, was thrown out by the electorate in favour of the newly formed People's National Movement led by Dr. Eric Williams. Williams had made a name in political science at Oxford University and Howard University, Washington, D.C. He subsequently served with distinction on the Caribbean Commission until he was summarily dismissed for no clear reason. This injustice provoked his sense of destiny to be his nation's leader. He offered the people a respectability that the rabble-rousing Uriah Butler would never achieve. Around him Williams gathered dedicated supporters like the experienced Dr. Patrick Solomon, southerners Dr. Winston Mahabir and Gerard Montano, young A.N.R. Robinson from Tobago and the influential Moslem Mohammed brothers, Kamaluddin and Sham. Apart from the sugar-belt Hindu Indians, this represented a good cross-section of the community, even though it was clearly dominated by middle class negro attributes.

Dr. Williams was a witty speaker with a pedantic academic style. Statistics were listed in numerical sequence giving an air of schoolmasterly authority to an electorate long accustomed to being told what to do. This was part of the "colonial heritage" which was trotted out as a scapegoat whenever the failings of Trinidadian temperament required rationalisation.

From 1960 onwards Eric Williams widened his political base at the grass roots level. In time his supporters also became known for their wide base, the "Fat Arse Brigade" of mainly negro matriarchs who revered the undemagogic and austere negro academic. The negro-dominated unions of the Port Authority, Telephone Company and Civil Service Authority were also solidly behind him.

Lined up against Dr. Williams' astute political manoeuvres were those who feared negro domination of the country, the professional and rural Indian classes led by Dr. Rudranath Capildeo, a brilliant mathematician but a political tyro. As leader of Her Majesty's loyal opposition, Dr. Capildeo had to back him such hyperbolic orators as Lionel Seukeran and Stephen Maharaj to vilify the PNM for every aspect of petty inefficiency - drains uncleared, potholes unfilled. Bhadase Maraj with a power base in the sugar workers union and head of the major Hindu religious organisation was reckoned to be the most dangerous force the PNM had to contend with.

Politics in those days was a parochial matter. The newly emerged nation of Trinidad and Tobago, cut off by the collapse of the West Indies Federation from its other Commonwealth neighbours, was finding its feet. The colonial heritage of a well organised civil service, education and economic systems were left intact, and those in their jobs continued in the competent and dedicated manner in which they had grown up. Graft and corruption were not prevalent.

## Independence

Following a middle-of-the-road political line, careful not to antagonise the United Kingdom, Canada or the United States by flirting with the socialist bloc, Dr. Williams plodded forward. A small recently independent country was a sitting duck for international con-men. Trinidadians recall with embarrassment, the Scotland Bay sod-turning ceremony for a massive tourist hotel and marina complex by the then Chairman of the Industrial Development Corporation. A senior peer of the British realm, the Marquis of Bristol, accompanied by an East End gym operator of Jewish-Welsh background made headlines when they arrived in Trinidad to launch this project, and were wined and dined for weeks. To this day that first sod was the only one ever turned.

Five year plans, offering generous tax concessions, duty free import of materials for pioneer manufacturing industries, were successful in bringing a greater measure of self-sufficiency, albeit at the expense of quality and price. Foreign experts who had maintained the humid climate made it impossible to produce flour in Trinidad rapidly changed their tune when Government went ahead anyway, and offered their services on the design and construction of the mill. The idea of a car assembly plant for a nation of one million people was scoffed at as grandiose and doomed to failure. But the first assembly plant was rapidly followed by three others as the importation of cars was severely restricted.

The most notable initiative came from private enterprise. The dynamic South Chamber of Commerce in San Fernando sponsored a plan in 1965 for an industrial centre utilising Trinidad's energy resources to best advantage. Consultants decided that Point Lisas on the Gulf of Paria, 15 miles north of San Fernando and 20 miles south of Port of Spain was the ideal location. Sugar lands could be made available readily by state-owned Caroni Ltd for the ambitious industrial complex. A public company was formed, feasibility studies prepared and overseas partners sought for the projects.

The plan was well-conceived, being based on down-
stream products of the petro-chemical industry from fertilizers to plastics and industrial gases. Also included to take
advantage of the cheap energy available from natural gas was
a steel mill to serve the nation's modest needs. On the
recommendation of respectable Philadelphia bankers, a small
but well-established steel company of high integrity was
introduced for a partnership venture. The company bore the
Jewish name of the family that owned it. As luck would have
it another American company went directly to government
officials about a steel mill venture, also from the Eastern
Seaboard and with a slightly similar Jewish name with the
same initial, but devoid of the same high standing. Credit
enquiries revealed that the latter was a Bayonne scrap dealer
whose main interest in a steel mill could only be to provide a
captive market with his scrap metal. In the confusion the
authorities got the two companies mixed up, or thought they
were one and the same, and advised the Philadelphia company
to its consternation that the interest was no longer open.

For such reasons combined with the general lack of required
finance, the Point Lisas development was shelved. When the
petro-dollars started flooding in after 1974, Government
woke up to the fact that the South Chamber's company and
plans were ideally suited to their needs. They took over the
whole project by putting in more capital to give themselves
majority control. They also expanded the concept in line with
vast natural gas reserves being found off the East Coast.

With each election the opposition party, the Democratic
Labour Party, seemed less and less organised and resolute in
its objectives. So firmly was the PNM in the saddle that there
was little motive to try and unseat them. The Indian business
community was prospering modestly even though the country
as a whole had little forward momentum, its current expenditure bill growing steadily as the PNM created jobs for its
cohorts by increasing the ranks of the civil service.

The West Indies Federation had collapsed in 1960 when it
became an issue in the Jamaican national election.
Bustamante's party, which opposed it, won the election and
opted his country out of the Federation. This would have left

Trinidad and Tobago as the biggest component member on whom the financial burden would fall heaviest. Dr. Williams titillated his radio audience with his arithmetic, "One from ten equals nought!" and promptly followed Jamaica's lead. Dr.Winston Mahabir, who was Minister of Health at the time, attributes Eric Williams' loss of enthusiasm over Federation to the fact that the opposing DLP led by Hindu Pundit Bhadase Maraj won more seats than the PNM in the Federal elections. Many West Indians regretted the demise of the Federation and looked forward to something other than cricket to hold the English speaking Caribbean together. Instead each territory was exploring an individual path to independence. For Trinidad and Tobago, Jamaica, Guyana and Barbados this made sense. But how were the mini-states like Grenada and Dominica to stand alone? The Caribbean Free Trade Association was formed out of mutual convenience and after meeting with modest success was metamorphasized into Caricom, the Caribbean Common Market.

*The 1970 Uprising*

By 1970 the country had stagnated emotionally. Geddes Granger, a radical university student, found growing support for his inflammatory views involving demolition of the economic establishment. A new group, the Tapia Movement, named after the indigenous mud daub peasant huts, attracted sincere intellectuals. Marches into Port of Spain led by Granger won massive following. Then came the mutiny by one company of the three comprising the Defense Force encamped at the former U.S. base at Chaguaramas.

Rumours flew of foreign powers backing the Marxist Oilfield Workers' Trade Union. The mutinous contingent marched toward Port of Spain along the only coast road, and plans were later discovered for the mass execution in Woodford Square of all "enemies of the people". The police, loyal to the Government, were armed with outdated single-shot rifles. Had the well-armed mutineers reached Port of Spain the outcome could well have been a bloody military coup.

To the tiny coast guard force goes the credit for stopping the attempted takeover. Also based at Chaguaramas, it was commanded by David Bloom, a former merchant marine purser with more financial experience than military. It was he who made the decision to bombard the road at the point where it ran along the sea front with a cliff rising behind it. This effectively blocked all vehicular passage into Port of Spain and was enough to turn the tide. A state of emergency was declared with nightly curfew.

When the plot fizzled, stories came out how Dr. Williams and his Cabinet had planes loaded, engines running at Piarco Airport, ready for flight. U.S. marines were reported to be standing by in landing craft just over the horizon. The Venezuelan military, too, were supposed to be poised to intervene rather than find a Cuba-style revolutionary force within sight of their mainland.

After the event, recriminations as to who was to blame were to be expected. Gerard Montano as Minister of Home Affairs was a logical scapegoat even though Dr. Williams never allowed any of his ministers to take action without his endorsement. The facts are that Gerard Montano had repeatedly warned Dr. Williams well before the mutiny, of the social unrest that was building into a storm. Montano recommended the steps that should be taken by the police under his control to stamp out the general impression of Government's indecision, and prevent matters deteriorating. Dr. Williams overruled Montano on each step, preferring to trust that the ferment would subside of its own accord. This wait-and-see policy had proved effective in so many cases, the prime minister could not assess any difference in the current crisis.

Loyal to his party leader, Gerard Montano protected Eric Williams from blame by bringing out none of these facts. In return for his silence he was given a sumptuous exile in Brasilia as his nation's ambassador. He and his attractive, blonde, Canadian wife proved favourites in diplomatic circles,and won respect for the nation which had cast him into political obscurity.

After the 1970 uprising, Trinidad and Tobago as a nation was emotionally purged of bottled up hostility between differing ethnic groups. Whites would be spoken to with a new frank cameraderie by blacks as they passed by at street corners.

Gone was the former slightly truculent reserve. Many whites, of course, had fled. The number of expatriates had already declined steadily in the face of government's policy that locals must be trained to take over all jobs. Oil companies could no longer bring secretaries from overseas, nor banks their junior officials from Canada or England. With the 1970 crisis the pace of departure increased. Those that remained demonstrated their bonds with Trinidad and with its problems.

*Near Bankruptcy*

By 1973, the country's economic fortunes slid to their worst. But foreign borrowing had been modest and the country's credit was untarnished even by the unprecedented flurry of social unrest. The bulk of foreign revenue was earned from crude oil produced by land wells and off-shore drilling in the Gulf of Paria, but even more from the taxes levied on refinery through-put at the massive Texaco refinery at Pointe-a-Pierre, the largest in the British Commonwealth until the Milford Haven refinery was built in Wales. Pointe-a-Pierre's oil flowed in from the Middle East, Nigeria and Libya for refining into fuel oil for the North American market.

Sugar production was heavily subsidised. Cocoa and citrus earnings were minimal in the national budget. Trinidad's famed lake of asphalt which has unique qualities of endurance as a road surface, was exported in small quantities from the funicular cable jetty at Brighton. A massive capital injection would have been required to modernise the plant for expanded production. Even then foreign sales were not assured due to lack of marketing expertise.

Trinidad and Tobago's finances were eroded to the extent that it was commonly believed that there was sufficient in the Treasury for only one further government payday. Possibly a loan would have been floated abroad in desperation, but Government had announced no such action.

*The Oil Boom*

Out of the blue the guardian angel, reputed to watch over the innocent and the deranged, waved its wand over Trinidad and Tobago. Massive oil discoveries of an excellent ·quality were made off the East Coast. If that were not enough, the Middle East oil crisis flared up. Prices skyrocketed in October 1973, and overnight Government had money to burn.

After an initial period of shock when it all seemed too good to be true, Dr. Williams raised his sights to the bounty that the nation now found in its lap. With crude oil production increasing annually to a high point of 240,000 barrels a day foreign reserves accumulated rapidly, compounding at high interest rates in London and New York. Not a moment too late. The nation's infrastructure was badly in need of a going-over. Nothing had been done to repair, let alone expand the telephone system, still grinding along on its sturdy British GPO base. Old roads were broken up and new roads required to cope with the now rapidly increasing volume of traffic. The power supply was falling short of demand, providing no leeway for further industrial expansion. Water distribution was chaotic (few records had been kept from the colonial days as to which reservoirs supplied which mains) and inadequate, although the reserves were there for the taking.

Dr. Williams was inundated with foreign advisors who a few months earlier would not have given him the time of day. Dreams of complete economic self-sufficiency through an industrialisation programme could be realised. Swiss bankers advised on the acquisition of the smallest foreign commercial bank and its expansion into a comprehensive network throughout the two islands. The other commercial banks, all branches of international giants, breathed a sigh of relief that the spectre of nationalisation had faded away, and hurriedly heeded Dr. Williams' strictures about localising within five years.

### Pt. Lisas and the Aluminium Smelter

Eric Williams' great ambition had long been to bring heavy industry to Trinidad, particularly a steel mill, which to his British-trained mind epitomised the big-time. This was indeed achieved at massive cost, a cost which at present appears never ending. It was to be the largest component of the revived Point Lisas development scheme.

Within the Point Lisas project was included a plant

which would hopefully revive the ties of the lamented Federation. Both Jamaica and Guyana depended on the export of bauxite for the bulk of their foreign exchange. Trinidad had two transhipment depots at its western promontory where bauxite was brought from Guyana in shallow draft vessels to be stored in silos, in the case of Alcoa, and in a vast uncovered mound in the case of Alcan. From there it was loaded onto deep draft freighters for processing in North America. Neither Jamaica nor Guyana had sufficient energy available to process its bauxite into alumina or aluminium billets. Trinidad did, and Dr. Williams saw a simplistic means of binding three major units of the West Indies together with an aluminium smelter as part of the industrial complex at Point Lisas.

From the start Jamaica and Guyana were lukewarm to the idea. Apparently fearing they might become controlled by Trinidad's key role, both carried on negotiations to subvert the plan. Jamaica preferred a liaison with nearby Mexico. Guyana wanted to develop its hydro-electric resources to power its own smelting plant, and would cooperate with Trinidad only as a stop-gap measure. Despite this, feasibility surveys were prepared by an Argentine aluminium company. Tenders for turn-key contracts were invited from French and Austrian giants in the aluminium world. Though the odds greatly outweighed the chance that a smelting plant (with all its attendant ecological dangers) would go ahead, the staff at the Point Lisas Development Company's headquarters who gave tours over the complex to business visitors and school-children, referred to it as an actuality.

For several years trading relations between the island states of the British West Indies went well and Caricom looked like being a success. Trinidad and Tobago, Barbados and Jamaica did a thriving export trade to each other in clothing, stationery, appliances and furniture. Then matters turned sour. Guyana ran out of foreign exchange and credit. Jamaica, in a sorry state generally in the last years of Prime Minister Manley, left importers' bills unpaid by refusing to allocate scarce foreign exchange. Barbados and Trinidad were jealous, each thinking the other was doing better at its expense. Some smaller islands flagrantly turned a blind eye to the rules about local content, often re-exporting foreign goods to which had been added a Caricom label of origin.

Trinidad and Tobago had suddenly become the "rich boy on the block." Generous loans were made to its less fortunate neighbours from its bulging purse. Petroleum products were supplied at an artifically low "neighbours" price. These were only interim measures. Trinidad was envied for its windfall prosperity and derided for its extravagance.

To give Jack his jacket, as they say in Trinidad, Dr. Williams' technocrats made sincere and well-thought-out plans for the investment of Trinidad's surplus funds. While oil reserves had passed their peak and production was on the decline, natural gas was found in large amounts off the East Coast where oil had been expected. The "drive mechanism", to use oil drillers' lingo, of the economy would have to come from the gas reserves which would last an estimated forty years. Rather than burn up the gas in providing cheap energy, as much as possible would be used as a raw material for fertilizers, ammonia, chlorine, methanol and ethanol. The gas itself could also be compressed at huge expense into LNG (liquified natural gas) for export in special tankers to North America or Europe. The country's electrical power production would be doubled by gas turbine generators. For its treasured steel mill the new Direct Reduction process would provide Trinidad with a mill that would serve not only its own needs, but permit the earning of significant foreign exchange from exports. The only catch was that the steel mill would not be viable unless it exported 80% of its 150,000 ton annual capacity. Moreover the only source of supply for the raw material was Brazil.

### A Time of Scandals

After twelve years of penny pinching it could hardly be expected that the spending of tens of millions of dollars on new projects would not place irresistible temptations in the way of all those who could influence decisions as to which foreign firms would be involved. Rumours of bribes and deals became rampant. The former schemes of bringing down re-conditioned machinery invoiced at new prices (the difference going to a Miami account) were petty compared to the creaming reputed to have gone on over the purchase of wide bodied jets for the national airline, a steamer for the Tobago ferry, the choice of electrical generators, telephone systems etc. Everyone shared in the wealth as the nation's largesse was lavished on new cars, houses and yachts. Too much money was chasing too few products, with inevitable inflation resulting. Lavish subsidies were granted by government to avoid the unpopularity they feared higher prices for staple products would bring.

Disclosure of financial scandal seemed always in the air, but no one expected punitive reprisals to be taken. Dr. Williams, by then sinking deeper into academic reclusion, appeared oblivious to the scurrilous stories circulating. He gave every evidence of being too pre-occupied writing books to dip his hand in the pot like so many leading figures in his government were reputed to . It was only several years after his death when his daughter Erica was listed among the top handful of the world's wealthiest women, that there was reason to think otherwise.

Prior to this prosperity Trinidad and Tobago suffered little corruption, as has been mentioned. Bribery was not the usual way to get business done. The police were straight if occasionally over-zealous in the "body music" dished out to lower class suspects. The judges and lawyers were above reproach. If a customs officer accepted a bottle of scotch to expedite, but not suborn his efforts, it was "no big thing." This was a far cry from the practices in the great majority of lesser developed countries. With prosperity, cynicism seeped into all levels of society; integrity became suspect from cabinet ministers on down.

Foreign exchange controls were part of the colonial heritage intact from the post war Exchange Finance Regulations of 1949. These were amended only after nearly twenty years of independence when an Exchange Control Act was passed. For ten years after independence there had been no restriction on sending funds throughout the sterling area, still the Mother Country financially. The anomaly of this eventually dawned on the authorities, and despite widespread apprehension of what was to follow, all currencies were deemed "foreign". The annual travel allowance was $1,200 at its lowest, and despite a generation of inflation and two devaluations, still stands at only $2,500. With their love of travel and the certainty of friends or relatives to stay with in New York or Toronto, it was to be expected that Trinidadians would treat exchange control with contempt, evading it where possible. When politicians boasted of the nation's huge foreign reserves, the logic of exchange controls was lost on the public.

Kickbacks and "agent's commissions" invariably involved placing funds outside the Trinidad banking system and thus the inquisitive eye of the tax man. This, of course, contravened exchange control regulations if one accepted that the funds had been "earned" in Trinidad.

## The Growth of "Bobol"

A former government minister of European stock exemplifies to the Trinidadian all that happens behind the scenes of power. He was a confidant of Dr. Williams, who seemed so blind to the scandals that buzzed around his friend's head that it was conjectured he must have had some blackmail hold over the prime minister. When appointed to a special commission, large sums were likely to be spent under dubious circumstances. Should the subsequent uproar prove too embarrassing a commission of enquiry would drag its heels until the public no longer cared about the outcome. This was certainly the case with a delapidated ferry boat bought from enterpreneurs in Venezuela for the Tobago run which broke down on its well-publicised maiden voyage. Major repairs in Venezuela proving unequal to the task, it was eventually returned to its Dutch builders for refurbishing at a cost substantially greater than that of a new vessel. This former minister was well known to have close connections with horse racing and cock-fighting interests. Although cockfighting is illegal in British-oriented Trinidad, he was famous for breeding and fighting his birds, and had been pictured on the front page of the daily tabloid with the unforgettable headline, "Johnny Mounts Plane Cock in Hand."

The ferry scandal was not enough. A newly elected member of the elite Steward's Committee of the Turf Club had the effrontery to flout the hallowed colonial etiquette and appear in a white guayabara locally called a "shirt-jac", instead of the mandatory coat and tie. The shirt-jac was by then accepted at cocktail parties and even for bank clerks as acceptable national dress, but the transgressing steward was asked to leave the stand for being improperly dressed. Subsequently standing his ground on the dress issue he was disbarred as a steward. Dr. Williams was no turfite but had long recognised the Turf Club as the bastion of reaction. Here was an ideal opportunity to clip their wings. Purportedly to decide whether racing should continue at the Grand Stand on the Grand Savannah or be centralised along with other turf clubs at a single location, a Racing Commission was appointed. Its two members were none other than the shirt-jacked ex-steward and his crony the cockfighting ex-minister.

*Horses before Houses*

Horse racing has been held regularly on the Savannah since the meeting in 1853, for which a grand stand was built to accommodate the throngs of aficionados. The adjacent stables became inadequate for the popular sport which attracted an increasing number of owners who enjoyed the tax-deductible and prestigious thrills. Precisely what the Savannah should be used for was vague, except that it should be for the use of the people and not the racing elite. It was even suggested that Carnival bands should use George V Park for the judging stand instead of the Grand Stand. There were other race courses at Union Park, San Fernando and Santa Rosa Park, Arima; both would also be terminated once a single racing complex was agreed on and built. Only the humble track in Tobago would stay open. The two-man commission selected a site on the Caroni Plains geographically equidistant from the various centres of population but close to none of them. They invited designs from architects for something as splendid as those in Caracas and Puerto Rico where they gambled with their Latin confreres.

At a time when Trinidad and Tobago was rolling in

petro-dollars, the escalating cost, first $120 million, then $180 million, $240 million and ever upward was taken in stride. All those with a vested interest in racing or the construction of the complex whitewashed the disadvantages of a site which would require new roads and bridges to reach. No longer could the poor folk stroll from their barrack yards of Belmont or Marabella to watch and bet on the local race meetings; everyone would require vehicular transportation.

The racing complex would be sumptuously appointed with the latest technology in computerised pari-mutual facilities. Even the stables were to be air conditioned. The newly formed opposition party of outcasts from the PNM, calling themselves the Organisation for National Reconstruction (ONR) saw in the air conditioned stables a juicy weapon for their cause. "Houses before horses" became their rallying cry, and made the man in the street aware of the extravagances from the public purse for a sport that had operated very efficiently under private control for over a hundred years. Had it not been for the furore which resulted, the Racing Complex would have gone ahead at an expense to the nation estimated even before final cost escalations, at over $400 million.

Informal investigation uncovered irregularities in the tendering procedure for Racing Complex contracts with the odour of much worse. Dr. Williams predictably appointed a commission of enquiry to defuse the nation's outrage. Petro-dollars which up to this time had seemed limitless were fully committed to large projects and the ever-increasing bill to pay the civil servants would soon make it necessary to decide which projects would have to be curtailed as each one spiralled higher in cost.

Only after two years of procrastination, rationalisation and prevarication did government reluctantly back off from the Racing Complex. $120 million had already been incurred for land preparation, foundations and drains. The authorities fired the U.S. contractor for bribing their own cronies and refused to settle outstanding claims. Evidence clearly implicated the cock-fighting ex-minister who, despite weeks during which the police could have apprehended him, emigrated at his leisure to Panama with whom there was no extradition treaty. His shirt-jacked sidekick abandoned his medical practice and also opted for the security of Panamanian nationality, although both mixed freely with Trinidadian friends in Toronto.

Despite all this, and assurances that the completed infrastructure will eventually be used for sporting facilities there is a fatalistic belief that the Racing Complex will emerge like a phoenix from the dust, whether or not the stables are air conditioned.

This was only one of the more flambouyant projects in which graft had evidently played a large part. It seemed as if the guiding philosophy was "The more it costs, the more we can milk it." No effort seemed to be made to introduce basic cost effectiveness or relate expense to the public need. This is not to say that every project entailed bribery. Dr. Williams developed a policy intended to remove the risk of underhand deals known as "Government to Government" negotiations. The prime minister decided which country's contractors should handle which project. The French got the hospitals, the Austrians the cement plant. The elaborate Hall of Justice was put out to competition for design, and the result to international tender. The massive Financial Complex, ill-advisedly sited on the reclaimed area of the former schooner jetty, was also put out to international tender. Some were cost-plus contracts, open-ended as to the eventual cost to the nation. The results were not necessarily rip-offs by contractors, or entailed graft. That was more likely to find its way into the "prime cost" sums for nominated sub-contractors supplying costly specialist equipment. The question should have been asked, did the country really need such grandiose facilities, and in the long run could it afford them?

## ISCOTT *(Iron and Steel Corporation of Trinidad & Tobago)*

Everything depended on Point Lisas where by far the biggest concentration of capital was being poured. The world market for steel and fertilizers was badly depressed. What had looked at the start to be sound projects were now only marginal - given efficient production. The steel mill, known by its acronym ISCOTT, rapidly proved to be, if not a national disaster, so costly that it would be obsolete before profits could ever offset the initial investment.

Dependent on pellets of iron ore from Brazil, the first product of the mill would be DR (direct reduced) pig iron which would be re-exported to energy-short Brazil for its industrial needs. While it was known that DR iron was highly volatile and that any intruding moisture would start a chemical fire which would have to burn itself out, creating a poisonous gas in the process, it was overlooked by the consultants to provide a cover for the open-air conveyor belt which ran half a mile from the factory to the dock. Loading could only take place during fine weather until the conveyor was covered. Even with this oversight corrected, exports of DR iron were only a fraction of projections.

The mill's second product was steel billets of 100 mm section. These could not be used by the single existing rolling mill which had produced reinforcing bars for several years from imported billets. Its machinery could only handle a 40mm size. Until another rolling mill was set up, ISCOTT would be wholly dependent on the export of its billets into a world market already saturated with over-production and spare capacity.

The third item ISCOTT could make was coils of extruded steel up to 3/4 inch in diameter, suitable when straightened and cut for reinforcing purposes in the building industry. Four firms were established for this purpose. Aided by German technicians, production of the intended quality was achieved. Meeting the targeted volume of production was equally important, and selling it abroad entirely another matter.

It had been blithely projected that ISCOTT's billets and coils could be readily sold to the U.S.A. In fact the U.S.A was its only potential customer. What had not been taken into consideration was the reaction of the powerful U.S. steel industry, itself fighting for its life with largely outdated plants. U.S. legislation precluded the import of dumped goods, or goods artificially cheapened by government subsidy. The steel industry lobbyists argued successfully that ISCOTT was getting its natural gas, a major cost component, from the state at an artificially low price. Whether they took into consideration the value of government finance to ISCOTT is not readily ascertainable. At any rate ISCOTT found to its consternation that its only customer was closed to it.

For a while limited production continued, but then the problem as to whether to continue on a loss basis was resolved, in a manner of speaking. Maintenance at the mill had been so poor that after two accidents the plant was closed down for yet one more enquiry. The official report showed that largely due to inadequate protective maintenance, a massive sum would have to be spent to put the plant back on its feet. Rumour had it that ISCOTT was losing $350 million a year. This was scotched by official word that losses were "nearer half that amount." The enquiry went on to suggest that it would be more prudent to mothball the vast plant until the world price of steel went up sufficiently to make operations profitable - several years hence.

## The Death of Dr. Eric Williams

By this time Dr. Williams had died. Again in Trinidad-fashion it was passed around that the shock of his chief technocrat's revelation to him that ISCOTT was a fiasco had been the final blow to his weakened constitution. He had done his sincere best for his country as its leader for over twenty-five years. While he had in most ways let circumstances set policy for him, he had not committed any major blunders. His canny control over his colleagues had prevented any effective opposition to him either within or outside the party. The resultant stability had gone a long way to letting the country develop from an agricultural backwater into a middle class nation with considerable small manufacturing diversity. The natural advantage of oil wealth, for which Dr. Williams seemed to claim the credit, had been misspent, not so much in the projects to which they were allocated, so much as in the manner the funds were drained away.

Dr. Williams was long held to be a pillar of political wisdom, yet his policies played little part in the country's lurch forward in living standards. Any other leader might have done much worse, but might well have done much more.

It must have come as a crushing disappointment to him that the assurance of continuing prosperity from wisely invested windfall petrodollars which he had intended to leave to the nation as his legacy, was in serious jeopardy. The confused and rumour-ridden details of his last hours never suggested that he died from a broken heart but rather from a diabetic coma. Ironically his confidants were to the last afraid to take action without his express consent. By the time they obtained medical aid it was too late.

It fell upon the President to appoint Dr. Williams' successor, as Eric Williams had resolutely abstained from grooming anyone to take his place. To the contrary, any minister who showed too much initiative and gained popularity was viewed as a potential rival, and evicted from power. There was widespread speculation who would be chosen. President Ellis Clarke's speeches at Rotary lunches had provided a semblance of national leadership that Dr. Williams' reclusion rendered impossible. It was suggested that the President might wish to take over. His selection of the least charismatic and physically inocuous of the three contenders added fuel to these suspicions. George Chambers was a seasoned if lacklustre cabinet minister who lacked the respect felt for Errol Mahabir and the staunch Kamaluddin Mohammed. But they were both Indians, and Trinidad society wasn't ready for that.

Chambers made an effort to show that, like many men of small stature, he meant to get his way. But with the financial tide on the wane, he was helpless. Just as Dr. Williams had been projected fortuitously forward on the crest of oil-price inspired prosperity, so George Chambers was dragged down by the drop in oil revenue. He had time to bite the bullet and impose austerity measures while there was still time, but did so only timidly. He shirked the unpopular step of cutting down on government expenditure. The fat attitude which the PNM had fostered during the years of profligacy continued.

For the first time people speculated how long Chambers and the PNM could remain in power, and what the alternative would be. There were those who felt Chambers would be the lamb sacrificed to keep the PNM in power. There were fears that the PNM would split into its two dominant factions, the

"Black Power" group and the Indian-dominated "other." Waiting in the wings were former senior PNM ministers, ANR Robinson and Karl Hudson Phillips, victims of Williams' fear of rivals. "ANR" ruled the legislature in his island home of Tobago, but had little backing in Trinidad for his Democratic Action Congress (DAC). "Karl" had formed the hard-working Organization for National Reconstruction (ONR) which received encouraging voter support in the 1981 election even though it won no seats. A coalition of these two forces with the Indian rural party, remnants of the DLP led by trade union lawyer Basdeo Panday, seemed the only solution.

Press polls indicated widespread voter support, but many doubted that such a coalition of convenience would work if it were elected. Despite this, dissatisfaction with years of inefficiency and graft by the PNM made the people opt for the uncertain alternative of the National Alliance for Reconstruction (NAR). Under Robinson's leadership, the NAR won by a a landslide in the 1986 election. The PNM could retain only three unimportant seats. Robinson inherited a bankrupt treasury that left him with no room to manoeuvre. Devaluation of the TT dollar was inevitable; to sustain the confidence of the IMF on whom the country was now dependent, unpopular medicine would have to be swallowed.

Suffering a major decline in living standards by a people renowned for their love of highlife has already created serious dissatisfaction. The political marriage with such unnatural bed-fellows as the populist John Humphrey and union-oriented Panday has already been breached. Trinidad and Tobago has not accepted its loss of prosperity, and sees the new government as the scapegoat. One cannot envy Arthur Napoleon Raymond Robinson the difficult road that lies ahead.

*Classics on Steel*

# Chapter 11

━━━━━●•◉•●━━━━━

# *The Arts and the Artists*

Blessed with a unique creative bounty in the music of calypso and steelband which extends into the exuberant fantasy of Carnival, it would hardly be expected that an island of one million could make a showing in the fine and performing arts as well; yet Trinidad has a creditable record.

In the field of literature, Trinidad has produced one giant, the novelist Vidia Naipaul, universally regarded as one of the great writers of our day and a potential Nobel laureate. In his shadow until the latter's death in 1985, was his brother, Shiva Naipaul. Both turned their backs on the island of their origin, despite using it for material, and became very British. C.L.R. James was known throughout the sporting world for his cricketing literature. Had he not been suppressed, for a while to the extent of house arrest, by his former boyhood friend, Prime Minister Eric Williams, for his radical politics, his historical and political works might have received greater fame. He died in 1990. Apart from these with novelist Samuel

Selvon, the Trinidad literary scene has been dominated by St. Lucia-born poet and dramatist, Derek Walcott. Now he too is a celebrity and spends most of his time in the United States.

## Music

A cornucopia of calypso tunes pours onto the local scene each year. Young and old sway and jump to an indigenous music. Classical music is not likely to appeal to a people that love to dance. Small wonder Trinidad cannot field a full orchestra. With most residential areas resonant with corner panyards, where youths spend hours picking out tunes by ear, there is unlikely to be much interest in the more rigid discipline of learning the violin or oboe. For the handful so inclined there are precious few teachers. When orchestras have been garnered together from time to time, they have usually depended on a foreign-trained string section. The Police and Regiment bands are in effect the only groups that can provide musical accompaniment for the extravaganzas staged at the Grand Savannah.

Music as an academic discipline, flowers every two years at the Biennial Music Festival. This is a legacy from the colonial past with British adjudicators imported to sit in judgment over local efforts. A respectable number of musicians and singers have succeeded on the international scene such as the Nathaniel sisters, Sandra Browne, and the Gomez sisters. Throughout the year The Recital Club, comprising music teachers, performers and aficionados provides a stage for mainly foreign-trained talent. Their monthly concerts, supplemented by the occasional Rotary Club-sponsored visitor, keep classical music alive. The several ballet schools thrive with termly displays of nubile daughters to their proud family. Every so often a locally produced "artiste" will return and give a single concert to show "we local gyul make good in London"; but this is only a ripple on the Trinidad musical pond. It would be a brave impressario who would bring down a classical pianist to fill the Queens Hall as they did up to the 60s. Mass audiences are for the soul, pop and rock stars these days.

With this background, it is all the more surprising that

steelbands should be able to attain such extraordinary heights when tackling classical music. The origin for this goes back to the musical "bomb" which steelbands would drop on the judges as they inched their way down Frederick Street on J'ouvert morning. Breaking out of the calypso tune, steel bands would suddenly switch to "Fingal's Cave Overture" or the "Flight of the Bumblebee" with marvellous effect.

The Bomb Competition as part of J'ouvert has long been replaced by the more formal setting of a separate stage where the judging can be more exact. Instead of the hundred-strong "street side", a select more highly trained "stage side" bows primly to the judges and audience in colourful uniforms designed specially for the occasion. This is the biennial Steelband Competition held at the sports stadium. No orchestral work is too hard to tackle. Witco's Gay Desperadoes astounded the world with a rendition of Bach's Chaconne recorded in a New York church. From that time all leading steelbands have responded to the challenge of classical music. Many lean on the expertise of trained musicians such as the erstwhile painter, Pat Bishop, who arranges the music and conducts the steelband with all the panache of a Toscanini. This serious steelband music has nothing whatever to do with Carnival. This does not prevent it from receiving avid mass support. Through such tortuous routes is the finest in music made palatable to the man in the street in Trinidad.

The area of music besides steelband in which Trinidad has achieved greatest success and recognition is with its chorales. These also emanated from the music festivals to which British adjudicators are still invited to sit in judgment. Dance and music find a natural outgrowth at every weekend fete, from bottle and spoon to cuatro parang. With the addition of academic discipline, the lovely swaying bodies of a chorale such as the Marionettes, produce choral music of the highest standard. A number of racially diverse groups, looking like tropical blossoms, have toured abroad successfully. The lilting musical cadence of Trinidadian "parlance" is often compared to Welsh. In its facility with chorales another parallel with the Welsh can be drawn.

## The Stage

Prior to Derek Walcott's "Basement Theatre" named after its cramped quarters in the Bretton Hall Hotel, the expatriate-dominated Phoenix Players was nearly the only group to provide Trinidad audiences with dramatic presentations. Rival offshoots were formed, playing at the reconstructed Little Carib Theatre, an interesting fare of West Indian plays. The Irish wife of a local pediatrician, Helen Camps, exemplifies individual achievement in this area.

Belmont's enterprising Pelham Street Theatre burned to the ground and ceased operations. Other theatrical companies have risen, metaphorically speaking from its ashes - the Bagasse Company, Strolling Players, Trinidad Tent Theatre, Playhouse Company, The Space and others.

The Little Carib Theatre was founded by Beryl McBurnie in the converted house of a relative in Woodbrook. Through her untiring and often quixotic efforts to provide Trinidad with a permanent dance theatre, she has become a living local legend. From the time she returned from a British Council scholarship for folk dance, she has devoted her colossal energies to little else than the Little Carib Dance Theatre. The makeshift theatre was open to the rain and neighbourhood distractions, but flourished from the late 50s until, after many such threats, it was torn down by the health authorities as a fire hazard in 1969. Governor Sir Edward Beetham and his entourage were regular habitués, giving it a vogue with local aesthetes and visitors. Beryl McBurnie used local music and rhythms as a basis for dance variety shows which were touted as a cultural "must" in tourist books. When the makeshift theatre was demolished it was in anticipation of its rebirth as an architect-designed steel framed structure squeezed onto the same two lots of land, and still with insufficient room for the performers to change.

It is widely known that Miss McBurnie borrowed money in her personal capacity for the theatre, repaying it from her salary as a teacher. Fund raising efforts supplemented her own. So much of her energy went into the building project that her dance company faltered. But the theatre for which she condemned herself to a life of poverty, flourishes as a venue for a variety of theatrical and dance productions. Her heroic efforts to provide a stage for the performing arts have not gone unrewarded even though it has been in the form of a medal, The Hummingbird - Gold, rather than the monetary support for additional equipment that she would probably have preferred.

In his own way, Prime Minister Eric Williams' initiative of the "Best Village Competition" did a great deal too, to take the performing arts down to grass root level, even if in a less sophisticated way. Dances by village troupes might follow in the stereotype of African drummers, but at least each group was trying to "do its own t'ing." Drama is reduced to declamatory burlesque skits of the most homespun genre; but the efforts have brought a sense of participation in theatre to every Trinidad home. These dramatic efforts overflowed when they won prizes, onto the television. Other more professional groups took their place, backed by a nationalistic motive to do with less imported programming. Gradually the quality of locally written and performed TV dramas has improved. The excruciatingly amateurish has given way to a respectable professionalism of which such a small country has good reason to feel proud.

## Graphic Arts

Michael Cazabon, whose life is described in another chapter, is often cited as Trinidad's first artist. He was a Paris-trained academician who has nothing to do with today's artistic scene. Central to post-war painting in Trinidad, was the Art Society's annual November Exhibition. There was no permanent gallery, only a small sampling in a wing of the dusty national museum. The November Exhibition was held for many years at the Woodbrook Market on French Street from which vendors of fish, fruit and ground provisions formerly sold their wares. A hard core of artists such as "M.P." Alladin, Sybil Atteck and Carlisle Chang supported by Margeurite Wyke and the Rawle sisters comprised the heart of the artistic community. Others such as Pat Chu Foon and Isaiah Budhoo went "away" on art scholarships to return in due course as teachers.

Among those painters who returned from Britain during the 1960s was the talented Boscoe Holder who, with his wife Sheila, had enjoyed success as nightclub performers in various parts of the world. Boscoe had originally formed a dance troupe even before that of Beryl McBurnie, and took it abroad on tour with Sheila as one of his dancers. They later developed into a nightclub singing duo. It had been Boscoe's natural talent as a teenage pianist that had made him much in demand for colonial social functions in times when it was unheard of for a local black man to be accepted into society as an "artiste."

Boscoe's younger brother, Geoffrey, proved to be equally talented in a variety of fields. Unlike Boscoe, he veered to New York where today he has become a household name as a painter, designer, actor, dancer and even author of a creole cookery book. While he will always be the quintessential Trinidadian, Geoffrey only returns to Trinidad for brief family visits, and is sadly not a part of the local art scene.

Both Holder brothers are internationally known for their sensuously glamourous studies of black nudes with long necks and languorous smiles. Less known is their equal facility with tropical beach and mountain scenes. Perhaps Boscoe's most common subject is his wife draped in an ever changing fantasy of lace and ruffles. He takes equal delight in dressing her in finery for social occasions and has developed her costumes into an art form of their own.

The use of bright vibrant colours runs as common thread through the work of most Trinidadian painters, whether they be representational, abstract or in between. Perhaps the intense light and vivid hues of the Caribbean make more muted tones ineffective. This bold use of colour stands out clearly when one visits a gallery in Puerto Rico or Caracas, equally tropical Caribbean settings. There one will see a far greater variety of techniques. Against such a backdrop, the common denominator of Trinidadian painting would readily stand out.

Even in Japan few artists are reported able to support themselves solely by their painting. Inevitably the same is true in a small island society. Nearly all have jobs as teachers, commercial artists, or civil servants. Willie Chen was even a baker. Some who showed great promise like Audley Sue Wing and Pat Bishop dropped out to concentrate on other activities. So too did Carlisle Chang of a broken artistic heart after all his works submitted to the prestigious Sao Paulo Exhibition went astray in transit and were never recovered. Thereafter Carlisle devoted himself for many years to the commercial artistry of dolls and tourist souvenirs, besides Carnival band costume designs for Stephen Lee Heung. Only recently has he emerged again to provide leadership to the artistic community filled with a fresh crop of young talent.

It is a popular conception that lack of local support stunts the development of local artists. Yet individuals and business entities snap up the best of each annual crop. With a population no greater than a medium-sized metropolitan city, Trinidad has as respectable a number of buyers, as it does of artists. Buying such paintings cannot be viewed as an investment as in London, Paris or New York. Without international acceptance it is impossible to say whether the work of any of the fifty or so familiar names will appreciate in value. It is true that when Edwin Hing Wan died after a life as a cripple painting beach scenes at Mayaro, there was a rush for his work by those who recognised an opportunity; but this is rare.

With so many painters having established a local reputation over the years, and so few pre-eminent, it is hard to know how they are best mentioned. Should they be grouped according to genre? The abstractionists - Pat Bishop, Leroy Clarke, Willie Chen, Audley Sue Wing, Glen Roopchand and Harris. The realists - Dermott Louison, Mervyn Lynch, Neal Massy, Bascombe, Jackie Hinkson and of course Jose Mosca's exquisite bird studies. The primitives - Marcelio, Leo Basso, Samuel Ishak, Rolle and even Adrian Camps Campins. The semi-abstract - Isaiah Budhoo, Leo Glasgow, Knolly Greenidge. Water colourists - Noel Vaucrosson, deceased Nan Richards and ex-banker Trevor Rostant.

Others in categories of their own are Mark Savage who uses linear monochrome to weave complex political commentary reminiscent of the Mexican muralists when he is not doing signs for Guinness stout; Akong's scratchboard studies of shacks and tropical plantlife; and the adopted Trinidadian architect, the late John Newel Lewis, whose manneristic studies of gingerbread houses adorned (in reproduction) the waiting rooms of doctors and dentists when little else local was framed.

Some help has been provided to artists by shops that sold paintings on commission alongside a range of tourist souvenirs which did more to pay the rent. Only in the 80s did several galleries emerge with full commitment to the artists displayed. Of these Clara Rosa de Lima's on St. Anns Road is the largest and features one-man shows more frequently than the others. Artists complain nevertheless that the disposable income of the oil-boom did not go into art works, so much as electronic extravagances and the inevitable "Benz".

Sculpture does not have the same participation as painting. Apart from Pat Chu Foon's outdoor works, few of which withstand vandalism by the mentally deranged (the Kew Place statue of Ghandi was demolished in 1986, the Pan Players at the Wrightson Road end of Independence Square is periodically savaged) sculpture in Trinidad is best known for the work in clay, wood and stone of the husband and wife team of Ralph and Vera Baney. Perhaps because Trinidadians do not have mantlepieces and periodically remove all furniture from living rooms for fetes, the idea of having breakable statuary has not caught on. Equally likely is that Trinidad's exuberant vitality does not have time for anything as static as sculpture.

Overflowing as it is with native talent, new stars such as one of the latest, Wendy Nanan, will continue to flash into the public's eye. One can hope they will receive enough support to persevere and not fall by the wayside like so many talented predecessors.

*Cipriani Statue, Independence Square*

## Chapter 12

# *The Square That Is Not*

Those fortunate enough to approach Port of Spain by sea in the early morning, gain a beautiful impression of the wooded hills, rising steeply behind the city's tall buildings stretching off to the east. This impression is destroyed upon landing at an unlovely waterfront and dock area. Cruise ships have been provided with special berths in an effort to minimise the effect, but there is still a long hot walk from the docks, dodging traffic across busy Wrightson Road to the western end of Independence Square.

This is not a square at all but the open space between the east and west bound streets leading for nine blocks to the western door of the Cathedral of the Immaculate Conception. Originally the area was called by the Spanish "Plaza de la Marina," evolving into Marine Square as land was reclaimed from the sea steadily to the west. The name was particularly appropriate as the southern edge of the square was the original marshy waterfront. The waterfront was filled in first to South Quay running parallel with Independence Square, and subsequently to its present line. Marine Square's nine blocks were shaded parks with paved footpaths running down the centre. A roundabout was made at the foot of the main shopping street, Frederick Street, and the bronze statue of the political hero and mayor, Andrew Cipriani, was erected in its centre.

The needs of an expanding society encroached inexorably. The Legion Hall, "temporary" wooden wartime offices and electrical sub-stations were allotted space. Then the pressure of parking needs rose with the country's prosperity, until today, only the trees and the central footpath remain of the former park areas, apart from the new plaza facing the new financial complex.

Tall buildings on the southern side bear testament to Trinidad's oil wealth. Behind the seamen's club at the corner with Wrightson Road, rise the mosaic walls of the cable company. When the international Cable and Wireless Ltd. was responsible for telegraphic needs, they made do with cramped quarters in the ground floor of the businessmen's Union Club. Once Government took over, a suitably splendid monument to the national ego was naturally required. The six-storey building was generous in its space allocation. One complete floor was allocated to private offices for the directors who attended one meeting a month. The ground floor office was adequate to handle the volume of cables but not the crowds who were subsequently obliged to use it for public overseas telephone calls. For some reason smelling of political in-fighting, the cable company, Textel, volunteered to take over this function from the telephone company. Those who sit shoulder to shoulder on benches and sweat despite the air-conditioning can regret that the architect was never forewarned of this expansionist possibility.

Towering over Textel's building are the twin towers of the new financial complex rising sixteen stories into the sky. Since the site chosen was filled waterfront of the former St. Vincent Street jetty pictured in Cazabon's engraving, the foundations gave the construction firm a nightmare. Directly across on the northern side of the "square" is the Treasury

Building and former General Post Office in the stern straight lines of GPO modern architecture. This was the site of the rum bond which burned spectacularly in 1932. With independence in 1962, besides changing Marine Square's name, the time had çome to expand the duties of the Treasury and build a new post office building. The new post office is convenient to the dock area but too far for downtown pedestrians and in the heart of the worst traffic for those with cars. Even with the post office removed there was insufficient room for the new Central Bank's expanding duties and staff. The decision was taken to construct the new Financial Complex on a scale so large that many floors would have to be rented out to private firms or stand empty.

Unfortunately the pedestrian visitor from the docks has to admire these imposing structures from an unshaded pavement until reaching the first welcome balcony after Abercromby Street. Their tall, slender cast iron columns provide shelter from rain and sun. In the days of the Spanish cabildo which ruled Port of Spain, it was a city ordinance that buildings should have overhanging balconies to protect the citizenry. Such a practical approach was discarded by later town planners as a historical anachronism.

Up to the 1970s these sheltering balconies started at the historic Ice House on the corner of Abercromby Street. They continued the whole block to Chacon Street. It was from the mansarded turret of the Ice House that signals were telegraphed via Fort George lookout to and from North Post on the cliffs at the head of the Diego Martin valley. Early notice of approaching shipping a full day before they would reach the harbour, was critical intelligence to the canny merchants during times of shortage. Ice was brought down from St. Johns and Halifax for storage in the building. Before the days of refrigerators this was a luxury of which the city was proud. The upper floors were occupied by the Hotel de Paris, a social oasis for generations of visitors to the city. More modern hotels forced it into a steady decline. At the end the only signals relayed from its windows by the drying panties of the occupants were of a very different nature.

Unconcerned by activities upstairs, the ground floor was

tenanted by a Canadian bank until they built a prestigious marble edifice at the foot of Frederick Street. The Exchange Control Division of the Central Bank occupied the ground floor of the former Ice House in a squat modern building, until moving into the Financial Complex. Only the wooden kiosk of the Ice House taxi-stand facing it recalls the past. Gone too are the slender columns supporting the balcony above Yuille's Printerie. Eating a Chinese lunch on that balcony gave an absorbing view of downtown activity. The utilitarian office building which took its place has one saving grace; a wide eave sheltering the pavement below.

Two of the older buildings alone remain, those of Muir Marshall Ltd., booksellers and John Hoadley Ltd. - "The Don," men's outfitters. They deserve a comment as the introduction to the architectural tidbits found throughout Trinidad but primarily in Port of Spain. Several writers have assumed that the cast iron columns and balconies, reminiscent of New Orleans' French Quarter, must be of French derivation. France was the dominant culture, after all, from the influx starting in 1783. However it was a Scotsman, George Brown, who was responsible for the upgrading of Port of Spain at the turn of the century after the Great Fire of 1895. Making use of the cast iron structural steel and ornamentation then available from Glasgow, the former French and Spanish colonial buildings with low ground floor storeys and taller upper ones were replaced with graciously tall ground floors supported on slender columns. It is these old facades which gave downtown Port of Spain and the Grand Savannah its unique character.

Facing this block on the south side of the square is another of George Brown's creations, the Union Club, a lunchtime haven for Port of Spain's businessmen. The three-storied building has two tiers of cast iron balconies supported on delicately ornamented cast iron columns. Shops and offices occupy the ground level but three terrazzo steps lead through frosted glass doors with gleaming brass handles into the 19th century. Broad mahogany handrails lead up the staircase to the spacious dining room where the tables are decked in white linen and business gossip is traded back and forth. To the right is the bar, beyond it the gloomy billiard room, and furthest away the men's room. It is the main reading room that captures the full flavour of the club's antiquity. Deep leather armchairs, dry and cracked in the tropic heat are for the most part empty. The days are gone when the planters rested here before setting off in their horse drawn carriages after having transacted the morning's business. But the stained and faded mezzotints of the Edwardian era they admired are still on the walls, *The Times* and *Tatler* still on the library table as if awaiting their return.

Before it was refurbished during the oil boom of the 1970s, the Union Club was a ghostly period piece. Eighteen-foot high ceilings created a cathedral quiet. Upstairs were rooms where up to 1963 the planter could board for a modest $75 a month while his family was on cold climate leave in France or England. A veneer of modernity has been applied with carpets, air conditioning and vinyl chairs, but the echoes of the past cannot be stilled. Membership in the club is open to all but on a selective basis which keeps a predominance of European faces at the luncheon tables. The selection process is not one of bias so much as to ensure that new members can be trusted to follow the mores of the club. And that, right or wrong, is what such clubs are all about.

From the number of banks in the area it is not surprising that the next part of Independence Square is known as Bankers' Row. Far more surprising is the eyesore that stands in the middle of the square between the banks. This is an area of squalid wooden shacks where rasta-headed leather workers make and sell their sandals and handbags. The air is thick with burning incense (not to be mistaken for marijuana, or "ganja" as it is called in Trinidad, besides its many other metropolitian names). "Ganja" is an Indian word and goes back to the time before World War II when country groceries might have a sign above the entrance "Licensed Seller of Ganja." To a visitor unaccustomed to the matted and unkempt "dreadlocks," the aggressive familiarity of the artisans, the congestion of the booths and their unsanitary smells may send him scurrying back to his cruise ship. Taken in its stride it is a picturesque and unique experience more likely to be found in the soukhs of Marrakesh or Zanzibar.

How did this anomaly of town planning ever come about? The empty area had fallen into neglect, occupied only by weeds and broken concrete paths. In 1968 the sole British bank got together its banking neighbours and the shops which at the time faced it to fund the creation of "an oasis of peace and quiet" in the heart of the commercial area. The authorities formally sanctioned the project. Concrete block troughs were built for shrubs, trees were planted and benches placed in their shade. For a brief period the revived park provided what its sponsors intended. Then came 1970 with its racial tension. Vendors had long sold their wares on the pavement of Frederick Street, known as "The Drag." Scarves and trinkets were peddled throughout the year, giving way to apples and grapes during the Christmas season. The City Council decided they had become a nuisance and should move to the abandoned buildings of the old Eastern Market on George Street, far from Frederick Street's shoppers.

Instead the vendors opted for the oasis of peace between the commercial banks. Overnight they put together stalls that soon became more and more substantial. The vendors began to live in them despite the absence of sanitary facilities. The embarrassed city fathers got no support from Goverment in moving them out. Timid to antagonise a group with highly racial if not tribalistic overtones, Government did nothing but murmur promises of alternate sites. More than twenty years later they are still there, and the alternate sites are still being contested by the squatting vendors as unsuited to their trade. One feels sure that Andrew Cipriani whose statue overlooks the squalor would never have permitted such a development while he was mayor of Port of Spain.

Behind Cipriani's statue at the foot of Frederick Steet, the wide thoroughfare appropriately called Broadway leads to the waterfront. Parked cars now line its centre but it was not always so. Before the southern edge of Independence Square was reclaimed from the sea, Broadway was a mole of land jutting out into the harbour with the lighthouse at its end. Tall almond trees shaded the gentry on their customary promenade known as Almond Walk. Only when the broad

road was paved in 1906 did the grateful store-keepers petition successfully for a grander, if less romantic name.

Provision dealers occupy most of the rundown and smelly buildings fronting it, except for the unexpected corinthian columns of Trestrail's facade where a treasure trove of equestrian equipment, chandler's goods and hardware lay piled in gloomy dank storerooms. The restored fortifications of Fort San Andres stand on the western edge beyond South Quay, complete with cannons and cannon balls. This was Port of Spain's only defense against the invading British in 1797. It proved useless when Sir Ralph Abercrombie's force marched along the coast from Mucurapo and entered Port of Spain from behind the small fort. There was no battle, and only one British officer died in the brief skirmish. The two-storey building behind the ramparts of Fort San Andres was the home of the police Traffic Branch. For many years the upper story was occupied by the Chamber of Commerce, but with general prosperity they were able to purchase their own building on Frederick Street overlooking Woodford Square. The expanded Traffic Branch took over both floors.

The lighthouse is Trinidad's humble version of the leaning tower of Pisa. Heavy traffic along the waterfront has caused the foundation to sink on one side so that the lighthouse is noticeably more than five degrees askew. Unlovely commercial signs stating "Lean towards export..." used to adorn the tower alongside posters of past cinema shows. It is regrettable that concerned citizens did not maintain it in better shape by painting it afresh in its former black and white stripes. No longer used for shipping but very much a landmark for the heavy traffic which passes, it is a shame to be ignored.

Beyond the lighthouse is the schooner jetty. Sturdy craft from Grenada, Barbados and St. Vincent with masts thicker than telegraph poles lie alongside rusting motor vessels from Guyana. They bring much-needed cargos of fruit and "ground provision", the root vegetables of eddoes, tannia, sweet potato, yam, and dasheen which with rice and Irish potatoes make up a large proportion of the local diet. Dieticians say this accounts for a high incidence of chronic constipation. Why does a country as fertile as Trinidad need to import? The soil is adequate, but the cost and availability of local agricultural labour make it much cheaper to import. It is a fine sight to watch a schooner leaving Port of Spain harbour under sail in the sunset, assisted by its powerful engines should the breeze be contrary. Adventurous travellers may persuade the master to take them as deck passengers. They should know that it is not rare for a schooner to sink without a trace.

It is hard to believe that in the 1960s the largest pig farm in Trinidad occupied a small muddy island across from the schooner jetty. It flourished until bureaucratic disaster struck. Hogs are routinely vaccinated against hog cholera. Through a lapse on the part of officials in the Ministry of Agriculture, supplies of the vaccine ran out. The farmer was refused permission to import his own vaccine. He watched his fine herd come down with the disease and be wiped out. To forestall his threats of legal action he was compensated with a long lease over an abandoned U.S. army camp site which over a number of hardworking years he turned into one of the largest contract broiler chicken farms in the country. He was not going to risk his livelihood a second time on pigs and official incompetence. The island reverted to mud.

Across Broadway from Fort San Andres is the imposing but deserted railway station and bus terminus building. Trinidad was graced with a railway as far east as Sangre Grande and south to San Fernando and Princes Town by 1886. The U.S. forces built two arterial highways for their needs and after the war, the Trinidad Government saw no need to support the dwindling railway system with perennial subsidies. The line to San Fernando was closed with due ceremony, the cars packed with sentimentalists singing Lord Kitchener's famous calypso "Last Train to San Fernando". That left only the commuter line to San Juan and Arima. Despite the infrequency of trains and their leisurely pace, travellers and pedestrians were killed regularly through carelessness or bravado. In December 1968, the Arima line was closed, and with it the age of railway in Trinidad. It was left to the same enterprising scrap dealer who had bought the massive steel buoys of the wartime submarine net, to buy in situ the miles of railway line. It was removed for sale abroad or conversion into reinforcing bars at a handsome profit.

Overlooking Cipriani's statue stands the Salvatori Building. This was the first modern office block in Trinidad, heralding the new age of air conditioned comfort. The Salvatori family were one of the many Corsican stock which came to Trinidad during the 19th century. In 1972 the building was sold and the head of the family retired to the comforts of the Cote d'Azur. The building changed hands before being acquired by Government at a price which enriched the entrepreneurs by several million. Each year before Carnival a large steel frame stand is bolted together opposite the Salvatori building on the space intended as a park. Each year after Carnival it is taken down and the area reverts to littered concrete paths. It is at this stand that the mayor of Port of Spain officially opens Carnival as we have seen in that section.

"Bankers' Row" is now past. Unless they are burnt down by the time this writing sees the light of day, the buildings on both sides of Independence Square are curious, some former cocoa warehouses, some stores, lacking any architectural distinction but interesting remnants of a by-gone era. Particular note should be made of Mario's Pizzeria building which occupies a former hardware store. It was recently renovated in the original Turn of the Century style and stands out as a gem. Port of Spain must indeed have been an attractive city filled with such elegant buildings. Beyond them at the head of the elongated square stands the Catholic Cathedral of the Immaculate Conception.

Port of Spain's first church, made of timber, occupied the area behind the present cathedral, Tamarind Square. The Protestant Governor, Sir Ralph Woodford, was conscientious and sensitive in his government of a predominantly Catholic populace. Under the Spanish law adopted by the British at the Capitulation, the Governor had considerable ecclesiastical powers over the Catholic Church including the approval of church appointments. He showed none of the Protestant bias which was so often in Trinidad's social history to cause friction between what could be termed for the sake of generalisation, the British and French factions. It was on his initiative and with his financial support that Woodford's secretary, a qualified architect, Phillip Reinagle, was commissioned to build a stone church to replace the delapidated wooden one, starting in 1816. The colony had become more prosperous from cocoa and sugar exports and deserved a suitable church. Sir Ralph, who was a young man of 29 when appointed governor, regularly attended the more important masses at the Papist altar he had caused to be built as part of his gubernatorial duties. Upon his death his benevolent role was commemorated with a suitable plaque in the north trancept, a unique distinction for a Protestant. In the 1970s, Tamarind Square was nearly turned into a parking lot. It was only when an alert historian pointed out that, as the site of the original church, the area was consecrated ground; the plans for parking were dropped.

Consecrated or not, Tamarind Square and Columbus Square behind it are now a haven for elderly derelicts, the pavement dwellers who resist all attempts to place them in suitable institutions. They prefer the anarchy of their cardboard bivouacs, eating scraps of food cadged at the back doors of Chinese restaurants. The sight of these unfortunates is distressing to those who live in Port of Spain and are accustomed to seeing them wander the city begging for change, but far more so to visitors who do not know of the efforts made to improve their lot. So benign is the climate that like their canine counterparts, these human strays flourish for years in their squalor. With the easy permissiveness of Trinidad, they are tolerated as a harmless eyesore.

Patrick Leigh Fermor dismisses both the Cathedral of the Immaculate Conception and Trinity Cathedral, also designed by Philip Reinagle as "servile imitations of English models of the time of Pusey and Ruskin." In this he is giving little credit to colonial history and is showing a superficial knowledge of architecture, particularly seeing that Ruskin was still a child when both cathedrals were built, and Pusey only in his twenties. Professional architects credit the Catholic church with a refined charm. The forecourt fenced with magnificent railings and gates, was not in the original design. George Street crossed in front of the western door. The commanding site at the head of the elongated square could, in retrospect, have used a more splendid structure; but in 1816 who was to know this?

Behind the cathedral across the East Dry River gleams the reflecting glass of a fine new skyscraper. "Riverside Plaza" was built to absorb the ever-increasing ranks of civil servants who were scattered in scores of offices throughout the city at high rents.Placing this building on the border of a slum is a brave effort to upgrade the area. In the early 1960s, Besson Street Police Station across the tiny square would be besieged` for days at a time by gunshot sniping from the local residents. Demolished was the Vasco da Gama bar where generations of labourers drank neat rum each afternoon with a chaser of Madeira wine before climbing the hill to their shanties. Civil servants in Riverside Plaza deplore the squalid walk to Frederick Street's "main drag" but in time the effort to decentralise the downtown area will be accepted. This is the old part of town where Port of Spain saw its origins. The Spanish lay-out of the streets now bearing princely British names - Duncan, George, Charlotte, Henry and Frederick, has held good to the present. Eminent 19th century visitors commented favourably on the town planning with its grid of streets. Traffic congestion blinds us to these merits today. The impression is one of noisy confusion and detritus. Every night scavenging crews clean the streets of orange peel, coconut husks, chicken-and-chips boxes and sweet drink cans; but every day negligent throngs litter them again.

*Angostura Bitters*

A few yards from the Catholic cathedral north up George Street is a long white warehouse now occupied by a variety of tenants. This was the block-deep premises extending throughout to Duncan Street where Angostura Bitters were made in secrecy for 150 years. The company moved to modern facilities at the outskirts of the city in Laventille in 1973 taking with them the secret formula and the gloomy family portraits of the Siegert forebears.

Dr. J.G.B. Siegert concocted his aromatic bitters primarily to aid his medical practice in 1824. It is still widely used as a prompt remedy for upset tummies. The distinctive crinkle-topped  label which catches dribbles down the side of the bottle, tells us that it is not made from Angostura bark, so is no kin to quinine or mauby. Its name comes from the city of Angostura in Venezuela where Dr. Siegert practised medicine until revolutions made him seek the political stability of nearby Trinidad. Angostura will not be found on today's maps of Venezuela. The word means "narrows " and is the city now known as Ciudad Bolivar occupying the narrows 240 miles up the broad Orinoco River where Sir Walter Raleigh and Antonio de Berrio travelled in the 16th Century in their search for El Dorado. Angostura, then Venezuela's fourth largest city despite its remote location, was honoured in 1846 with the name of the country's liberator, Simon Bolivar. Angostura had been the seat of the bishopric of Guyana which had religious authority over Trinidad until Protestant Governor Woodford's representations to the Vatican put matters right, and gave Trinidad its own vicar-apostolic in 1820.

The city's name is retained only by the bitters which give a unique flavour to pink gins, rum punches, and countless recipes around the world. Again the label, anxious to conform to modern day requirements on the labelling of ingredients, assures us that it is a "preparation of gentian in combination with a variety of harmless vegetable spices and vegetable colouring matter". Gentian is a plant genus with nearly 300 species, but the most commonly used one is "Gentiana lutea," going back in medicine 500 years. The Encyclopedia Britannica confirms that gentian "is one of the most efficient of the class of substances which act upon the stomach so as to invigorate digestion and thereby increase the general nutrition, without exerting any direct influence upon any other portion of the body than the alimentary canal."

Gentianin, the key component, is soluble in alcohol and this has been the source of many problems in promoting Angostura's bitters sales. Our crinkled label tells us that the alcoholic content is a potent "44.7% Gay Lussac," roughly equivalent to 90% proof. Although it would be scarcely possible to drink enough bitters to benefit from the alcoholic content, unlike many cough medicines and gripe mixtures, Angostura bitters have always faced the same prohibitive barriers as alcoholic beverages like rum and brandy with the resultant duty increase. For many years the company's directors have campaigned in North America and Europe to have their bitters recognised as a flavouring instead of a spirit, do away with the high duty and enable prices to be dropped substantially for the housewife and bartender.

The Siegert family with young blood of the new generation still control the recipe but the rum empire they also built up is now part of the Schenley Group. "Old Oak" their best known rum is immortalised in many calypsos and typifies the high calibre of Trinidadian rum. Jamaica's heavy navy rums, the amber rum of Barbados and the syrupy Demerara rums of Guyana are for some reason better known. To a rum drinker any Trinidad rum compares favourably to Bacardi and the best Puerto Rican light rums. In fact the House of Angostura now produces Bacardi under franchise in Trinidad, so high is its quality. During the prosperous oil-boom years a love of style made the majority of Trinidadians feel nothing but Scotch was good enough for them, and "deluxe" at that.

*The Lunchtime Limers*

# Chapter 13

━━━●•◉•●━━━

# *The Main Drag*

Every city has its main shopping street. Large cities may have several shopping areas competing with one another for leadership. In Port of Spain, Frederick Street has no rivals either for shopping or for the centre of social and commercial activity. It is the nation's carotid artery running down the centre of the downtown area to the statue of Andrew Cipriani on Independence Square. Fancy air conditioned malls may have attracted a high proportion of the luxury trade but in sheer volume of pedestrian activity, the number of stores and the amount of business transacted, Frederick Street is way ahead, and looks like it always will be.

We have seen that it was not one of the city's first streets. Only after the St. Ann's River was diverted down the present East Dry River was the area drained for development. Its Spanish colonial name was Calle de San Carlos. After the influx of the French it became known as Rue des Anglais, the Englishmen's Street, after the number of English sailors who would carouse there, while on shore leave. Only after the British captured the island in 1797 was it renamed after Prince Frederick, son of George III. Exactly which son is unclear. George III had nine sons, four of whom had Frederick as a Christian name. It was the second son, Frederick, Duke of York who the street is most likely to commemorate. George III seems to have had trouble thinking of names. Four of his sons also bore the name Augustus and of his six daughters, two were called Augusta. Frederick Street only applied for the first two blocks to Prince Street. Above that it was St. James Street for a further two blocks, finally becoming Clarence Street for the upper portion beyond Park Street all the way to the Grand Savannah. Perhaps out of consideration for the economies of sign-making this profusion of names echoed in all the north-south streets, was later pragmatised into a single name for the whole street.

Before George Brown brought style to Independence Square and Frederick Street at the end of the 19th Century, a succession of undistinguished wooden buildings burned down periodically. But neither Chacon Street to the west, which terminates abruptly at the Anglican cathedral, nor Henry Street to the east could compete with Frederick Street. Henry Street's stores to this day, while busy, are cheaper in rent, lower in quality of merchandise and in the clientele. Even more marked is the contrast of Charlotte Street running parallel one block east again. Here the lowest economic levels ply their trades in gloomy stores and on pavements. Run-down Chinese stores and restaurants do a thriving business at the bottom of the economic scale. (The epitome of degredation is to become a "Charlotte Street whore" - pronounced for the edification of those attending a calypso tent, "ho.")

Charlotte Street cannot be lightly dismissed. In many ways its squalid dynamism is more picturesque than the pretentious stores of Frederick Street. While a visitor will stand out like a sore thumb wandering the pavements, it is an experience for nose, ears, and eyes to jostle the throngs spending their pennies on cheap enamel utensils and ground provisions sold on jute bags on the pavement.

"Come, dahlin' look meh sweet zabocas (avocados). Try one,\

nah. Only a dollah."

"But, eh, eh. What you doing here chile? Dress up so nice you should be in Hi Lo (the main supermarket chain). Tek care you don't step in no mess!"

In a friendly but somewhat patronising way it will be made clear to you that they know you are slumming. You may not make out what is said in broad creole, but the smiles or mock fierceness will reassure you. Charlotte Street has the vitality of a North African soukh. The people are close to the earth, without pretensions or style, otherwise they would be "posing up" on Frederick Street.

George Brown gave more than style to Frederick Street. With thick dividing walls and cast iron steel frames, he introduced fire resisting standards still in use. The cast iron balcony of Stephens and Johnson, until its liquidation when the economy collapsed, the largest department store, and the columns of Glendinnings are all that remain in the first block walking northward from Independence Square. Go through to the Chacon Street side of Excellent Stores (formerly Woolworths) for one of the finest cast iron balconies. Is it a clause in their lease to keep it so spick and span? Further up Frederick Street there are many other samples of cast iron balconies to enjoy, but in the first block many new buildings have taken over. Glendinnings alone is unchanged inside from what it must have been in 1936 or 1906. Slender columns supporting a mezzanine around the perimeter of the building with a high glazed well of the "lantern roof."

Despite the effectiveness of George Brown's measures, fires continued to leave great gaps in the downtown streets. Arson finds a way to demolish the most modern concrete structure, and the social unrest of 1970 and after took its toll. So too did overloaded wiring and the air conditioning ducts through which a small fire could spread so rapidly. While fire hydrants stand at most corners, they were found to be mere decorations when it came to fighting fires. Water distribution inadequacies were most marked when it came to fire-fighting. "No pressure," was the oft-repeated cry.

At multi-million dollar expense, a new salt water main system drawing its supply from the sea was introduced in the

late 1970s. Traffic, always bad, was made much worse as
every street was excavated to lay the lines, and was poorly
repaved thereafter. Even with endless sea water, the fire
department seems to have problems with its pumps or the
condition of its hoses. Hardworking though the firemen may
be, it is rare for a fire to be snuffed out in its early stages. All
too often bystanders watch it gather strength until the building is a raging inferno. It is considered a success if firemen can
wet down the neighbouring buildings to prevent the fire
spreading. The incidence of commercial fires has become so
bad in Trinidad over the last fifteen years that insurance
premiums have sky-rocketted, and international re-insur-
ance companies are getting cold feet about accepting Trinidad
as a risk.

Until they failed in 1988, Stephens and Johnson shared
premises as a single enterprise. Johnsons formerly competed
with Stephens directly across the street, offering the best
quality goods in town until its modern, escalatored building
burned down. A glossy conglomeration of a mall has taken its
place, rents so high that one fears from their anguished sale
advertisements that the tenants cannot survive. The same is
true of other stores. Elegant Habib's Man Shop for which top
international designers were used, has given way to a mundane shoe shop. Stylish Aboutique making the most of its cast
iron columns, had new fretwork made to set off its quality
fabrics. It too burned down, and in its solid concrete replacement is another shoe shop.

With prosperity from oil, a brashness descended on
Frederick Street which is yet to leave. The pavement vendors
were moved initially to Bankers' Row on Independence Square.
The second wave of vendors that replaced them were provided
with quarters on the group of burned out premises above
Queen Street. A new wave of vendors has taken over, touting
incense, cheap scarves, stainless steel bangles and illegally
imported blouses. These new salesmen are likely to be towering "rastas", open dashiki shirts jangling with a life-savings
of golden chains, eyes glaring aggressively as they waylay the
passersby with their huge arms. One is glad to get to the oasis
of greenery at Woodford Square.

Shopkeepers on Frederick Street will tell you that the flood of people is no indication of their buying intentions.

"They just come out to lime," complain many. Every store front has its neatly clad young men leaning in rows against a store front, commenting audibly on the passersby. Girls come in for most of the "heckling" and soon learn to turn a deaf ear to the provocative, witty and salacious blandishments murmured expertly to them as they pass. Many will see friends and stop to chat, even joining the lime for a time. With an hour for lunch and the boss probably coming back late, there is plenty of time for sport on the pavement before returning to a mundane desk job. Only occasionally does the verbal molestation become physical in the Italian fashion. That is likely to provoke a torrent of shouted abuse, quickly drawing a crowd of onlookers eager for scandal. The stentorian voice of an evangelical preacher declaiming to everybody or nobody from across the pavement is ignored in the general hubbub.

The limers watching the girls pass have every reason to enjoy their pastime. With their love of style, colour and a natural sense of "theatre" all the girls will make the most of their natural talents, and the young men will offer good competition. Those generously endowed will have no fear of making the best of it. Jeans may be specially fitted to hug every generous curve. Hair will be styled weekly whether it be in cane-rows with beads, Michael Jackson curls or whatever the passing fad. What is in fashion this month cannot be seen the next. Youths will spend a week's salary on the latest style in shoes. Even those working on building sites will quite likely be wearing a $150 Gucci jersey. Chances are they have been seen in it at two or three fetes and it cannot be worn again in public. To all appearances the youth of Trinidad, like the Teddy boys of post-war London, are prepared to squander the bulk of their earnings for the sake of appearance.

This pride of appearance is a remarkable trait. Should you happen to pass by a modest unpainted wooden shack in an unfenced yard on a Saturday evening you would very likely see a gorgeous girl, made up like a tropical blossom, hair fresh from the parlour, in the latest avant garde fashion from tip to toe, emerging carefully across the muddy path onto the road.

She may be one of a family of eight who somehow or other live three to a cramped room; yet can all manage to wear immaculately laundered and tailored clothes. Moreover each will have spent half an hour bathing in the cold outdoor shower before dressing; for the cleanly personal habits of Trinidadians generally matches their outward appearance. Small wonder then that Frederick Street should be a constant source of voyeuristic entertainment. Everyone is out to be seen, as much as to see. They make sure they flaunt what they have.

Woodford Square is justly named after the governor who saved it from becoming a church yard. The Catholics dominated religious life from the earliest days of the colony, but with the English at the start of the 19th Century came their Anglican religion and the need for a suitable church. The earliest name of the square was Place des Armes from a reputed Carib battle there. When the British took over it was named Brunswick Square, and retained as the plaza intended by the Spanish in their town planning. When the garrison chapel on the south side of the square burned in the fire of 1808, the new church commissioned was sited slap in the middle of the square. By the time Woodford arrived to take up his post construction had advanced to the stage that the roof was ready for installation. A petition of the proprietors around the square persuaded Woodford that the square had been given in perpetuity to the public. Moreover, the proprietors pointed out, they had been required to pay a premium for their lots because of the protected outlook.

Amazingly the twenty-nine-year-old governor gave the order to demolish the church and rebuild it to a new design on the southern side of the square. He took the opportunity to let his secretary, Philip Reinagle, handle the design at the same time as he was doing the Catholic cathedral. Trinity Cathedral sits on a charming site, except for the eastern side conceded to car parking. Its little octagonal spire seems too small for the square tower on which it sits as if money ran out and economies had to be made. It lacks the imposing presence of a true cathedral, but this is appropriate in a land where the Anglicans, despite many running political battles, between the creoles and the "English party", have always played second fiddle to the Catholics.

Facing Frederick Street across the full width of the square lies the massive legislative building known from its brick red plaster as the Red House. Now this is a building of which any city would be proud, as imposing in its columned mass as New York's Central Library. It is dominated by a tall central storey topped with a square copper dome, hollow to the now waterless fountain on the ground floor. The former parliament building designed in 1844 by Richard Bridgens was separated into two sections by Prince Street which then ran through it. It was first painted red to celebrate Queen Victoria's diamond jubilee in 1887. It was burned to the ground in the Water Riot of 1903. This was a serious affair arising out of an intended metering of water which resulted in sixteen deaths and forty-two injuries when the police opened fire on the crowd.

Daniel Hahn, a German-trained architect, was commissioned to design the replacement. He retained a public walkway through the building but otherwise linked it into one building. The red exterior was also kept. With understandable pride the *Port of Spain Gazette* anticipated, as it neared completion, that it "will perhaps be the finest structure in the West Indies." Certainly it gives an air of grandeur to the city, raising its whole architectural morale. To think of Port of Spain without the Red House is unimaginable.

On the north side of Woodford Square the curious old Lucien Building was demolished to make way for the block-large complex of the modern Hall of Justice. This was completed in 1985, the first of the oil boom extravagances. One of its features is a triplication of facilities to prevent jurors talking to witnesses, or judges speaking to either on their way to and from court. There are separate sets of lifts, fire escapes and toilets for each. The air conditioned courts will be welcome to jurors and witnesses accustomed to sweltering in jackets in the midday heat. Respect for the law is clearly to be encouraged, and "improper dress" in a court of law cannot be tolerated. Shirt jacs do not meet the conservative standard set by judges and lawyers who wear the wigs and gowns of their Temple brethren. For the many country people who own no jacket one can readily be rented from hawkers on the pavement outside.

Alongside the Hall of Justice is the Public Library built of the yellow London brick used as ballast on the return voyages of sugar boats. Its modest facilities are well tended and appear to suffice for a nation of people who prefer to perform the arts rather than read about them. Next door is the modern City Hall hollowed out into a patio from which rises a staircase. Carlisle Chang's mural, "Conquerabia" - the name we are told the Arawaks had for the area, does little to give the building much distinction.

Commercial activity on Frederick Street peters out along Woodford Square where Greyfriars Presbyterian church stands beside its hall, available to social groups at a modest rental. The pavement at this point is unfortunately littered with professional beggars. To those who pass them every day they are taken for granted. They are a part of the local scene which has resisted official efforts at removal. To visitors they are a shock and a human tragedy which they view with abhorrent dismay. How can so wealthy a country permit it? This is not Calcutta. Non-committal about criticism from tourists, no more stringent efforts are made to remedy the problem.

Dr. Eric Williams referred to Woodford Square as the "University of Woodford Square" from the political meetings he held there during his heyday, and the education he gave his listeners from the bandstand. Soul music and reggae were more commonly heard blaring from loudspeakers in later days of political indifference. There is always a handful of self-inspired orators declaiming to passers-by how the wrongs of the world should be righted. This is the Hyde Park Corner of Trinidad, a safety valve for extreme views.

Above Woodford Square, commercial Frederick Street takes on a new lease of life. Above and below the broad cross street of Park Street new buildings sport a variety of boutiques and dress shops. These end at St. Mary's College, at present the most prestigious place of secondary education. It is also known by its initials, CIC - College of the Immaculate Conception.

The upper blocks of Frederick Street still have examples of the older quaint fretwork architecture. One block is taken up with the tall yellow wall and entrance gate of the Royal Gaol made famous in Sparrow's 1962 calypso. Destined for destruction should the multi-million dollar facilities at Golden Grove be completed, the Royal Gaol has primitive conditions which have led the inmates to riot more than once in recent times. One or two even threw themselves to the ground from the tall walls rather than continue to suffer.

At the top of Frederick Street stands the Victoria Institute looking across at Memorial Park. The museum is housed in the Dutch-inspired building conceived by Daniel Hahn, architect of the Red House and Queen's Royal College. A galleon's rusted anchor, unlikely to have come from Columbus' fleet, and a pair of rescued cannons stand outside. The ground floor long contained dusty showcases of stuffed animals and factory models. Upstairs is a small collection of Trinidad's foremost artists, including a group of Cazabon's coloured etchings. In recent years the museum has been much improved.

One of Trinidad's most famous sons, the artist, Jean Michel Cazabon, illustrates the early multi-racial nature of Trinidad society. He was born in 1813 to parents who were free negroes. At the age of nine he was sent to boarding school in England, moving to Paris when he was old enough to study medicine. Instead, the artistic life attracted him more, and he worked successfully there and in Rome as an artist. It was not until he was thirty-seven that he returned to Trinidad with his family for ten years. During that time he painted the scenes of Trinidad, reproduced as the coloured etchings now so prized by collectors. He moved to Martinique for ten years, returning to his birthplace for the twilight of his life as art teacher to the boisterous pupils of Queen's Royal College and St. Mary's (at that time affiliated to each other). He died at his easel, aged 75, after enduring eighteen years of classroom indiscipline.

The annual November Exhibition of paintings and sculpture is displayed in the same room. Critics may discern a common denominator in Trinidadian painting whether by African, Indian, Chinese or European. Representational, brightly coloured and unsophisticated, many Trinidadian painters would seen naive in a Puerto Rican gallery.

Sharing space with the paintings is a tableau of Carnival costumes, dusty and pathetic out of the context of the band from which they came. Missing is the exuberant movement of the masqueraders who played in them for two glorious days. To those unable to witness Carnival they may be of some interest for the workmanship and imagination, but not to anyone else. The only display of costumes that does them any justice is put on right after Carnival at the Hilton Hotel. They are then still fresh in memory's eye and unspoiled by dust. There has been much talk of a better display of Carnival to out-of-season visitors, but it is probably a waste of effort. Carnival is a living experience needing the music, the crowds, the sunshine and flasks of rum and constant movement to give the costumes any validity.

*The Boissiere House*

# Chapter 14

━━━●•◉•●━━━

# *The People's Playground*

Copenhagen's Tivoli Gardens are held to be the most versatile park area in any major city. Port of Spain's Grand Savannah, officially still the Queen's Park Savanah, must come a close second. Unlike downtown Port of Spain which has retained the original Spanish colonial layout, the Savannah has nothing to do with the Spanish legacy. By the end of the 18th Century, today's Savannah was Paradise Estate and belonged to the Peschier family, one of the first French families to take advantage of the Cedula of Population of 1783.

Young Governor Woodford could not afford to purchase for his new residence the nearby estate of Champs Elysees, now the Trinidad Country Club, because official funds were tied up settling American negro ex-soldiers into settlements in the South. It is just as well. Instead he purchased from the Peschier family, Hollondais Estate adjacent to it to the north for his own residence and the Botanical Gardens. The Peschier family were allowed to keep their family cemetery, occupying 6,000 sq. ft. in the middle of the Savannah provided they maintained it themselves. It is still there. Woodford laid out the 199-acre Savannah as a common for the public grazing of cattle and general recreation in 1820. The public wasted no time in putting it to good use. The first informal racing took place in 1828. According to Cazabon's engraving of the first formal meeting in 1853 there was even a cast iron grandstand. Other sources indicate Governor Harris organised an earlier race meeting in 1846.

As the city grew, so jealous eyes viewed the Savannah for real estate development. They nearly succeeded. In the 1890s the Governor, Sir Napier Broome, Knight Commander of St. Michael and St. George, had in mind to sell off 24 acres from the lower section of the Savannah in a line from Marli Street to Jerningham Avenue for residential lots. (It was not called Jerningham Avenue at the time, of course, as Jerningham succeeded Broome as governor). An employee in the Crown Lands Department, Thomas Potter, is given credit for having "sweet talked" first his boss and subsequently the governor into reconsidering the plan. His prescient view was that in years to come the city would need as much recreation space as possible. Thank you Mr. Potter.

The Savannah is shaped like a left ear, rounded along the eastern side with New Town carved out of the lower western portion. Apart from the sunken Hollows at the northwestern corner, it is flat, sloping gently from north to south. Standing on the "pitch walk" in front of the site of the mansion Woodford built for his residence, the blue of the Gulf of Paria can be seen between the taller buildings. The pitch walk around the outer edge of the Savannah was, as one would expect, made from the natural asphalt from the Pitch Lake at La Brea. Benches are generously interpersed along the Pitch Walk. They are well frequented by the thousands of people who use the Savannah each day. These days the benches are made of cast concrete with green wooden slats. The Victorian cast iron benches identical to those in London's Hyde Park have not survived the ravages of hard usage. It is more manly to sit on the back, feet scraping the slats of the seat. You are then on eye level with the girls you intend to heckle.

Very little remains of the iron fence that once prescribed the Savannah's edge. Nothing so fancy as railings to keep out lovers and vagrants after sunset, merely two horizontal square bars supported each twelve feet by small pillars, ideal for sitting on with heels hooked over the lower bar. When cows grazed on the Savannah, this fence kept them in, but it also served to stop children straying in front of the wheels of the Savannah tram making the rounds up to 1950. Two turnstiles remain in the stretch of fence on the northern perimeter. The rest went, not to the War Effort like British fences, but piece by piece to negligent abuse. Many of today's older citizens recall the trip around the Savannah on the tram with their nanny as a special treat.

Being the hub around which the life of those in Port of Spain revolves, there is outspoken interest and concern about the Savannah. Should the fence be removed altogether or be replaced with a sturdy low concrete block wall? Horrors, a wall for rapists to hide behind. Never happen! But it nearly did. When the Water and Sewerage Authority built an ugly block shed to house a pump in its never-ending battle to keep up with prodigal usage, concerned lovers of the environment shrieked in letters to the editor about despoiling their heritage. The shed still stands, but the next effort by WASA in compromise was a small fenced pump with no shed. Great steel pylons appeared one day at key points around the race track. These were for TV cameras on the dozen days of the year that races are held. Another outcry. The top sections were removed, gulling the critics into thinking they had won. But the stubby towers remain for TV cameras to capture for the stewards, any foul play by jockeys.

Cars are allowed to park on the Savannah around the Grand Stand on designated occasions like Carnival, race meetings and special events. Signs warn it is against the law at any other time. With the upsurge in car ownership, more and more cars edged onto the Savannah at all points for lunchtime chicken and chips or an afternoon picnic until it began to look like a parking lot. Another outcry and temporary respite when the newly introduced ticketing system provided a suitable weapon.

Horses still enjoy pride of place on the Savannah. There is stable space for 206 race horses but more is needed. This was one of the arguments for moving racing to one central location in the Caroni plains. If the Racing Complex ever achieves the removal of horses from the Savannah it will be regretted by owners who enjoyed slipping down in shorts before breakfast to see their prided animals exercise, and swap knowledgeable speculation with grooms and trainers. Children too, love to watch the horses galloping around the large sand track. It is possibly their only chance to see horses run. The race track itself prescribes a smaller circuit in front of the Grand Stand and is grassed.

Interspersed around and between these two tracks are 28 cricket pitches allocated to sporting clubs and public schools. With the start of the rainy season, cricket gives way to soccer. Soccer pitches and two rugger pitches find space on the large grassed area. Tall trees shade the outer Pitch Walk, mainly with pink and yellow poui with occasional young samaan. There is a double line of tall pink poui forming an avenue carpetted in pink blossoms at the end of the dry season in front of the mansions known as the Magnificent Seven. Within the Savannah there are few trees. The patch of shade that these few provide are commandeered by batsmen so they can lie in groups and "old talk" or on a weekend fete-match, "fire grog."

A complex bureaucracy rules the Savannah. The pitch walk and its benches fall under the Ministry of Works. The trees around the edge fall under the aegis of the Ministry of Agriculture as does the Hollows. The interior is controlled by the City Council. Getting anything done on the Savannah requires the keen brain of a lawyer to keep the red tape untangled. The iron railing if nothing else provided a clear line between opposing controls.

The Hollows at the northwest corner lie across from the turrets of Stollmeyer Castle and the Ministry of Agriculture. Decorative concrete pools stocked with lilies and fish give endless entertainment to toddlers with proud parents and bands of mischievous youngsters. The older generation will tell of the keeper of the Hollows who guarded it like Cerberus.

Should any youngster tamper with the pools or risk breaking a branch by climbing the logwood trees he would appear with a roar from concealment over the bank, causing the boys to flee in fear of their lives. Evading him was half the fun. Today's youngsters would show scant regard for such devotion to duty. In all probability they would stand their ground and "stone" him.

Between Christmas and Carnival, the Hollows' natural amphitheatre is used for several out-door steelband concerts on Sunday evenings, courtesy of a leading commercial bank. Many hundreds gather in their smartly turned out family units, lovers' arms entwined, to sit on the grass banks or stroll about, sure to encounter friends. When darkness falls a corner of the Hollows will be used for a small revival meeting lit by a hurricane lantern hung in a tree. Concrete benches will be illicitly moved into a miniature chapel grouping.

Much larger religious functions are rented space at the diametrically opposite southeast corner. This is a wasteland between the Grand Stand and Queens Park East where Carnival bands entering the Savannah have pounded the soil into a surface so hard that even weeds are unequal to the struggle. A broad swath has been tarmacced to let the wheels of steel bands pass more readily. Adjacent to the public toilet facilities used primarily by grateful derelicts who spend their lives nearby, a large canvas tent is pitched for evangelical gatherings, promising miracles of healing and a new spiritual life. When the crusade decamps, the appropriately named Paradise Fun Fair may take its place for a month or two. Carousels and other stomach-churning contraptions, bright with a thousand lights, will provide an irresistible appeal.

It is on the Pitch Walk that most activity takes place. Just as this book makes numerous reference to the Savannah, so the people of Port of Spain seem to return to it or drive around it several times each day. Until 1982 traffic around the Savannah was two-way. One of the only two traffic lights created a few weeks storm of criticism against Prime Minister Williams who had declared "Massah Day Done!" It was placed outside his office at Whitehall so that he and his ministers could emerge safely into the current of traffic. Was this evidence of executive privilege the thin end of the wedge for a new massah? As the volume of cars grew, the Savannah's capacity to deal with it sagged. On a Friday afternoon, particularly if it was raining, traffic would freeze up at each corner roundabout into a monumental traffic jam.

The residential valleys of St. Anns and Cascade have no other means of access but the Savannah. All the Maraval and Long Circular Road traffic spews out at the Hollows roundabout. Residents of the congested valleys of Belmont flow naturally out onto Queen's Park East. So too Lady Young Road brings the Morvant residents to the city and with them all those from points east and south trying to by-pass the downtown jams. St. Clair and Newtown have alternative routes but seldom resist the arterial flow pulsing around the heart of Port of Spain. Even if traffic is often slowed to a crawl there is plenty to watch. Young mothers pushing prams, the clique of white-haired Portuguese on their customary bench, occasional camera-slung tourists with pallid buttocks peeping out from shorts, and joggers, with a bit of luck, well-endowed.

With a bold move in 1982 the Traffic Branch introduced a radical change to the city's bloodstream. The Savannah was to become one-way running clockwise. A giant roundabout. It was purportedly a three-month experiment, of course. To make it permanent off the bat would smell of dictatorship. But the populace knew and accepted that, like most trial periods, it was a foregone conclusion it was there to stay. What author of the scheme could accept the loss of face by reverting to the status quo? It is 3.7 kilometers around the Savannah, but despite many gloomy predictions, the traffic flows smoothly. While it may not be the largest roundabout in the world - Brasilia's vast verges must be larger - it must surely be the largest for a city of comparable size. Cramming four lanes of traffic onto the road, in places narrow, requires precision driving. No self-respecting Trinidad driver, male or female, would let this slow him/her down. With the reckless yet skilled sangfroid that leaves visitors aghast, but surprisingly few drivers in the mortuary, cars slip in and out of lanes with an intuitive understanding of each other's intentions.

Getting into the rapidly passing stream is the hardest part. Once in, you jockey for your place with the same ease children learn at the fun fair's dodgem cars.

This constant and rapid flow makes it hard for pedestrians to reach the sanctuary of the Pitch Walk. Additional traffic lights have been installed to give pedestrians a sporting chance. They can again reach the carts of the coconut vendors and enjoy a cool "jelly nut" guaranteed good for the kidneys. Or in the evening buy from the oyster vendors whose jars contain varying degrees of fiery red sauce. Corn on the cob comes in two forms- charred on an open coal-pot ("roasted" as it is called), or boiled over a coal-pot in a tall pan of seasoned water that has replaced the old "sweet oil" tin. On a race day or at one of the pre-Carnival events, itinerant vendors provide a greater variety of diet. Sweet drinks of virulent hue, hamburgers and above all, snow-cones.

The block of ice is no longer shaved by hand. A machine rapidly grinds a mound of snowy crystals which are piled into a paper cone. Violet, orange and yellow syrups are poured over it, quickly absorbed into the crushed ice. Sucking it may freeze your teeth, but it is sure to refresh you.

Folk art finds a place on the vendors' carts. Several of these are left on permanent display with negligent trust at the corner where steelbands enter the Savannah. Hours of devoted imagination have gone into the staring-eyed puppets on the carts, embellished with terse statements of earthy philosophy. Every surface has its figures set on a canary yellow background. Do their makers prize them as much as passersby? It is their personal year-round Carnival display. Just because they are left in the midday downpours does not mean they are thrown aside like the Carnival costumes.

How best to savour the Savannah's delights? Little by little. It is too much for one bite. As a human carousel it is most comfortable to sit in the shade of a poui tree letting the tide of humanity flow past in the golden rays of the setting sun. For recreation either in the dawn's freshness with the joggers and walkers, or the late afternoon when the heat of the midday is done and the playing fields are busy. Cricket has been adapted into a version known as "windball" played by both men and women. The leading women's teams play on the two asphalt paths leading into the grand stand when it is not busy with race meetings or other exhibitions. Although no pads are worn as in normal cricket, the women dress in brightly-coloured uniforms, turquoise slacks topped by yellow tee-shirts versus green slacks topped by orange tee-shirts. Instead of the hard leather or cork ball, worn tennis balls are used. Even though these may be dipped in water to give them more weight, they cannot be bowled in the regular straight arm action. Instead they are lethally "chucked" after a running wind-up. Stumps and bails do not suit the asphalt wicket. An oversize board wicket supported by a prop behind is used. Male supporters give a vociferous commentary on the errors and  heroics of the contestants.

Sunday afternoon entertainment is provided by the police or regiment band playing  in the bandstand in front of the president's mansion. The current crop of calypsoes will be interpreted to a martial beat while families in their "Sunday best" stroll around the grounds. More formal entertainment is provided at the Grand Stand. You may not be a "turfite" but can you resist the annual dog show or horticultural exhibit where fountains gurgle through fern-festooned gardens as a backdrop for one of the world's finest displays of orchids? The space underneath the bleachers of the stands is used for this and many other similar displays. North American stage stars for whom the Queen's Hall was too small, could perform to massed crowds on a stage erected in front of the Grand Stand until the Stadium was built.

But it is the score of events leading up to Carnival when the Grand Stand comes into its own. An equally large stand is built facing it on the northern side. Instead of the uncomfortable metal chairs whose curved back and seats create a most unorthopedic agony, the hurly-burly aficionados of the North Stand have wide wooden bleachers on which cooler chests and bars can be set up. Pickpockets crawl beneath the supporting framework on the lookout for protruding wallets. Flasks of scotch and cameras can equally easily slip into their hands.

Wooden fences are erected for Carnival to channel the flow of masqueraders across the stage. Rickety eyries are built for

TV cameramen and the press. Along the south edge of the Savannah, vendors' huts are hurriedly erected. In former years these were left to the individual construction skills of the vendor and his family. A motley line of shacks resulted. To improve appearances the Carnival Development Committee announced it was seeking the help of local architects in providing a suitable design for a collapsible unit. A prize would be awarded. Come Carnival season, ugly booths scarcely better than those built by the vendors sprouted up. Another outcry. Was this the best local architects could manage? The architects' professional body declared that their honour had been besmirched. It was not an architect's design at all, but the work of some enterprising but ungifted petty contractor who had been commissioned for the work by officials scared of missing the deadline. Next season it was better. Pre-fab units built of locally grown teak were neat until the vendors started decking them out with the usual beer and sweet drink signs and Christmas decoration tinsel.

After Carnival, the units were offered for sale as modest housing units, work sheds or whatever. Perhaps the price was too high. There they remained until it looked like a conspiracy to leave them permanently. One more outcry. Eventually the sheds were dismantled. Pre-fab units are now used, but each year lovers of the Savannah grow nervous that the authorities will try and slip one over on them by putting up permanent stands and sheds. Vigilantly they watch for the first signs of demolition. It is in the best Trinidadian tradition to have reservations about those in authority and keep them in line by periodic furores.

*Around the Savannah*

If the Savannah is a constant source of diversion to its people, how much more so to the visitor are the buildings which skirt it. Despite the heavy traffic, encroachments of commercialism have been restricted. The Savannah is still residential in character even though many of the fine old homes house insurance offices and government departments. To many tourists they are merely curious old-fashioned buildings. To the architecturally conversant they are more.

*Mille Fleurs, Queen's Park West*

A long catalogue of noteworthy buildings can make dreary reading. But let us follow the highlights around, just as the traffic does. The elegant silk cotton tree below the Hilton Hotel makes a natural starting point. The cafe on the corner of Belmont Circular Road long catered to the lower middle class residents of Belmont. The family that owned the ugly concrete structure made their own excellent ice cream. Beyond are some quaint little houses trimmed with turn-of-the-century wooden fretwork. The RAF Association occupies one of them. The Central Library Services building housed an extensive library until the late sixties. The roof received inadequate maintenance and a series of downpours drenched the stacks of books. The library was closed "until further notice." That was over fifteen years ago. The library staff are employed elsewhere. The books have presumably dried out. But whether the building should be renovated and upgraded, or the library moved to grander quarters is a dilemma which the authorities appear unable to resolve. The public library on Woodford Square is barely adequate for the public's needs.

Half way down the eastern side of the Savannah is a substantial excavated foundation. Placards along the front boast of luxury condominiums, naming the professional firms responsible. This project teetered on the edge of success at the height of the oil boom. Every appeal to high price snobbery was tried to sell the units. But even a penthouse overlooking the Savannah could hardly justify a million dollar price tag. Why, for that a man could buy two Mercedes .

Some large gingerbread houses continue down to Memorial Park. One of them claims to offer "Indo-Chinese" cuisine. Those wishing to savour the lost delights of Saigon will be disappointed. The food served is Indian curry and roti, or regular Chinese. An insurance company and a computer firm share a modern concrete office block which replaced one fair old lady in gingerbread skirts. This is taken to be a sign of progress. But were the gingerbread houses so impractical? Let us look at their fretwork facades more closely. Was all that work put into the building merely because labour was cheap? Far from it. There were advantages which were unnoticed for fifty years. Study now shows that the fretwork barge boarding breaks rainfall and filters the light and air. The cast iron cresting was not an extravagant way to keep the pigeons away but served to anchor the roof. The wooden finial jutting up at the ends of the steeply sloping roofs secured the ridge ends and the rafters could be tied structurally together by the religious-looking cross-brace below. Ornately carved wooden brackets helped stiffen the slender wooden posts supporting the porte-cochere and gallery. It was even found that the carved fretwork confused the bats' echo signals making them seek roosts elsewhere. Only when buildings are made without these features and the weather and bats wreak havoc, do the niceties emerge.

The late John Newel Lewis, a noted local architect and artist who did more than anyone to keep alive in his coloured drawings, the merits of the old buildings, put it this way:

"They cannot be faulted from a technology standpoint as a closer inspection would reveal a full understanding of good construction related to local climate. The assembly of the building components has been faultlessly carried out. The roofs are usually very steep, the high pitch allows the water to be disposed of quickly. The joints in the buildings are well protected. These are very vulnerable connections which can suffer early attrition.

"The exposed ends of main bearing timbers are battered by the weather, high winds, water saturation and earth tremors which can loosen key connections. The use of heavy finials tie the gable and hold down the end of the roof. The weak joints which take water penetration are fully protected by cills, heads and architraves, fretwork boarding, string courses, hoods, louvres, trim and cover strips. Every single piece of fancy work has a practical reason for being there. Every decorative item has its origin in functional protection. The houses are well built and sensibly engineered."*

It has been claimed that there are only six different basic motifs used in the fretwork designs. Undoubtedly a comprehensive study would reveal a much greater variety than this. The carved boards were mass produced locally on a production line basis before modular construction had a title. Was this a parochial architecture or a deliberate attempt at style? The same Scots builder, George Brown, who changed the face of the downtown area with his elegant cast iron columns and balconies, must be given much of the credit.

The signpost that used to stand at the corner of Queens Park East and Memorial Park which read "Queens Park East/ Queens Park West" sadly no longer stands. Where better than Trinidad does East meet West so appropriately? Memorial Park was set apart from the Savannah to site a fine British cenotaph commemorating those Trinidadians who fell in World War I. A marked reminder of Trinidad's colonial past, it would be equally at home in a Hertfordshire town. There is no need to remove it. It is a fine example of its genre, and nothing of comparable quality would take its place.

Proceeding west from Memorial Park past an ugly walled basketball court, we reach the abandoned site of the old Princes Building, marked by the lonely fountain that still stands in front. This large assembly hall was built in a hurry in 1861 to provide a suitable venue for a ball to honour Prince Alfred, Duke of Edinburgh, Queen Victoria's youngest son. Amazingly, the building was thrown together in five weeks, using among other things, bricks from the ruins of the governor's former residence on Belmont Hill. Small wonder that Charles Kingsley of "Water Babies" fame who was spending a few months in Trinidad at the time, should point out that it lacked architectural merit. Prince Alfred actually cancelled his visit because of a smallpox scare, but the large hall earned its name at last when Queen Victoria's grandsons, Prince Arthur and Prince George, later George V, came to Trinidad

*John Newel Lewis, *Ajoupa* by kind permission of the author

in 1880. Besides being used for concerts, it housed Queens Royal College until the present building, one of the Magnificent Seven on Queen's Park West, was built at the turn of the century.

No doubt remembering the concerts of his childhood, Lord Kitchener, "The Road March King" prevailed on the authorities to rent him the hall for his calypso "tent" during the late 70s. Otherwise the building was vacant except for assorted pavement dwellers who lived in nests of cardboard in the foundations. And we must not forget Miss Dalrymple.

Miss Dalrymple operated a small snack bar below the eastern gallery. Generations of tennis players from the nearby courts would gather there for her refreshing but bitter home-made mauby.

The imposing Princes Building was a casualty of prosperity. Government announced grandiose plans for a Performing Arts Centre, with a generous prize for the winning design. The site was in the immediate vicinity of the Princes Building. Clearly the old building was in the way. In a curiously inevitable way a small fire started in the foundations and was, not surprisingly, wetted down so casually that the fire spread and the historic building was destroyed. Will we ever see our Palace of Fine Arts with its various art galleries, stages and auditorium? Highly unlikely as it was to have cost over $50,000,000 and has a low priority in today's constrained economic circumstances.

Beyond the derelict site of the Princes Building where a magnificent samaan used to spread a vast umbrella of branches, stands "Knowsley", a gracious mansion which occupies the entire block at the corner of Chancery Lane. It was built by William Gordon Gordon who had come to Trinidad as a junior clerk with Colonial Bank. Among his duties was the delivery of shipping documents to the gloomy warehouses of importers. His canny Scots eye quickly formed and educated picture of what stocks were in short supply, and on which a price rise could be expected before new shipments arrived. He soon went into business for himself, building a merchant empire which included his own small bank. The building now houses the Ministry of Labour which must be given credit for repairing the outside without destroying the integrity of the building. The conical tower which is its main feature could not have slates replaced, but asphalt shingle is an acceptable substitute. At the back, rising above the Dundonald Street wall was a fine dovecote, occupied by grateful pigeons until its demolition.

At the top of Victoria Avenue stands the famed Queens Park Hotel, now largely demolished. The original portion was built by George Brown for the son of the great Chief Justice, Charles Warner, whose Protestant pro-British rule over Trinidadian affairs spanned seven governors and was the bane of the French creole faction. On the further corner, George Brown built his own house. His descendants continued to occupy it until it was sold to an insurance company in 1987. The firm had little regard for architectural sentiment and announced plans to tear it down to make way for a modern office building. This outraged the coterie sensitive to the nation's heritage. They picketed the building and protested in· the press. Never before had there been so much outcry over an old building. Happily the insurance company accepted a suggestion that their new building could as readily be built behind George Brown's house, leaving it intact.

One must duck down Cipriani Boulevard at the next corner to see George Brown's first known house. This is the residence of the Boos family owned, occupied and well maintained by Olga Mavrogordato, authoress of "Voices in the Street." Rather untropical in its battleship grey paint, it is a fine house set in a garden large enough to do it justice. George Brown's three other notable Savannah houses are on the western side of the Savannah among the "Magnificent Seven."

"Gingerbread" decoration reaches a state of the art at 12 Queen's Park West. So ornate is the carved tracery around the edges that one expects a fairytale witch to be waiting inside instead of the elderly and devout Misses Boissiere. One imagines that time has stood still for them and that the interior of their charming home will be a tableau of by-gone Edwardiana.

At the corner of Marli Street stands the first building on the Savannah, All Saints Anglican Church which was built in

1846. It looks across at the modern, utilitarian American Embassy with its large waiting area filled each morning with those seeking visas. Even before the oil boom turned to bust, masses of Trinidadians had relatives in Brooklyn whom they wished to visit. Now they are likely to be trying to make their visit permanent. Small wonder the embassy authorities screen applicants so cautiously.

Modern apartment buildings are interspersed with old houses until one reaches the roundabout at the corner of Maraval Road. It is here the celebrated western edge of the Savannah starts with its line of buildings known nowadays as The Magnificent Seven. The first is Queens Royal College, a boys secondary school designed by the same Daniel Hahn responsible for the Red House parliamentary building. The college's florid facade of beige and rose pink stripes has a certain ugly flair, but the main feature is the central clock tower. Two modern concrete bunkers flank the main building and do nothing to enhance the overall impression. It was here that Dr. Eric Williams, Vidia Naipaul and many other of the country's notables received their schooling.

Next to it stands the least magnificent of the Seven, even though it was built by the esteemed George Brown in 1910, the Anglican bishop's residence, "Hayes Court." It holds its own in such majestic company, but if one were to rearrange things, "Knowsley" would be more suited to the spot. Next door is another George Brown creation, "Mille Fleurs," originally the home of the Prada family and subsequently the Salvatori family, who like the Ciprianis, the Agostinis, the Majanis and others, originated in Corsica.

With the servant shortage starting in the 1970s such a house was scarcely practical. It was sold to a group of Syrian businessmen who intended to use it for a social club. To this end they rebuilt the servants quarters at the back with Spanish tiles. They had not allowed for the whims of Dr. Williams, however. All the houses in this part of St. Clair are on 999 year lease from the Crown, now the State, with strict covenants about single family residence and no business on the premises. This was used to suppress the Syrian club plans. It was rented out occasionally for weddings for which

*The Archbishop's Palace, Queen's Park West*

the old home was a suitable setting, albeit hard on the building. To resolve the impasse, Government acquired the building, no doubt at a price which compensated the Syrians for their disappointment. It is now used to house the Ministry of National Security, despite the naive statue of two coy children playing under an umbrella in the pool at the entrance. Apparently being a ministry does not constitute a business, so far as convenants are concerned.

Fourth in the series, suitably centred, is the queen of the queens, the old Ambard House better known as "Roodals Mansion." The multiplicity of intricate slated towers and turrets above the glorious white decorated ironwork of balconies and brackets must be seen to be believed. Any attempt to describe it would make it sound a hodgepodge instead of a serene gem looking across the Savannah. It is the only one of the Seven used as a private family residence by a daughter of the Roodal's, who is both a physician and a theatre magnate. The present name, "Roomor," is a combination of Roodal and Morgan. The swimming pool is a recent addition.

The rose pink castle across the next street is the official residence of the Roman Catholic Archbishop. Another masterwork of George Brown, the use of cloisters conveys a suitably ecclesiastical tone to the building, which with its turreted tower and spiral staircase, lacks any homely feeling. Small wonder then that the present archbishop, first one to be of local stock, should have opted for humble parish quarters in preference to this palace, which had been specially modernised with engraved glass screens in anticipation of his occupancy. With a blind eye turned towards convenants, the palace serves well as an ecclesiastical office building.

"Whitehall" the sixth in the Magnificent series was appropriately the office of the Prime Minister and the site of Cabinet meetings. It is hard to think of its busy Corsican moorish walls inhabited by a single family, the Agostinis, as it originally was. Guards stand at the two gates controlling the constant to-ing and fro-ing of traffic aided by their private traffic light. Before the present traffic congestion it seemed anomalous that this, the most important of government offices should be so far removed from the others. Nowadays there has been an exodus to the traffic free avenues off the Savannah, and the location of the Prime Minister's office proved perfect until renovations necessitated a move to the modern Financial Complex.

Last of the Magnificent Seven in the line but not in effect, is "Killarney" better known as Stollmeyer's Castle from the family who built and lived in it until 1974. "Family" is misleading. Old C. C. Stollmeyer and his blind widow lived alone in it, except for one or two retainers. The three daughters and one son had long since married. Upon his death Mr. Stollmeyer's widow staunchly determined to remain in her home despite her handicap until her death a few years later. It was built for C.C. Stollmeyer's Germanic father by the local firm, Taylor and Gillies in 1904. Turrets were borrowed from Balmoral Castle in the design, and the name came from Mrs. Stollmeyer's wish to visit Ireland at the time of construction. A museum piece such as this, accompanied by the rigid covenants of the lease, make it very limited in marketability. After remaining empty for many months, it was disposed of in frustration for less than a three-bedroom bungalow in the suburbs would cost six years later. The buyer never used it, but had it lovingly restored to its original condition, the roofs being replaced slate by slate after new rafters were installed. Goverment then added it to its collection. If the intermediary owner did well on the deal one cannot hold it against him, after preserving an important part of the nation's heritage. There it stands today, still unoccupied despite the overall need for bureaucratic office space. Undoubtedly the fine building will benefit from eventual occupancy as buildings always do. It is to be hoped that its character will be retained as well as it has up to now.

So there they are - the Magnificent Seven, lined up like precious porcelain on a mantlepiece. It is the sequence of them from one corner of the Savannah to the next, and the setting across from the Savannah which gives them their stately charm. Were they not fronting on the Savannah they would seem too large for their one-acre lots, each one asking for grounds of its own reached along a sweeping drive.

Government reflects and determines the temper of the people. They do not wish the newly independent nation to be cowed by reminders of the colonial past. For this reason there is still no National Trust to protect the architectural heritage despite enduring individual efforts. Every month sees some fine old building demolished to make way for a cost-effective but sterile replacement. Only in the Magnificent Seven is it accepted that there is some merit in the vestiges of the colonial past. From these seeds perhaps a greater acceptance that what is old is not automatically unwanted can be nurtured into full bloom. But little time remains.

Our circuit of the Savannah is nearly done. Only one building remains, that of the President's mansion on the site selected by Governor Woodford. It is remarkable and a delight that for a stretch of nearly a mile along the northern edge of the Savannah there should be trees, shrubs and gardens on both sides of the busy throughfare.

Facing the Hollows on the start of this stretch opens shady Lady Chancellor Road leading up Emperor Valley. The name comes, like Lady Young Road by the Hilton and Lady Hailes Avenue in San Fernando, from wives of former governors. The road was built with convict labour and was opened in 1920. It passes up to the head of Emperor Valley named not after any historical personage but for the profusion of Emperor butterflies. These brilliant turquoise and black members of the morpho family savour the flesh of overripe mango. Their habits are strangely regular, lolloping along the same route at the same time each day. The first house on Lady Chancellor Road was built by a keen butterfly collector on a premontory above the valley. Just beyond this house is a hairpin bend turning up to Poui Hill from the top of which is the finest panorama of the city, the gulf and the plains beyond to San Fernando Hill. The upper stretch of Poui Hill is barred to cars, but is well worth the ten minutes puff to the top reserved, it is said, for a hotel site. After winding through the hills with only the occasional house perched on either side, Lady Chancellor terminates at a lookout. This was the parking lot for a restaurant famous for its wild meat of quenk, lappe, agouti, tatoo - the local name for armadillo, and tiny deer. The elderly jewish couple, refugees from Nazi Europe, have gone down into local folklore, but not for their food. When the husband died, his widow grieved so much that within a few days she too had died of a broken heart. The empty restaurant was soon burned by vandals.

The Emperor Valley Zoo stands at the foot of Lady Chancellor Road across from the Hollows. Its inmates relax in the tropical warmth customary for them. The lions have felt so much at home that they have produced many litters, providing the zoo with good swaps of animals from other zoos. Adjacent to the zoo are the Botanical Gardens, spaciously laid out by Governor Woodford on 63 acres around 1820. While not the oldest in the Caribbean, the maturity and diversity of plants come from the great interest being expressed in tropical plants in the early 19th century. Guides will offer their services for a stroll through the gardens and identify outstanding trees and shrubs. If one does without their services it is better not to stray too far into the bush up the hillside. The St Anns Mental Hospital is not too far distant, and weirdos are not uncommon.

Ferguson was the architect of the last fine structure of our circuit which, alone of the mansions around the Savannah, has enough grounds around it to avoid the cramped appearance of the others. It replaced a rambling structure which Governor Woodford had built 50 years earlier and is today the presidential residence. In a cottage behind it Charles Kingsley wrote "At last! A Christmas in the West Indies." After Trinidad and Tobago gained independence in 1962 it was considered too grand for the governor general and was made the home of the national museum. There was pitifully little to display in the large rooms and when Queen Elizabeth paid a visit to Trinidad in 1967 and needed a suitable lodging place, the museum was hurriedly transferred back to the Victoria Institute facing Memorial Square, so that the mansion could be refurbished for the governor general's occupation. Thereafter Sir Solomon Hochoy, the Governor General, lived there in style, as did his successor, Sir Ellis Clarke, who stayed on as president (having reverted to Mr Clarke) when Trinidad and Tobago decided on republican status.

In front of the president's mansion sits a bandstand in which concerts were performed by the police or regiment band on Sunday evenings to the delight of passersby in their Sunday best. From here it is two minutes walk back to the roundabout below the Hilton Hotel, past a modern marble monument. The circuit of the Queens Park Savannah is complete. Surely it was worth the exertion to see the heart which sets the pulse of the city and its people?

*Sunday at Maracas Bay*

## Chapter 15

# *Let's Go to the Beach*

Look at a map of Trinidad and you will assume that the people in and around Port of Spain swim in the Gulf of Paria on which it stands. Unfortunately the beaches of the Gulf are not inviting. The water is muddied by the outflow of the giant Orinoco River across the Serpent's Mouth to the south, and by the red mud washed down from the valleys of the Northern Range in midday downpours.

Far better to drive fourteen spectacular miles through the lush mountains to Maracas Bay. Climbing up to a shoulder of the Maraval Valley, Saddle Road passes through a narrow cutting in the rock before dropping in hairpin bends down into the citrus and cocoa estates of the unspoiled Santa Cruz Valley. But our route is to the left just before this cutting. Stone pillars mark the start of this road which was built during the Second World War by the US Seabees. Up to that time there was no motor road to Maracas Bay. The only way to reach it was by hiking over the steep trail from Maracas

Valley on the south side of the Northern Range. Hence the beach and the valley on the other side sharing the same name.

The view back down the Maraval Valley as we start on the road to Maracas is magnificent particularly in April when the mountain immortelles are sporting their canopies of brilliant coral orange. Far down below are the emerald greens of Moka Golf Club and Trinity College. Tourist taxis pull onto the verge for photographs to be taken. Those enterprising tourists who seek out the few buses that travel this route have no such opportunity. Rented cars or taxis are the customary method of travel for visitors.

All signs of human habitation are left behind as the road passes through the abandoned cocoa estates festooned with tree ferns overhanging the road. There are occasional glimpses down into the Santa Cruz Valley until, dramatically, the brilliant blue of the Caribbean Sea appears a thousand feet below us on the left.

When cocoa was king, estates wrested a good living on these precipitous hillsides. The cocoa beans were collected by sea or taken out on a donkey's back. The mountains rise just as sharply above us on the right. For many years after the road was completed, it was common for heavy rains to bring down a great tree across the road. Bathers would be stranded at Maracas until the road was cleared, perhaps the next day. Today this seldom happens, as earth-moving equipment is standing ready at the only building we pass.

This Caribbean corniche winds along the forested cliff face for eight spectacular miles. Faint hearts will shrink back from the sheer drops into the tree tops far below. At one point only does a shoulder of the hillside permit a lookout space for cars to pause. It is from here the precipitous descent is made to the secluded "Timberline" guest cottages in an abandoned cocoa estate. A fruit vendor has mangoes or oranges set out on a box; a gaily shirted troubadour pretends he is a genuine calypsonian as he darts out to the latest tourist arrival and plucks at his cuatro. Looking back to the west, the mountains of Venezuela seem to merge directly into the Northern Range. To the east, if recent rains have cleared the haze, the faint outline of Tobago can be made out on the horizon. More winding road through the jungly foliage until, rounding a bend we see the tall coconut palms fringing the broad beach of Maracas Bay deeply enclosed within two projecting promontories.

"We reach!"

The plunging slopes of the mountains are thickly forested. In the valley below, a few galvanized roofs mark where farms have been started. Above looms El Tucuche, the second highest peak, by one metre, on the island. One could be a hundred miles from a populous city, not fourteen.

You never know until you reach Maracas what the weather will be like. It may have been cloudless when you left Port of Spain, but be rainy at the beach, or vice versa. Even during a chill rain storm, the sea water is pleasingly warm to bask in until the sunshine returns. This uncertainty adds a dimension not savoured when a beach is predictably the same.

Every Sunday, rain or shine, the broad mile-long beach is thronged with families from all parts of the island. Finding a space to park will not be easy. The open huts built by the tourist board are redolent with shark-and-bake being fried over a charcoal pot by a vendor. Each family will bring a large cooler filled with "sweet drinks", beer and rum punch. The menfolk stand in groups for a relaxed "ol' talk," away from their languorous wives lying on the sand. Their children frolic in the gently deepening water, safe from the boisterous breakers further out. The full spectrum of Trinidad's multi-racial society can be studied in all its very attractive flesh. The girls are gorgeous in their brief and stylish bikinis. Where do they find these latest fashions? The youths, lithe and muscular, show off their skills with a soccer ball. A cricket game will start using the stem of a coconut frond as a bat, but the tennis ball will do little harm when it lands on nearby picnickers. The extended families of the Indians are to be found at the eastern end of the beach where the ohrni-clad mothers dish out paper plates of pelau to paunchy patriarchs all the way down to skinny toddlers barely able to paddle at the water's edge.

Bored taxi drivers lean against their cars and gossip together while they wait for their passengers to finish their swim. They have changed in the facilities provided by the

Tourist Board, and will feel greatly outnumbered as they stand, absurdly white and pink, among all the locals. If they had come on a weekday it would have been different. The long beach of pale golden sand would have been deserted. There would only be a single life guard instead of six, herding people to bathe away from the lines of strong outgoing current marked with red flags.

Wading across the river at the western end of the beach we can reach the fishing village of Maracas and its little church. Ugly black vultures, the corbeaux, stand around the fishing boats sunning their outstretched wings, waiting for the next catch. They will do you no harm. Behind the beach is a modest hotel. There were, and perhaps still are, plans for a grandiose resort hotel on the hill above, complete with cable car to the beach. Despite intermittent press announcements over the years, financial constraints and bureaucratic hurdles have prevented it becoming a reality, a common story for hotel projects in Trinidad, and one for which the visitor used to mass tourism elsewhere will be grateful.

Maracas Beach is best enjoyed at night in the light of a full moon when a "lime" has been arranged for a beach party. A large bonfire will offset the chill night breeze and may be used to barbecue chicken, hot dogs and hamburgers. There is sure to be music. Every other Trini seems adept at the cuatro, but a bottle and spoon and a makeshift scraper will do to accompany the songs at a pinch. A "boombox" may be brought to play tapes of the latest calypsos, but it is ten-to-one the fetesters will make their own music. A swim by night will be daringly taken when the moon is bright. The waves, if we are lucky, will dance with a glimmer of luminescence as they break. Everyone has brought "grog" and ice. The paper cups run out before the drink.

It is late when the fete breaks up. The full moon is low over the silhouette of the mountains. A lot of liquor has been drunk but the drivers know the winding mountain road back well, and there is no traffic. Better not linger on the beach alone. The days when a couple by themselves at the beach was safe, are now gone. Be prudent and stay with the group.

If solitude is sought by day, however, no problem. The

nearby beach of Tyrico, really an extension within Maracas Bay, is likely to be uncrowded, even on a Sunday, and the waves will not be as big. Four miles further along the un-spoiled coast we pass a mere handful of wooden shacks and arrive at Las Cuevas Bay. This beach is longer, whiter, its water safer and bluer. There is a parking lot and a small fishing village. The infrequent buses turn around here to return to the city. Why then are there so few people in this paradise? The answer is sandflies! These are the same barely visible demons known in Florida as "no-seeums." They are a menace in many locations around sunset, but at Las Cuevas they are waiting for you at all hours. No bigger than a grain of ground black pepper, their bite will make you squirm. But do not scratch. Doing so will make it worse. Remember to rub citronella oil or some other potent repellent onto your ankles, elbows and wrists beforehand to keep them at bay.

Sand flies can be so bad at Las Cuevas that they follow you into the sea. Visiting scientists claim that Las Cuevas has the "purest cultures" they have found; that is to say, more of them. Yet strangely enough there can be days when they are not around. On these rare days Las Cuevas is indeed the paradise it looks at first glance. There have been plans for a large beach hotel here since 1960. The land was owned by a wealthy Chinese businessman who was keen to go ahead. Government kept putting obstacles in his way until he got the message. He was finally forced into selling the land to the government. This did not resolve the question of a hotel. We can thus still enjoy Las Cuevas in its unspoiled beauty - but remember the citronella.

The adventurous can drive still further down the coast to Point Filette. This new road is even wilder and more traumatic than any part of the coast road so far passed. A dirt road used to pass along this stretch, but it kept being washed away down the precipices after heavy rains. The new road passes along a higher route and is made to last. At Filette the old road from Blanchisseuse is reached. We are back, relatively speaking, in civilisation and have linked up to the chapter describing the north-east of the island.

Visitors seeking other fine beaches have the whole length

of the Atlantic-facing East Coast to choose from. Salibia Bay, Balandra Bay, Matura Bay, Manzanilla and Mayaro together form over forty miles of fine golden sand interrupted only by the rocky headlands that divide one from the next. Beach houses are intermittently dotted among the dense coconut palms that border these beaches, and they are popular for an extended stay. The ceaseless breeze has a soporific effect. It is easier to laze in the shade than to scramble in the surf. Swimming is hard work compared to the more sheltered bathing of Maracas and Las Cuevas. Because the East Coast beaches are so extensive they are never crowded. Trinidad is generously endowed with fine beaches which will remain sparsely used until, perhaps, tourists eventually descend en masse. Trinis are sociable and love company; that is why when a Trinidadian says, "Let's go to the beach," he probably means "Let's go to Maracas".

*Dasent House, Phillips Street, Port of Spain*

# Chapter 16

# *Around and About*

Where are the residential areas where the people of Port of Spain live? The hotels, the public buildings, the shops and the landmarks are far removed from the suburbs where the great majority spend their domestic lives. A taxi tour of the city for cruise passengers is likely to include a ten-minute circuit through the fine homes of Ellerslie Park beyond the Kapok Hotel. Most of Ellerslie Park's residences house ambassadors, chief executives of companies and other "big shots" unrepresentative of all but the highest strata of Trinidadian life style. It reflects what Trinidadians can aspire to, like a "Benz" to show the community they have made it. Only by looking at the various suburbs of Port of Spain is a more typical picture obtained.

The Savannah, being the hub of the wheel around which life in Port of Spain revolves, is the concourse onto which the valleys around it empty their tide of cars each morning filled with commuting parents and their schoolchildren. The roundabout below the Hilton Hotel is as busy as any. Onto it debouch the residential valleys of St. Anns and Cascade and the mini-suburb of Coblentz Gardens between them. Coblentz Gardens was originally a single estate dominated by Coblentz House. Legend has it that a former estate house on this site was built with "excess materials" salvaged or purloined by the clerk of works supervising the construction of the St. James barracks. The fine estate house later built was still there until 1985, but was less impressive after it had been divided into apartments. The acres of grounds that formerly surrounded it have long given way to substantial homes whose gardens are filled with fruit trees and flowering shrubs.

St. Ann's Church is tucked up a cul-de-sac. Across from it is a convent occupied by a dozen or so cloistered nuns. Until the last few years they could never leave the convent's grounds. Visitors could speak to them only through a wooden grille during the limited visiting hours. Despite this they managed to keep well-informed on current affairs and much of the local gossip. Several are aged, but others are young and bubbling with life. It seemed anachronistic that they should continue a tradition going back to the Middle Ages. The rare visits they are now permitted to the outside world must have been a traumatic change. It is not for us to criticise their choice of solitude. It is ironic, however, in view of the frugal conditions in which they live, growing their own vegetables and fruit to attain near self-sufficiency, that they should occupy 600,000 square feet of prime residential land worth no less than TT$3,000,000.

Beyond the convent the streets leading up to the left contain sedate middle class homes. Very soon the valley narrows and the calibre of the houses declines as the road hugs the edge of the St. Anns River. The mental hospital, next reached, is a large institution handed down from British colonial days when the need for such facilities was much smaller. Demand for places now greatly exceeds availability with the result that a great many unfortunates who would be institutionalised in a metropolitan country are handled on an out-patient basis. As a result it is only too frequent that the mentally disturbed walk the streets. Not all are harmless. Talking to themselves fiercely, they may well work up a rage and start belabouring a lamp-post or a car with a two-by-four. Although there are now health officers responsible for these cases, they seem to have little effect on the problem. Neither the police, the ambulance service, the hospitals or even the fire department wish to take on the problem of removing persons, sometimes naked and raving, from the vestibules of offices or the halls of banks.

It would be wrong to give the impression that there are mad men and women walking all the streets, but equally wrong not to admit that it is unusual not to see at least one or two different ones every day. It is a problem, like that of the pavement dwellers, that Trinidad never came to grips with even during the years of its greatest wealth. Most people attribute this to the *laissez faire* attitude which can be found in so many aspects of Trinidadian life. Harmless Craig, reputedly a former schoolmaster, strolls Frederick Street dressed in a sackcloth toga. He holds up his eruditely worded message to the world and gazes passively at passersby with his shrewd round eyes. Tourist Annie, perhaps not mad at all, used to sit in a doorway sporting a Carmen Miranda headdress of tropical produce with a colourful shawl and skirts. She was there to be photographed - for a fee - by tourists. Woe betide if they should not pay, or any bystander cross her for an imagined slight. A torrent of obscenities would ring through the streets. Although cursing is a chargeable offense, no action would be taken by the police standing by. Annie was around for over twenty years. What's the point? These are the harmless ones. As for the others, best steer clear..

St. Anns Valley seems to peter out into shacks at the bridge beyond the mental home, but takes on a second lease of life at the swanky area of Fondes Amandes. Its architect-designed homes on hill sites commanding views down the valley are a surprise so deep in the valley. The main road below Fondes Amandes follows the river past a busy junior school occupying the former Monte Cristo estate house. This is reached by a covered bridge across a deep ravine that fills with water after a downpour. The daily traffic jam of air-conditioned cars on the narrow valley road when the children are collected in the afternoon, makes one doubt the sanity of the planning authorities for permitting a school to operate here. Beyond the school is a further surprise - a modern idyllically laid out restaurant which reflects the best in contemporary architecture, harmonising with its tropical setting. Unfortunately the same can no longer be said for the food. Half a mile beyond this restaurant the houses become sparser and more cheaply built, until the road disintegrates into a track and finally a hunter's path leading into the "bush." Further hunters' trails lead up through the hills, some climbing over the steep ridge of the mountains into the Santa Cruz valley.

Cascade Valley is much the same. Good houses give way to meaner dwellings, then, in patches, high quality developments with well tended gardens. Beyond them a steady decline, with rotting bodies of derelict cars abandoned at the edge of the road. Finally a track leading into the bush.

*Maraval Valley*

Maraval Valley, off the north-west corner of the Savannah, is different. It is not a cul-de-sac like most valleys of the Northern Range, but has access to Diego Martin and to the unspoiled Santa Cruz valley; alternatively one can turn left where the road drops down into the valley and take instead the glorious scenic road to Maracas Bay, Las Cuevas Bay and beyond to Blanchisseuse.

Just beyond Boissiere Village at the corner of Saddle Road is the Trinidad Country Club, still popular with the expatriate community but attended by the five thousand local members mainly for the big fetes of Old Year's Night (New Year's Eve) and at Carnival time. For many years this club was the symbol of European elitism. Professional men of all races were allowed to join on a very selective basis, causing resentment to those who could afford the modest dues, but were refused entry. The crowning humiliation was that expatriates on a work permit could get in immediately. There was little that could be done. The club is not a members' club, but is privately owned by the same enormously wealthy owner of the Queens Park Hotel and goodness knows how many other properties. For the politicians to threaten that the club would be closed down held no fears for the owner and would only whip up the antagonism of the business class which dominated its membership. Gradually the position eased as greater numbers of darker skins were seen around the pool and at the Saturday night barbecues. There was a furore when a negro couple from New York staying at the Hilton went there to play tennis. They were told at the club that they would have to be introduced by a regular member. This formality had invariably been waived for other (non-black) guests of the hotel.

Since then the club declined in popularity and became so run down that it was no longer the bone of racial contention it once was. Dark skinned members no longer feel they are a conspicuous minority. It has taken time, but over a period of twenty five years, racial integration advanced into the last bastions of the formerly privileged.

Saddle Road continues up Maraval Valley from the Country Club past large and small supermarkets, hardware stores and bakeries interspersed with blocks of flats providing the clientele. The Maraval River on the left, often reduced to a gurgling stream and the steep slopes of the mountain on the right, often leave room for only one house on each side of the road. A bend reveals the Spanish tiled roofs of luxurious homes and condominiums set out in a well-ordered development.

This is "Fairways," the former St. Andrews golf course, remembered only from the names of the roads that took its place - Eagle Crescent, Birdie Drive and the like. It is in Fairways that architects were given free rein and purse to exercise their skills. Mortgages were easy to obtain and "money was no problem." Individual taste often approaches noveau riche ostentation.

After Fairways and its nearby satellite areas, the valley closes in at a picturesque little reservoir. The village of Maraval just beyond it has little to do with Port of Spain and cannot be considered one of its suburbs. It is a country village which has been enveloped by the growth of the city. Its striking Romanesque church, facing the intersection of Morne Coco Road, sits high above the road on a knoll, dominating with its architecture, the crumbling stores of the villagers. Morne Coco Road winds through abandoned cocoa estates and forest across a mountain ridge to the dormitory valley of Diego Martin. It is gradually becoming built up, and the days are gone when car thieves would use the solitude of its shady clearings to strip stolen cars. In those days this was the closest place to Port of Spain to show visitors what dense forest looked like, with spectacular views from the winding road over the valleys.

A little way up Morne Coco Road from Maraval is a fork to the right leading to Paramin. The people of that area are of Venezuelan descent and patois is still spoken. These are not descendents of the colonial Spaniards of Trinidad but of the 19th Century influx of Venezuelans who settled surreptitiously in certain remote mountain plateaus of the Northern Range to raise cocoa. There they remained with their language and life style unchanged, and with minimal contact with the outside world. Even up to 1965 there was only a donkey trail, and the community had no electricity or piped water. By chance the general manager of the power company was a keen walker and from time to time would stop with his companions for a barely cool beverage in the little Paramin store. Knowing he was the key to receiving electricity, one of the elders of the hamlet asked one day.

"Mr. Finch, sir, you is in charge of the electric? What we have to do to get electric in Paramin?"

He told them that to bring power to Paramin would take time, as no funds were then available to put poles for the line. Unsuspecting, he told them,

"The poles are no problem, We have them in stock. Its the labour of digging the holes."

"You let we dig holes for you?" he was asked.

"Certainly," he replied, "if you dig the holes, there would be no problem."

He was probably counting on the fact that in Trinidad cooperative efforts frequently fail because there is too much "ol' talk" and too little action. He had not taken into consideration the unusual community spirit of Paramin. To his astonishment he found a delegation of Paramin elders waiting outside his office dressed respectfully in unaccustomed dark suits usually reserved for funerals.

"Good morning, gentlemen," he said, thinking they had come with a further request in which he would be unlikely to help.

"Good day, Mr. Finch, sir. We has the holes ready for you jus' like you say, oui. Now we ready for the poles you promise."

The whole village had got together over the past two weeks digging the holes at the prescribed distances. So impressed was he with their effort and loath to back down on the assurances he had given them, that the order was given to install the poles and take power for the first time to the remote community. The grateful villagers had no sooner got electricity than the delegation went back to his office.

"Mr. Finch, sir, you help we well. We much appreciate. But sir, we need you' advice. How we get pipe water in Paramin? We have long walk to river in valley, and in dry season t'ings muy malo."

He put them in touch with his counterpart at the Central Water Distribution Authority who gave a similar outline.

"The problem is the cutting of the trench. That will require considerable outlay for which we have no provision in this year's budget. The pipes are no problem and we may be able to manage the pumps."

"You let we dig trench, sir?" they asked.

"Well, I suppose so. But its several miles and a lot of work."

"Perhaps we manage, sir," and back they went to Paramin.

Confident that he would hear nothing further the CWDA chief forgot about them. Three months later they were back.

"We ready for you, sir."

"Ready?"

"Yes, sir. Trench she finish. Mucho trabajo, but we finish. Now we get water like you say, oui?"

Unfortunately water is always a problem and although efforts were started to take water to Paramin it was not as promptly supplied as the electricity had been.

If the cooperative effort demonstrated by this little Spanish enclave and others like that at Cumaca, high on the Platanal beyond Arima, could be harnessed throughout the island, many problems would be overcome. Unfortunately the opposite has been the experience. Despite Trojan efforts by Government to get the cooperative movement into a viable force, the results are dismal. Dissension and a natural inclination to lose interest after the initial spurt of enthusiasm frustrates most projects. Negro communities are reminded of the communal house-building of African villages. Cooperatives are the African tradition, they are told. It does little good. Indian villages are likely to fare no better. There is sure to be factionalism and disputes with one group subverting the efforts of any other. The colonial heritage used to provide a handy cop-out. As Dr. Williams used to say, "You are too used to being told what to do by your colonial masters to make decisions for yourselves!"

But Paramin is living evidence to Trinidad of what a small community can achieve when it gets together with dedicated purpose.

Beyond Maraval, across the wide but minor bridge that took three years to complete instead of the scheduled six months, another upper income residential community is laid out. This is a stronghold of the French creole community, Haleland Park. The spacious bungalows are set out in shady gardens that show the area is not a new one, though new homes are being built on the few remaining vacant lots. Above on the hillside with dramatic views all the way to the sea are more grandiose homes, perched on ledges cut out of the hillside. Houses were unlikely to change hands here for less than US$200,000.

When Haleland Park was started there was little prospect that the St. Andrews golf course, now Fairways, would be relocated at Moka Estate half a mile beyond Haleland Park. This residential area accordingly, now has one of the most beautiful courses in the Caribbean on its doorstep, watered by an irrigation system for the valley put in place generations ago by the Spanish colonists. Haleland Park may seem remote from the heart of Port of Spain when unfamiliar with the road, but it is only seven minutes drive from the Savannah, given favourable driving conditions.

At the end of Maraval Valley was Perseverance Estate with its magnificent estate house. In its later years this became Perseverance Club which in its heyday competed with the Country Club for social pre-eminence.

## Belmont and Woodbrook

Much closer to the Savannah across from its eastern edge is the crowded lower middle class suburb of Belmont. Although not situated in a valley, it is enclosed by hills. As one approaches these hills, the homes give way to ghetto shacks overlooking rushing foliaged streams. Attempts were made to impose a grid of streets on Belmont but much remains a maze of winding alleys and cul-de-sacs. Names like Zampty Lane and Roget Place confirm its grassroots origins. Houses are cramped together on tiny plots that never contemplated the garaging of a luxury such as a car. Many of the original wooden houses remain, but many are being rebuilt to the original design in concrete block. Feared by most Port of Spain residents as an unknown area, Belmont had very respectable residents besides virtually tribal areas.

It was behind Belmont's lanes that a truly African encampment was established, lasting for many years. It was founded not by blacks disgruntled by a white-dominated society, but by a community of "Radas" fresh from French Dahomey in 1868. On property bought by their tribal chieftain, the huts of the little commune were laid out to continue the pattern of life to which they were accustomed. Fascinating as it is to learn of tribal Africa transplanted intact to the western world, it would be out of place to describe it at length here. Full details are available in social study papers.

Alongside Belmont are the hills of East Dry River, Gonzales and Laventille. These are lower class areas occupying hills overlooking the city. Many of the homemade shacks of salvaged boards and rusted galvanized roofing are reached up a flight of steps. It is a dense area filled with gang antagonisms. These were exemplified in the clashes that used to take place between the steel bands that were nurtured in cramped back yards. Now that commercial firms sponsor most steel bands and they are responsibly controlled by their leaders, these "clashes" on the streets of Port of Spain at "jouvay," the dawn of Carnival, have ended. Wickedly sharpened cutlasses and rows of sweet drink bottles for missiles are no longer concealed under the carriages of the steel pans.

Atop Laventille's squalor, Our Lady of Laventille church shines golden in the evening sun against a backdrop of eggshell blue sky. Not far from it on the ridge stands renovated Fort Picton, built by the first British governor to dominate, not the approach to the harbour by foreign invaders, but the French and Spanish citizens in the streets below.

Woodbrook's background is tame by contrast. A former sugar estate at the fringes of the city, it was developed into rectangular housing lots of 5,000 square feet by the City Council. The original wooden bungalows raised up several steps to provide air circulation beneath, are still much in evidence. Increasingly they are being upgraded and modernised. This is to be expected when one considers that the Syrian community, small as it is, concentrate for the most part in this flat suburb. Some wealthier Syrians have moved into snobby neighbourhoods, but the majority have chosen to remain in Woodbrook and rebuild their houses with enclosed galleries and central air-conditioning. It is only in Woodbrook that grape vines can be found. It is too wet in Trinidad during the long rainy season for vines to survive mildew and fungus; but over the sunny concrete driveways of Woodbrook the air dries quickly enough for a family vine to flourish, not for its grapes but for its leaves. How else could the Syrians feast off grape leaves stuffed with spiced meats?

Running parallel with Woodbrook to the north of Tragarete Road is prestigious St. Clair. The Magnificent Seven of the Savannah are the easternmost of St. Clair's homes. Beyond them stand the other large old-fashioned houses on large lots which have largely outlived their former appeal. Those that have been modernised at substantial expense are suitable for embassies; but Saturday auction sales in the homes forced by death or infirmity to give up their old way of life, reveal that in many ways living was far from gracious. Huge bedrooms with primitive bathrooms above antiquated kitchens and living rooms echo hollowly without the servants on which life in them depended. For those who live in the more modern St. Clair houses, life can still be luxurious if there is adequate finance to maintain the large garden and dust the staircases and fretwork.

Behind St. Clair is an interesting complex of parks and playing fields with the paved bed of the Maraval River running between them. George V Park used to be an idyllic area even though it was adjacent to the throngs watching first class cricket at the adjacent Queens Park Oval. Like the Oval, considered one of the most beautiful test match sites in the cricketing world, George V Park was renowned for its mighty umbrella-shaped samaan trees. In 1967 Government decided, for valid reasons, that George V Park could be put to better use in providing much-needed recreational amenities for the nation's schools. There were apprehensive murmurings from the residents of St. Clair. Where would they take their leisurely evening stroll with the family dog?

Then began the unbelievably confused series of events which are still to be resolved. The park was fenced, concrete practice nets built for cricket at one corner, and a small stand for spectators was built along the southern edge. Schools used the new facilities during the day without problem. Then towering floodlights were added to permit nighttime soccer matches. The St. Clair residents became incensed at this invasion of their tranquility, not so much by the bright lights, as by the gangs of youths walking the area at night and misbehaving the way gangs of youths do. The Prime Minister turned a deaf ear to these protests. They came, after all, from a section of the populace that he loved to bait, and was admired by the masses for doing so. Yet mysteriously the lights were removed to the Public Service Association sports ground. Was George V Park to revert to St. Clair's residents? To the contrary. Plans were announced to build a proper sportsdrome with cambered perimeter athletic track, playing fields and courts. There would be a larger stand for the crowds.

Part of this rationale was supplied by one Ivan Williams, no relation to the prime minister, chairman of the Carnival

Development Committee. He felt that George V Park should replace the Savannah as the main judging "venue" for the Carnival bands. The former small stand was demolished. A large construction contract was awarded, earth moving machinery was mobilised and miles of reinforcing steel bars were bent into position. Whether it was Ivan Williams' fall from political favour or for other reasons, Dr. Williams drily announced to the nation which had watched work going ahead briskly, that the plans for the new sportsdrome had never been approved by Cabinet. Proper tendering procedures had been by-passed, and the hasty commencement of the project could be viewed as a mis-appropriation of public funds. Work stopped. Weeds grew. The contractor was rumoured to be delighted that he had been left in the lurch. A substantial rise in the price of steel provided him with more profit on the steel he had purchased for the cancelled contract than he would have made if he had completed it. No more was said about Carnival bands leaving the Savannah.

For ten years the ravaged park lay idle, another monument to indecision and political rug-pulling. There was much talk of a full-fledged national stadium and where it should be. Jamaica had a stadium, after all, and they were broke. At long last another site for the national stadium was picked, on the foreshore of Mucurapo Lands. George V Park remained a wasteland. The fine samaan trees died from the damage by bulldozers to their roots. A "Save Our Samaan" committee was formed in the ensuing uproar. It did no good. One by one the proud samaans were cut down as they died.

Without warning a new plan for an intermediary size stadium was produced, and structural steel was again taken on site. That work should once again come to a halt surprised nobody. George V Park was evidently fated never to be developed. And so it is to this day, over twenty years later. Denuded of its magnificent samaans, carved up by bulldozers and disfigured by the partially erected stand, the park, no longer a park, stands unfinished.

Beyond George V Park and St. Clair, close to the exclusive homes of Ellerslie Park, lies Federation Park. This area was reserved by Goverment to house the ministers and senior civil servants who were to serve in the ill-fated West Indies Federation with its capital in Port of Spain. When the Federation collapsed few homes had been built. The empty lots were eventually sold off by auction. Attractive homes were built. Although they may not have the social appeal of Ellerslie Park or St. Clair, Federation Park's homes are in many ways more desirable.

Adjacent to Federation Park another large piece of land owned by Goverment, now known as the Flagstaff Hill Development, has been densely covered with luxury condominiums. It was Government's intention to use these units to house the expatriate families needed for Trinidad's myriad development projects. By the time the units were ready the projects were already completed that had been started. There were insufficient funds left to undertake the remainder. Instead the condominiums have been allocated for sale to the public. Occupying the hill in the centre of this project is the American ambassador's residence proudly flying the Star Spangled Banner.

*The Western Suburbs*

West of Federation Park and Woodbrook is the only enclave of East Indians in the Port of Spain area, St. James. Busy Western Main Road is its backbone, banks, shops and roti parlours lining its sides. From either side lead off streets with Indian names; Madras Street, Bombay Street, Calcutta Street, Dengue Street (of Dengue fever fame) and many others. For the people of Port of Spain, St. James has long been considered the place to buy the best hot roti, the curry-filled wheat flour pancake which has become to all types of Trinidadians, a staple comparable to British fish and chips. As we see in the chapter dealing with food, roti is cooked on a griddle known as a "towa" over a charcoal fire. Folded, it forms an envelope for the beef, chicken, goat, conch, shrimp or just plain potato fired up with pepper sauce. Care must be taken when eating roti with the fingers not to let the juicy contents dribble into your lap.

It is down the main street of St. James that the picturesque Hosay Festival parades. This ancient festival goes back even further than we know Carnival as it is today. It is a Moslem event but Hindus and non-Indians alike now join in the procession. One is not surprised to find a neat green and white mosque standing at the far end of St. James.

Leading off to the right of St. James up the hillside is the winding road to Fort George. This is best visited in the late afternoon when the sun is setting behind the Venezuelan mountains. After the hairpin bends through a valley of squatter housing, there is a fine if hair-raising view down over the harbour and the craggy coast line of Venezuela beyond.

Fort George was the largest contingent of British troops in the Eastern Caribbean during the 19th Century but they never saw active service. The days of territorial dispute over the Caribbean islands had by then ended. This did not prevent Fort George from becoming a *cause celebre* in British military history, albeit one of shame. Possibly out of boredom, the large garrison staged one of the few mutinies in the proud annals of British regiments. Details are so hard to obtain that there is reason to believe there is a continuing conspiracy to remove all mention of it from historical records. Perhaps some reseacher will unearth full details before they are lost. For the present only the regiments concerned know the facts and hide them. It is common knowledge that the British went to unusual pains and expense after the mutiny to dismantle the extensive series of forts ending in Fort Cumberland at the highest point where radio and television masts now stand.

A lookout and signalling station was retained by the coast guard until 1927 from which the signals of approaching vessels could be relayed from North Post on the cliffs at the end of the Diego Martin valley. From Fort George the messages were telegraphed to the look-out in the tower of the "Ice House" on Marine (now Independence) Square.

The large brass telescope through which the coast guard monitored approaching shipping can still be seen by visitors to Fort George. As late as 1969 an unfortunate coast guardsman used to walk all the way up each morning from the main road. Each evening, after fulfilling his tedious vigil, he would wend his way back. Nowadays, the Tourist Board supplies motorised transport for the staff of the lookout station which has been transformed into a pretty park with benches for lovers and children. A dungeon has been created for historical effect. The cannons, however, are authentic. All were rescued from the slopes below from former batteries by a dedicated former member of the same regiment disgraced by the mutiny. He made it his penance to restore some of Fort George's pride.

Besides a splendid bird's eye view over the Port of Spain harbour, the whole of the Diego Martin valley is laid out like a map below. This is the largest dormitory area for Port of Spain with many dense housing developments. The largest of these is Diamond Vale occupying an area where the bulk of Trinidad's ginger used to be grown. These were the first low cost homes built on a large scale. With reinforced concrete roofs they are sturdy enough to withstand anything short of nuclear attack. The original stereotypes were unlovely, but as the gardens grew, arches, galleries and upper stories were added to relieve the squat monotony. Today they fetch premium prices. One of the earliest buildings in this Valley was the huge boys reformatory built in 1890.

A new multi-lane highway leads along the river's edge past residential developments on either side. Without warning these revert to unspoiled countryside. At River Estate, until recently an experimental station for cocoa breeding, stands Trinidad's only remaining water wheel. The next turning to the right beyond it leads to Blue Basin. The walls of the valley close in above with lush foliage, and the road is damp with fallen immortelle blossoms or a sudden shower. A stream can be heard gurgling to the right and the energetic can clamber along the rocky bed of the stream up to Blue Basin. To those who know where to look there are freshwater crayfish under those rocks as they are in all streams of the Northern Range.

Blue Basin is a hauntingly magical place, purportedly an important site for Amerindian ceremonies. A sluice of icy water cascades over the lip of the rock face above, down the chute of solid rock it has carved over the centuries, and tumbles into the large pool below. Sheer rock surrounds this pool, festooned with creepers and ferns. Agile youngsters will clamber up to a ledge for a dive. Many more locals than visitors visit the pool. The Tourist Board has attempted to make it more accessible with an improved path but in recent times dreadlocked "rastas" have invaded Blue Basin claiming "Jah" intended it for them. Visitors may have a hostile reception when they endeavour to share the magic of the glen. Spiritual Baptists have long used Blue Basin for rituals eerily lit by candles on the surrounding rocks.

Instead of turning onto the Blue Basin road, most continue straight on to North Post. Before the road starts to climb, Patna Village emerges between the trees. As the name suggests, this is an Indian community which was only disturbed in its rural solitude when Diego Martin developed into a suburb of Port of Spain. The road winding upwards passes the wooden shacks of more than a dozen squatters before reaching the government radio signalling station of North Post. Even on the hottest day a stiff breeze cools those admiring the view far below, where the breakers foam against the forested cliffs. It is hard to believe that fishermen regularly climb down the steep slope to perch on the rocks above the swells. More than one has fallen off in a careless moment and been drowned. To the east march the peaks of the Northern Range; to the west, the mountains of the western promontory, the peaks of Monos, Huevos and Chacachacare, with the mountains of the Venezuelan mainland completing the panorama. On the landward side a different view casts a unique light on the ingenuity and adaptability of the Trinidad temperament.

Across the road from Patna Village, the Ministry of Housing established a low cost housing scheme. Several hundred unplastered shacks measuring twenty feet by twenty five feet, made of raw red clay blocks, were built on tiny lots of land, each house being spitting distance from its neighbour. They were cheap, sold readily to artisans and labourers who would have been hard put to find or finance anything better. Many of these houses are in their original condition, but more have been transformed into very presentable and attractive homes. Arches have been added, new wings attached, wrought iron grilles installed over the galleries and windows, the whole plastered and painted to reflect the same originality and style for which Trinidadians are famous in their daily dress and in their annual Carnival.

At the mouth of the Diego Martin valley is a good example of the most recent of Trinidad's phenomena, its shopping malls. Across the road are expensive modern houses competing with each other in architectural lavishness. Up to 1970 there was mangrove swamp along this stretch, with boys at the roadside holding up crabs for sale. The residential enclave of Goodwood Park is terraced into the hills above the former swamp. Bayshore and adjacent Shorelands along the shore below are older areas of luxury housing for the upper income group. Nearby for their motor boats is the "Yacht Club", now with scarcely any yachts. Nearly all yachts have gone to more sheltered anchorage at the yacht haven in Chaguaramas. The hills come right down to the sea along this stretch so that the road, passing through some squalid areas in Point Cumana, has sudden views of the sea front. This coastal scenery continues along the shore all the way to the reddened silos of Alcoa's bauxite transhipment depot.

Each year on St. Peter's Day (last Sunday in June) the fleet of fishermen's boats are blessed from tiny St. Peter's Church, perched out on the water's edge. The priest anoints the pirogues and the fishermen anoint themselves internally with far too much rum, against storms, lost anchors and poor fishing. The traffic jam of convivial fishermen weaving across the road to offer a swig of rum to all motorists who pass, should be avoided by all except the most forbearing of drivers. It is all part of the carefree scene which those accustomed to Trinidad's ways, take in their stride.

The suburbs of Port of Spain are behind us. All that remains is the "Base" as Chaguaramas and the western promontory are still commonly known. We see in another chapter how much that could have been utilised was pillaged and vandalised. Today the former officers' quarters form pleasant cabins for the Chacacabana Hotel. The largest building, formerly the VD hospital, was renovated at great expense with wall to wall carpeting and air-conditioning for a convention centre, used more frequently for meetings of the ruling People's National Movement than anything else. A hotel training school is flourishing in a building behind the former hospital. The nearby bay that had been the submarine haven during the war was turned over to the yachting fraternity. At first there was only a handful of yachts.\With the oil boom, yachts became one of the few ways that money could be spent for local enjoyment. Finer and larger yachts were imported, until today the fleet of cruisers is impressive. The pre-Carnival fete which is held for fund-raising purposes on the grounds of the Trinidad Yachting Association has become the most popular. Although still crowded, tickets are restricted and only those with friends who are members are able to buy a ticket.

Many buildings on "the Base" remain unallocated, but gradually the considerable potential of the area is being put to proper use. At the present pace it will be a generation before the area realises its potential and ceases to be a political preserve for businessmen with the right "contac'." Despite the wasted buildings and crumbling infrastructure, perhaps it is best that this area remain undeveloped and unspoiled. So many other parts of the country have been ravaged by opportunistic exploitation.

*"Down the Islands"*

# Chapter 17

# *"Down the Islands"*

Once you get tuned to the lilting musicality of Trinidad "parlance" which is often compared to Welsh, you are likely to hear young and old alike at fetes saying,

"Wha' happenin' Sunday? Maracas?"

"Nah, boy - down the islands for me."

"Cheups, you real lucky boy!"

As Trinidad is itself an island, what is the reference to these other islands? There is a Maughamesque suggestion of being removed from civilisation, and with some justification.

Go down to the Island Property Home Owners' Association jetty or the Small Boats marina on a Saturday morning. Both are on the coast road near the end of Trinidad's western promontory on what used to be the U.S. Navy Base. The parking areas are rapidly filling with cars. Scores of families lugging ice chests, hampers, crates of sweet drinks, bedding and assorted recreational equipment are gathering at the jetty. Sleek motor cruisers are lowered down the ramp into

*"Down the Islands"*

the sea by means of a tractor. With deft bravado, the captains of these craft manoeuvre alongside jockeying for a vacant spot. A line is thrown ashore. The baggage is loaded aboard followed by the eager family and friends.

Those not owning boats but spending the day at an island home will have to catch the eye of one of the boatmen who ply in their scarred wooden pirogues as marine taxis from the mainland across to Gasparee Island across from the jetty or Monos Island down to the west.

It was in these waters between the mainland and Gasparee, shown more correctly on charts as Gaspar Grande, that Admiral Sebastian Ruiz de Apodaca sank his five galleons in 1797 by setting fire to them rather than let them fall into the hands of Admiral Harvey's superior invading force. Governor Chacon urged Apodaca to fight knowing that Trinidad was otherwise doomed to capture. However as the British invading force had seventeen vessels backed by forty transport ships carrying a total of 6,750 soldiers, Apodaca clearly had little chance.

In 1859 a group of Americans used the latest word in diving equipment of the time in vain attempts to salvage the remains of the sunken fleet. They met with little success because of the strong currents that flow out through the first Boca even when the tide is rising. Even with more sophisticated equipment no one has been more successful. The secrets of the Spanish fleet remain undisturbed.

Today Gasparee is densely wooded except for the coastal fringes where a few dozen houses are perched on promontories and cuttings behind little shingle coves. In 1797 the Spanish had a battery on the island's high point. General Abercrombie captured the battery and called it Bombshell Hill. The bay it overlooked on the eastern end of the island facing Port of Spain became Bombshell Bay.

Generations of newlyweds who could not afford more exotic destinations honeymooned at the tranquil little guest house and its cabins on the edge of Bombshell Bay. In 1979, an ambitious condominium project got under way. The hillside was cleared and cabins of Guyana greenheart were erected in clusters. A jetty and marina were built. Initially the scheme fared well, but enthusiasm waned before all the units were sold. It resorted to time-sharing techniques, but this did not succeed. It has now been given new life as Fantasy Island Hotel.

At the other end of Gasparee, facing north through the First Boca between the mainland and Monos Island, is Point Baleine, Punta Ballena from the Spanish days when it was, as the name implies, a whaling station. Whales have not been sighted for many years, but schools of porpoise frequently play in the turbulent waters when the tide is changing. At night the explosive slap of giant manta rays leaping into the air are heard by fishermen.

Behind Point Baleine is a concreted path leading up through the woods to the Gasparee Caves. In 1980 the Tourist Board repaired the steps and handrails leading down into the vast cavern. A substantial house was built for the caretaker. Hundreds of youngsters would arrive from the mainland on Sundays for a picnic excursion to the caves. Under this onslaught the handrails became rickety and the gates to the caves were padlocked. In former years there was another entrance directly from the sea. Rock falls made this impassable, even though sea water still flows into the caves. A large sign advises that the caves are closed "until further notice", but latest word is that funds are being made available for the necessary repairs. The cave is of limestone, but there is not much in the way of decoration with stalactites or mites. It is the eery vastness of the cave that makes it well worth a visit. From sea level at the bottom one can look up over a hundred feet to the small natural openings in the roof above, through which entry is made.

Above the caves are two gun emplacements left intact from the days when they guarded against German submarines during the Second World War. Until 1980 the guns were buried in the undergrowth. Picnic tables have been placed in the clearings, but the tables themselves are being rapidly consumed by termites. Take care before sitting down.

Because all the homes down the islands are private there are few places for the boat-owning public to congregate. The most popular of these is across on the mainland at Scotland

Bay and its adjoining beaches. It is here the motor boat crowd carouse. Tents are pitched for overnight stays. Campfires are redolent with pelau being heated in a large pot. Yacht owners anchor in the centre of the bay and invite each other aboard for rum and coke or scotch and coconut water.

Across from Scotland Bay stands Monos, meaning "monkeys" in Spanish. Red howler monkeys are invariably heard roaring fiendishly by the Scotland Bay picnickers, but they are rarely seen. Monos Island has few monkeys these days, but in March the brilliant fluorescence of yellow poui in flower makes a memorable display. Monos rises to a greater height than Gasparee, but there are homes only along the water's edge. Even these are restricted to the eastern and southern perimeters of the island. Each home has its jetty for bathing, fishing and tying up boats. There are no homes on the exposed northern coast and few on the western coast looking across the Second Boca to Huevos Island.

Huevos means "eggs" in Spanish, and perhaps hungry buccaneers found those of sea birds in early days. Today it is isolated save for the island home of the Boos family who have the whole island on a long lease. Their island house stands at the edge of a sheltered bay fringed with coconut palms. For utter solitude this is as close to bliss as one could wish.

The last island, across the Third Boca, is Chacachacare, an original Carib name that the Spanish did not change. Its highest point is topped with a powerful lighthouse which guides mariners on their way from Grenada 80 miles north, and warns shipping coming along the coast to Venezuela. It is a good stiff walk up the path to the lighthouse from the sandy beach but well worth it for the staggering view over the Boca Grande to the deserted mainland of Venezuela's Guiria Peninsular six miles west.

Despite its sandy beaches - the only ones found down the islands, Chacachacare is virtually deserted. The extensive conglomeration of red-roofed buildings of the old Leprosarium are empty. Officially the Leprosarium is closed now that modern drugs can control the disease; but the cured lepers to whom it had been home for so many years refused to leave. Perhaps understandably, the buildings have been put to no other use. Here, possibly, is an opportunity for a ready-made holiday camp. The other homes on promontories around the deep bay appear equally deserted. This island gets almost no rainfall, being in the rain shadow of well-watered Trinidad. In this it is reminiscent of Molokai in the Hawaiian Islands, also a leper island movingly described in James Michener's book.

Water is in short supply in all the island homes. There are no wells or mains distribution. Only what rainfall can be captured in catchment cisterns is available for washing and cooking. Small wonder that only a handful of people live down the islands full time. Most homes are only opened on weekends. During the week the likely activity is the sporadic ejection by the old caretaker/boatman of an empty rum bottle from his hut onto the mound of bottles outside.

Apart from the Gaspar Grande condo development most of the island homes go back to the pre-war days. Few attempts have been made to modernise them. To do so would be against the code of utter timeless relaxation which is the rule. Before the war, families would move to their island home for the three months of summer holiday. Papa would arrive from the office on Friday afternoon and depart on Monday morning. Daily deliveries of provisions, newspapers and ice were made by a little steamer that called at every "bay." There was no electricity and some homes still have the old gaslight systems on their walls, and kerosene refrigerators.

The children would swim, fish from the jetty or go boating while the women folk fanned themselves in the shaded gazebo at the end of the jetty. Your boatman would row you out to a special bank where the red fish and grouper were known to be fattest. There were no outboard engines. While you fished, the boatman would lazily pull at the oars to "keep you on the marks" to avoid drifting off the bank.

With World War II came disaster for the island homes. The whole western promontory and adjoining islands were leased by the British to the U.S. government for use as a naval base and training camp. All homes were expropriated as part of the war effort. Summers and weekends down the islands were ended. Together with the army bases at Waller Field and Carlson field, the Chaguaramas "base" was a strategically important transhipment centre for tens of thousands of freshly trained recruits on their way across the Atlantic to North Africa and European war fronts. German submarines lurked in wait outside The Bocas. Thousands of young Americans lost their lives when their transport vessels were torpedoed en route.

Enemy submarines ventured inside the Gulf of Paria and sank three ships anchored in the stream outside Port of Spain harbour. To combat this massive steel nets were strung across The Bocas buoyed up by steel spheres five feet in diameter. After the war these buoys were sold as one lot in a war surplus auction to an astute scrap dealer who piled them like giant frogspawn in a nearby quarry on the coast road. The majority are still there, good as new; but scores have been sold as water tanks or to the off-shore oil companies for use as buoys.

Even after the war ended American occupation of the "base" continued on a reducing scale. They introduced a missile tracking centre and a radio telescope by stringing cables in a natural hemisphere formed by a jungled valley. Up to the late 1960s entry beyond the Chagville gate was barred by white helmeted U.S. marine police. The 20 mph speed limit was rigidly enforced on those who obtained passes to use the nine-hole golf course or the officers' club at Macqueripe Bay. The wealth of buildings and other infrastructure could have been a bonanza to the Trinidad government when Dr.Williams finally succeeded in forcing the Americans to hand back the Base. Newly independent Trinidad and Tobago had had nothing to do with Britain's original granting of the lease, and it had always been a bone of contention causing anti-American feeling.

Instead the VD hospital was ransacked, toilets ripped from adjoining quarters until nothing but gutted shells remained in nearly all buildings. At last a body was formed to develop the area and lease out the buildings. It moved at a snail's pace in allocating premises. Only a small proportion of the original assets handed over to the nation were salvaged. To this day a great deal remains to be done. Buildings deteriorate still pending allocation. The one area that benefitted from this lack of action was the wildlife which remained undisturbed by hunters or foresters for forty years. It is said that the animals of the Northern Range have sought its sanctuary providing the densest collection of fauna on the island.

When the owners of the island homes regained their premises they were allowed to enter the U.S. base as far as Staubles Bay to cross over to Gasparee and Monos. Gradually life down the islands reverted to its former idyll, except that families rarely go there for the summer. For one thing there was no longer a steamer to bring provisions.

There is electricity now, but keeping enough ice on hand for drinks is still a problem. Water is still scarce and a shower is a brief affair to wash away the salt water of bathing. Each bedroom is a dormitory crammed with beds to make as much room as possible for overnight guests. People sleep when it suits them, playing bridge or all-fours until the light of dawn marks the sky. For children the freedom is ecstasy after living in town where playing in the streets or parks is prohibited; too many madmen around these days. The ladies no longer fan themselves. The gowns of yesteryear have given way to the skimpiest of bikinis. They lounge gossiping, shouting from time to time to the children not to go too far out. Yachts come swooping past the bay, tacking before they get caught in the lee of the hill. Motor boats roar across from one island to the next, bikini-clad nymphets' hair flying in the breeze. The men drink steadily and maintain a benign tipsiness. Meals are served whenever someone is hungry. Time loses its meaning.

Then, as the sun starts to sink over the mountains of Venezuela, it is time to pack up. Sheets are removed, refrigerators emptied and refuse stored in black plastic bags to take to the mainland rubbish containers. Reluctantly the children are rounded up, the wooden shutter windows lowered and bolted, the front door padlocked. It is time to go back to the comparative hurly-burly of urban living until the next weekend down the islands.

On the way back let us join the motor boats leaping the waves as they race each other back along the coast to the Yacht Club in Bayshore. This will take us past the remainder of Trinidad's islands.

Kronstadt Island, formerly Creteau, has two contradictory

aspects. Speeding towards it by boat, the yellow silos of its industrial face stand out against their rocky background. It is a bustling quarry for barytes, a mineral essential to the oil industry. When drilling to great depths there is a strong upward pressure which would expel the drilling "mud" used to lubricate the drill bit. A very heavy granular material is needed to hold down the pressure - barytes. The dock at the quarry is used to import bagged barytes in its finished form for the local oil industry. As the quarrying continues a large plateau is emerging not far above the water level on which, it is rumoured, a resort hotel may eventually be built.

On the far side of the island as we pass between it and the jungled cliffs of Pointe Gourde is the island home allocated in former years to the colonial governor. It is presumably still available to the President, but it is hard to tell when it was last used.

Beyond Krondstat is the Alcatraz of the Caribbean, Carrera Island. Seen in the golden light of the setting sun it looks pleasant enough. Whitewashed walls line the dual stepways leading up the hillside from the jetty. "Carrera" is spelt out on the trimmed grass in whitewashed boulders. Up to the right are the residential quarters of the prison superintendent. To the left are the tiny windows in tall ominous walls of the prisoners' cells. Out of sight on the far side of the island is the hospitality bungalow for the Superintendent of Prisons' use when he makes a visit. Few visitors are allowed on the island. The prisoners who wave back forlornly as we pass below them in our launch, become agitated when visitors are on the island. To minimise the resulting discipline problems prisoners are taken by launch to the end of a jetty on the mainland to meet their relatives on visiting days.

It is natural to wonder how many have escaped by swimming the few hundred yards to the rocks of Pointe Gourde. Reportedly there are no attempts at escape because of the fear of sharks. But sharks did not harm the brave young seaman who in 1980 jumped off his ship in this same area to rescue a panicky horse which had thrown itself from the deck. He swam alongside the horse for an hour or two before the two were rescued. It is more likely the continually strong current that dissuades prisoners from making an attempt at escape.

Carrera Prison is to be closed as soon as Golden Grove Prison near Piarco Airport is upgraded to accommodate its inmates as well as those at the Royal Gaol on Frederick Street. One can picture living conditions on Carrera being not too different from those described on Papillon's Devil's Island. But after verifying the shark situation, Carrera could provide an interesting alternative to Chacachacare as a ready-made holiday camp on the "Club Med" pattern.

Only the "Five Islands" remain between Carrera and the Yacht Club. The Spanish knew these little patches of rock and scrub as "Las Catoras" but it is "Five Islands" they are now called. Small as they are, each has a name.

Nelson Island, the largest of the five, was used as a holding camp for East Indian indentured immigrants pending their distribution to sugar estates. The island gets its name from its owner at the time Dr. Thomas Neilson who called it "Bel Air." Officially it was shown in the records as "Stephenson's", probably a previous owner. Today all names are forgotten but "Nelson." At the outbreak of World War II it was used to intern Germans in Trinidad at the time. Ironically most of them were Jews who had fled Nazi persecution.

In the 1970 uprising when a mutiny by one company of the regiment nearly installed a radical regime, a handful of those left-wing firebrands considered responsible, were interned in Nelson Island's dilapidated barracks for several months. Subsequent oil prosperity gave the facilities a new purpose when refurbished as a youth camp. The remaining four clumps of rock are named Caledonia, Lonegan, Pelican and appropriately, Rock.

Our trip down the islands is over. The hazy inebriation of a weekend's conviviality and relaxation is a treasured memory. That grouper fried for breakfast twenty minutes after it was hooked, was a dish fit for a king. The lazing on the jetty, playing bridge and "ol' talking" made time fly. Small wonder that those Trinidadians who are able to seek its timeless ambience love it as much as they do.

*"The Dial", Arima*

# Chapter 18

——— ◉ ———

# East to Arima

Unless you are fortunate enough to have friends with a speed boat, the most comfortable way to see the Northern Range is from the deck of the passenger ferry on its Saturday afternoon run to Tobago. This ferry leaves Port of Spain at noon, and hugs the forested cliffs to take advantage of the Venezuelan counter current. Apart from the scattered fishing villages, there is little sign of human habitation. Most of the old estate houses which were serviced by the steamers "Alice" and "Arthur" on their calls around the island, have fallen into decay and are empty. The rocky coastline interspersed with scores of deserted sandy beaches, is a sight enjoyed by far too few. Even flying over the Northern Range from Piarco International Airport, one is impressed by the unspoiled forest and steeply-sided valleys, shrouded in cloud. Though the range only rises to a height of a little over 3,000 ft. at El Tucuche and Cerro de Aripo, the precipitous sides and dense jungle foliage give a challenge to the most experienced climbers and hikers, a number of whom have spent several days and nights lost in the valleys before stumbling out into civilisation.

From the southern side, the Northern Range is much more approachable, if less in its virgin state. From Port of Spain a series of towns form a solid chain all the way to Arouca along the Eastern Main Road, comprising what is called the "East West Corridor". The railway that used to bring commuters and school children into Port of Spain each morning was closed in the 1960s, and eventually, after nearly 20 years of dithering, an express road was laid on the railway bed, reserved for buses and government vehicles. The route taxis which so many prefer to use, still have to contend with the congestion of the Eastern Main Road. Barataria, the first town outside Port of Spain, has nothing to do with Don Quixote or Sancho Panza, so far as history can show.

It has always been a scruffy lower income area, only now benefitting from its proximity to the capital with the construction of more impressive business places. San Juan, next in line, seems always crowded and frantic with its crowds of commuters, vendors and tradespeople. The Croisee, pronounced "Quayzay" branches north into what becomes, after the clay block dwellings have dwindled, the most unspoiled rural valley one could ever wish for so close to a metropolitan center like Port of Spain, the Santa Cruz Valley.

The Town and Country Planning authorities must be given the credit for this. They have banned housing development along nearly all the valley in a possibly vain effort to maintain a green belt of agriculture close to the capital. The valley has always been famous for its cocoa, produced in such romantic estates as "La Regulada" and "La Deseada" owned by the same Stollmeyer family which built and until recently lived in the Scottish baronial mansion, "Killarney," around the Grand Savannah. There are two branches to the Stollmeyer family. Jeffrey, of cricket fame and his lawyer-cricketer and artist brothers are from the A.V. Stollmeyer branch. Jeffrey lived on the cocoa estate he managed in Bourg Mulatresse until praedial larceny, construction of a large government school and the encroachment of slum dwellers caused him to sell the estate and move into a Fort George condominium, where he was tragically murdered by thieves in 1989. It is the C.C. Stollmeyer side of the family that inherited and lived in "Killarney" on the Savannah and operate the large cocoa estates. The only son became a respected doctor, and it was left to the husbands and sons of the three daughters to manage the estates.

Driving up the Santa Cruz Valley, crisscrossing the little river that gurgles down its centre, is a step back into the past. There are only a few reminders from backyard auto mechanics' signs of the twentieth century before one reaches the top of the valley to pass through the rock cutting. There one can turn right to Maracas Beach, or return to Port of Spain along Saddle Road.

Back on the busy East-West Corridor, Petit Bourg is followed by Mount Lambert and Mount Hope where the Government has built a vast maternity hospital and medical complex with its petrodollar largesse. Pessimists fear that maintenance and staffing will not be sufficient to support the massive medical project. The road forks in front of a towering samaan tree whose trunk has been forever scarred from the impact, of a flashy sports car being driven at over 100 mph by the son of sugar union leader, Bhadase Maraj. The left fork leads up to the first Spanish capital of Trinidad, St. Joseph, a sleepy little town, remarkably unchanged by the population and economic booms that have gone on around it. Nothing is left of the original Spanish capital. The Catholic Church was built long after.

*Maracas Valley*

Going deeper into the Maracas Valley behind St. Joseph, the sides of the valley are marred by housing developments, the absence of which makes Santa Cruz Valley all the more appreciated. But these grow fewer the further on one drives, until incongruously there is a sign to the left that Valley View housing estate has been reached. Impressive architect-designed homes are tastefully placed on the rising hillside, reached by well-drained and paved roads that handle with ease, the heavy rains to which all these valleys are subject. This is the best in thoughtful and loving development by the

family which still owns and manages the surrounding cocoa
and citrus estate. At the highest point on a track accessible
only by jeep, there is a little family cemetery, from which the
Maracas Valley can be seen in all its forested splendour, with
only a few ugly red gashes where shoulders of a hillside have
been carved away to take advantage of the high prices for
residential land. Equally incongruous beside it are the grounds
of an evangelical theological seminary complete with commercial printing presses that benefit from the untaxed status
of the religious institution.

There is still much further to go up the valley along what
has been called from Spanish times, the Royal Road. The
valley widens out into grassy pasture and citrus estates in
places. Beyond one of the oldest churches in Trinidad, is the
turning to the right to reach the Maracas Falls. There is a
shady parking lot, squashy underfoot from fallen immortelle
blossoms in dry season, from which the footpath leads into the
forest. Care must be taken in the late evening along this path
which is one of the few places frequented by visitors where
there is a chance of encountering the feared bushmaster,
known in Trinidad as the "mapipire." There may be fallen
branches across the path, and it is in stepping over these that
the unwary may be bitten. Fear of snakes notwithstanding,
the thirty minute walk through the cool shaded forest is
idyllic. The occasional brilliant black and turquoise morpho
butterfly may come lollopping by, and the woods will be quiet
except for the metallic chunk of the anvil bird in a distant tree.

Except in rainy season, the Maracas Falls are a disappointment to those expecting a Niagara. Much of the year the fine
stream of water falling 312 feet disintegrates into a fine spray
by the time it has reached the rocky basin at its foot. It is the
shady setting in the craggy dell, and the shrines of half-burnt
candles and votive flower offerings which give the falls their
mystery. They are popular with youngsters on picnic outings,
as well as the spiritual Baptists for their hymns and prayers.
An early arrival can provide the magic of enjoying the falls
without the distraction of others taking photographs on the
rocks and playing the omnipresent reggae tapes.

For those who enjoy a hike, the Maracas Falls could have

been by-passed by continuing to the end of the Royal Road where the village of Ortinola nestles in the shadow of the surrounding hills. A footpath leads across shallow streams running through cocoa lands. It is in this estate that for many years the Cadburys grew cocoa for part of their chocolate needs. The path leads upward, getting rocky and pitted by the heavy run-off of downpours. After an hour of exertion, the saddle of the hill is reached and a much more gentle path leads through the forest upwards to the peak of El Tucuche, the second highest by a few feet on the island. It was one of the better aspects of the colonial heritage for such trails to be maintained for the hardy minority who liked walking. After the social upheaval in 1970, groups of youths sporting mottley uniforms moved into the hills as guerillas, often maintaining themselves by growing and selling marijuana. The trails were now dangerous for walkers and this provided a good reason to cease their maintenance by a government whose petrodollar extravagance was widely felt to have caused indifference toward routine maintenance.

The summit of El Tucuche has been cleared of trees, and there used to be a wooden hut in which hikers could shelter from the frequent showers. The view is a disappointment. Not only is the peak commonly shrouded in cloud; the slope of the mountain obscures the fine view of the north coast one expects. Should you climb El Tucuche during the rainy season, you might be treated to the sight of the rain running down the mountainside in such a volume that it builds into streams which jump across the path in a cascade under which you pass. This is when the large mountain crabs come out, and with them the folk of the hills with their bent wire crab forks and cocoa bags. Deftly they hold down and scoop the crabs into the bag, later to be cooked in a tasty stew known as "crab tea."

Before the American Seabees cut the present road to Maracas Bay from Port of Spain's Saddle Road, the only way to Maracas Beach was to walk over the lower part of El Tucuche trail, descending from the saddle. It was a three hour walk, but in those days youngsters thought little of such a jaunt. This is why Maracas Bay and Maracas Valley on opposite sides of the mountains share the same name.

*Curepe and St. Augustine*

If one keeps straight on at the scarred samaan tree which leads left into St. Joseph and Maracas Valley, the Eastern Main Road passes, below on the right, the largest and best Moslem Mosque in Trinidad. This is Jinnah Memorial set in a large grassed space below the road so that one is level with the freshly painted white and green minarets. Above it in St. Joseph is the Catholic church, and just beyond, set back from the road on the left is a good example of a Hindu temple. These three places of worship represent the best grouping of the three major religions of the country.

Across the Caroni River over an old steel Bailey bridge is the busy township of Curepe. At Curepe Junction was a railway station and the start of the Southern Main Road. This was the closest road access to the South from Port of Spain until improved roadbuilding technology permitted the construction of the Princess Margaret Highway during the Second World War. The Southern Main Road is still very busy. After crossing the Churchill Roosevelt Highway by the island's largest drive-in cinema, it passes an interesting cross-section of rural Indian homes. Older Victorian fretwork houses contrast with functional concrete, and the more recent wave of sumptuous and ornate two-storied homes with arches and balconies of wooden balusters.

Beyond Curepe is St. Augustine and the University of the West Indies - Trinidad campus, there being others in Mona, Jamaica and Cave Hill, Barbados. "UWI", as it is invariably called, was an outgrowth of the esteemed Imperial College of Tropical Agriculture, famous throughout the British Commonwealth for its experimental and development work. The original ICTA had been located at the northwest corner of the Grand Savannah in Port of Spain, across from "Stollmeyer's Castle," where the Ministry of Agriculture now has its offices. It moved to St. Augustine to have more space for its work, and has proved an ideal setting for Trinidad's only university. In common with many universities, UWI in Trinidad often appeared to be much more active in social ferment than in academic studies. This continually frustrated Prime Minister Williams who would make periodic threats to close it down by cutting off its funds.

The foothills to the north of the campus housed the teaching staff and other Europeans who wanted the greater spaciousness provided this far from the capital. Their little tennis club was multi-racial from an early stage, set a high standard of hospitality, and provided the best of the pre-Carnival Ole Mas' fetes, from which it was able to finance maintenance and improvement of the club.

Standing out among the low buildings of St. Augustine is one tall structure. The Scarlet Ibis Hotel could not survive in its appeal to visitors keen on nature study in the Northern Range. Gradually it evolved into a dormitory of efficiency units for students at the UWI campus over which it towered.

St. Augustine is ironically close to the Benedictine monastery perched up in the hills behind it. Mount St. Benedict is reached by means of St. John's Road, so long that it is also a community of its own. The road winds up to the school buildings long maintained by the Dutch fathers, together with their apiaries, dog kennels, church and guest house. Provided there is room, the public can stay at this guest house for a small sum. It is primarily intended for those in religious retreat or other emotional upsets such as would-be suicides. With its eternal tranquillity and striking view over the hazy Caroni Plains where planes can just be seen and heard taking off at Piarco Airport, the main excitement is the serving of the next meal, and the only noise the clank of soup spoons. The nuns who run it, not the Dutch fathers, have even managed to instill quiet into the Indian kitchen staff. It was a favourite spot for afternoon tea where home-made bread and the monastery's honey were served in the austere dining room open to a confused flower garden set against the rock mountainside. Sadly, teas are no longer available to visitors.

## *Tunapuna and the Eastern Dormitory Suburbs*

Next in sequence along the East-West Corridor is the mainly Indian town of Tunapuna with its busy Sunday provision market and song bird competitions. Substantial bets are placed on favoured birds to sing more often and longer than their rivals in the little cages set down on the pavement.

There are reports of thousands of dollars being paid for top songsters, and when hiking in the Northern Range the person one is most likely to come across is the bird catcher, his hands filled with cages. The song of the caged birds will help call down the hunted birds whose feet will be trapped in the sticky sap called "laglee." Beyond Tunapuna, El Dorado merges into it without a discernible break. The Caura Road strikes off to the north for the Caura Valley and tuberculosis sanatorium. Beyond the sanatorium is a lonely road dangerous to visitors from the car strippers known to frequent it, and latterly the guerillas and marijuana growers who favour its remoteness.

The next valley into the Northern Range welcomes not the tubercular or outlaws, but all those interested in 19th Century estate life. A yellow sign post indicates the turning, put up by the Tourist Board who in recent years have taken the Lopinot family home under their wing. Winding upwards along a fair road past modest shacks, today's visitor would no more expect the broad flat valley that awaits him than Comte de Lopinot did when he discovered his personal paradise around 1815. Architects have been employed to put the estate house and its outbuildings back into a state and appearance close to the original. Picnic tables are set out on the lawn shaded by the tall samaan trees. Children enjoy exploring the nearby river and can do so in complete safety. Snakes have long since found more secluded settings. It is heartening to see that the majority of the visitors are local. All too often local sights are taken for granted, ignored and mistreated by those who have the easiest access to them.

Back on the Eastern Main Road, the East-West Corridor is getting more sparsely populated, and sawmills indicate the rural surroundings as Cane Farm, Tacarigua with its large Anglican orphanage established in 1857, and Arouca are passed. At Golden Grove there is a road leading south to Piarco Airport, passing the largest jail in the country. Golden Grove Maximum Security Prison was one of the final flings of the petrodollar extravagance. The closed circuit television system alone was to cost several million dollars. The financial axe fell on the project mid-stream forcing many economies, but at least there was no public furore comparable to that of the Central Racing Complex. The Eastern Main Road leads on through scattered houses and occasional stretches of lush forest to the Royal Borough of Arima.

Running parallel to the Eastern Main Road a mile or two to the South is the Churchill-Roosevelt Highway paying tribute to those two great statesmen whose agreement to use Trinidad as a training and trans-shipment base had such an important effect on the island's development, not least of which was the construction of this main arterial highway to Waller Field army base beyond Arima. For three years there were over 20,000 able-bodied young servicemen in an island population of perhaps 250,000. The Americans, well paid, away from home for the first time, and heading for a war which they might not even reach, so many troop carriers were being torpedoed, probably outnumbered the local Trinidadians in the 18 to 25 age group. Inevitably their presence had a serious and adverse effect on local men who in calypsonian Lord Invader's immortal calypso saw "Both mother and daughter, Working for the Yankee Dollar." The hostility towards Americans lasted for 25 years by which time a new generation had grown up, many of them fairer skinned than would have been the case without the "Yankee invasion."

The northern side of the Churchill-Roosevelt Highway is devoted to light industry, and an impressive sight it makes to the visitor driving into Port of Spain from the airport. Even before the boom from oil prices, these factories and assembly plants were well established. The southern side of the road is subject to flooding and remains devoted to agriculture, sugar cane giving way to intensive vegetable farming closer to the city, with Indians watering and spraying tomatoes, lettuce, pigeon peas, sweet peppers and patchoi in the broiling sun.

They do well from their hard work and are not to be pitied as exploited peasantry. When the scores of factories end, hundreds of low cost housing units continue in a carpet from Trincity and Macoya to La Horquetta and Santa Rosa Heights, occasionally interspersed with agricultural land awaiting the bulldozer. It is here the government is providing housing for the young homemakers who fill the ranks of the civil service. Though the houses seemed cramped together until garden walls and trees appear, living standards are high. It will be rare to see a house without one car at least; colour television will be enjoyed in virtually every home. From these suburban dormitories thousands of children and their parents will make their way into Port of Spain for school and work in their cars, starting at 5.30 a.m. to avoid the traffic pile-up to be expected from 6.30 onwards. In the 1960s a higher income residential area complete with shopping centre was developed south of Mt. Lambert on both sides of the Churchill-Roosevelt Highway called Valsayn Park. Fine houses were built on the flat half-acre lots, and there was no problem commuting to the city. Even the widened roads built in the 1980s cannot contend with the flood of cars which ebb and flow daily into Port of Spain, and the Valsayn residents have to leave their homes earlier than they did twenty years ago.

Although the new housing estates are encroaching on the southern outskirts of Arima, and there are many factories established in the government sponsored O'Meara Industrial Estate, Arima itself is a seedy little town not yet awake to the explosion of development which will shortly engulf it.

## Arima and the Blanchisseuse Road

Just before reaching Arima on the Eastern Main Road is Cleaver Woods Park. This was opened in 1985 to preserve an unspoiled forested area from urban development. An Amerindian-style thatched hut, called an "ajoupa," was built to house an interesting display of Amerindian artifacts, tools and utensils, aided by anthropological maps, photographs and explanations. Efforts have been made to keep the surrounding forests as they were before the Europeans came. Barbecue pits in shaded glades make it a delightful place to picnic.

Arima, meaning "water" in Amerindian, was Trinidad's third town until the growth of Chaguanas in the 1970s. Even before the Spanish conquest it was an important Amerindian settlement. When nearly all the Caribs and Arawaks had been wiped out by disease, slavery or warfare, those that survived congregated in the Arima area which became recognised as a Carib preserve. That able and well-liked governor, Sir Ralph Woodford, used to ride out along the bridle path which is now the Eastern Main Road to celebrate with the few remaining Amerindians the festival of Santa Rosa de Lima. Queen Victoria honoured and in effect legitimised the Carib Queen with the gift of a bathchair! She also honoured Arima by making it a royal borough in 1888, the only one in the Caribbean.

The Santa Rosa de Lima festival continues to this day on August 29th, in the parish church of the same name. The handful claiming to be of Amerindian descent, congregate around their patriarch the Carib Queen, who is carried by poles on their shoulders in a simple throne - not the bathchair. Spanish influence over the centuries is evident in their aquiline noses and in their accented English. How pure the Amerindian blood flows in their veins is unimportant. This is Trinidad where blood has been mixed from the earliest days. A race meeting at Arima's Santa Rosa Park race course concurrent with the religious festival draws far bigger crowds than the church. It is a social gathering like the Siparia fete where families see their distant relatives, and maidens have a rare chance to meet eligible youths as husbands. It is a shame to think this may end if racing is centralised as Government intends.

Despite the factories of nearby O'Meara Industrial Estate and the encroachment of housing estates, Arima is still a sleepy little town and shows little sign of urban activity. Only a cycling velodrome and a few plate glass store fronts confirm that Arima is really in the 20th century. The highlight of the town is a four-faced clock known as "The Dial" standing in the middle of the main crossroads. From Arima, however, lead roads to the north-eastern corner of the island which rivals scenery anywhere in the Caribbean.

The Arima Blanchisseuse Road starts out as a broad drive along the river. It is busy with trucks collecting aggregate from the quarry operated by the nation's largest concrete block manufacturer. After a while the valley narrows and houses are few and far between. Once deep into the luxuriant forest with cocoa plantations and coffee trees, interspersed with citrus on either side, one is once again moving back into a bygone age. A small sign off to the left indicates "Simla" once the summer residence of the colonial governors, who copied the practice of imperial India. Spacious balustraded terraces look out over the rolling waves of tree tops. The residence is not a crumbling palace but an active natural history field station. It was founded by naturalist Dr. William Beebe and is affiliated to the Museum of Natural History in New York for which it does research. Dr. Jocelyn Crane, for many years Dr. Beebe's secretary and companion in the study of fauna in Venezuela, Guyana and Trinidad, took over administration of the field station upon his death. There are lengthy studies into the homing instincts of hermit crabs for which briny water has to be brought from the coast every few days; whether butterflies have the ability to detect colour and many such other.

Being devoted to scientific research "Simla" is not open to casual visitors, although students of natural history could no doubt write and explain their reasons for wishing to pay a visit in advance. At a dinner given by Jocelyn Crane for some visiting scientists and local friends including the head of the Virus Laboratory in Port of Spain, she produced a large hairy tarantula she was keeping in a glass box with the required vegetation and insects to make it feel at home. She told her visitors to treat the box carefully as the spider was fairly venomous. On this she was gently corrected by the American virologist. "Oh no, Jocelyn. I have tested their venom. It is quite mild. Moreover I couldn't get the spider to bite me at all. They seem to reserve their bites for things they know they can eat. However the hairs on their tummy will give you a rash like a stinging nettle. Any reports of tarantula bites are probably from these hairs and the shock." It is small comfort, perhaps, that an eminent natural historian could have a mistaken impression of the danger of the large loathesome spiders which commonly hide in banana plants to catch the insects going to the plant's flower. It is natural to give them a wide berth, but they die readily, collapsing into a pathetic jumble of legs if hit with a tennis shoe.

Beyond "Simla" along the Blanchisseuse Road, higher and more densely hidden in the largely abandoned cocoa estates, is another more famous natural history preserve, the

Asa Wright Nature Centre and bird sanctuary which was taken under the wing of the World Wild Life Fund upon the death of Mrs. Wright, an impressive Viking of a lady, in 1968. In former years, the fine Icelandic furniture she had brought from her birthplace graced the old estate house where she lived. It is now a commercially-run guest house for nature lovers who can accept with bliss the dilapidated rooms with twenty foot ceilings, and rudimentary plumbing in exchange for a unique experience in nature study. Seated on the large verandah, high power telescopes and binoculars watch a myriad of birds skimming from one treetop to another. Other birds can only be seen on foot exploring the trails and lookouts of the lush jungle. There is a natural bathing hole for swimming but the cool of shaded foliage prevents visitors from getting too hot. There is a sense of cameraderie among the visitors, most of whom are no longer young, that makes the Centre very popular.

After the Asa Wright Centre the well-paved but narrow and winding road continues its ascent with occasional glimpses through the tall trees of the rolling forested mountain tops. At last the top of the ridge is reached. A sign marks a road to the right, Morne Bleu, which if followed, leads to the most beautiful and largest, in terms of volume, waterfall in the island. The last few miles are reached along a narrow path to the top of Paria River where the falls cascade into the enchanting walled pool. More often this pool is reached from the sea side. At the Morne Bleu turning is a radio dish receiver which has largely replaced North Post for communications with all shipping in the area. The road descends into a glorious valley of cocoa and coffee, passing occasional small estate workers' and farmers' houses, picturesque with the only bright blue hydrangea to be found in the island. Apparently the coolness of the high elevation and the presence of iron in the soil provide the right conditions. Elsewhere this shrub, known locally as "bridal bouquet" is only seen in pink.

## The North Coast to Toco

Up over a smaller range of more open hills, and the charming village of Blanchisseuse is at last reached, complete with its wooden post office and police station perched above the sudsy breakers that give the name "washerwoman." Much more traffic comes along the newer coast road from Port of Spain than from Arima. If one is prepared to take a car on the picturesque cast iron and plank bridge across the Marie Anne River, one can drive a mile or two further before continuing on foot along the donkey path. After a testing three miles, the unspoiled and perfect beach of Paria Bay lies below. There are fewer sandflies than at Las Cuevas, making the beach, all in all, one of the best in the Caribbean that is yet to be exploited. At the eastern end the Paria River comes out onto the beach. There is a path along its bank which leads up to the unforgettable falls half a mile inland. Caution is recommended along this path which is frequented by the dreaded mapipire. During their breeding season, whenever that may be, they are more aggressive and do not slide off into the undergrowth unseen.

Paria Falls are well worth the exertion and risk of the hike. They can be heard long before they are seen, thundering down into the large pool where one can swim in the tranquil outer section, or be pounded by the falls themselves. Walls of rock enclose two thirds of the glen. Ferns festoon the steep sides, but most striking are the scores of morpho Blue Emperor butterflies flitting up and down the sides. Conditions are clearly ideal for them to be present in such numbers.

For the really hardy, the donkey track down known as the Paria Main Road continues along the North Coast, up and down rocky promontories, along fine sand beaches, sometimes half a mile inland, but mainly close to the shore. A party of oil company geologists were once walking along this narrow path, and were strung out so that not all could see the man in front. One of them had poor eyesight and wore thick glasses. He stumbled off the path, slithered down the steep slope to the rocks below where the waves were breaking against a tiny strip of shingle. His glasses were lost in the fall. He called out to his friends when he.estimated they were passing above, but with the clash of waves on the rocks his cries were unheard. Without his glasses he could see nothing, but could feel that the rocks above him and to the side were too steep to attempt a climb. Instead he opted to cling onto the rocks until his absence was noted, and help came. There he clung for the long night. The following day when a search party in a fishing boat came along the coast he was found. His friends had come back along the path for him the previous afternoon, but not spotted him below. Only by luck had they thought that a fishing boat might find him below the path out of sight.

After passing the beaches of Gran Taqueribe and Petit Taqueribe the Paria Main Road leads out into the wide mouth of the Matelot River and Matelot village on the further shore. This is the end of the vehicular road from the east, and makes Matelot the most isolated and underprovided village in the country. Electricity has only recently been provided on a reliable basis and the lack of traffic on the road has led the authorities to neglect it. Considering this, one is surprised to see so many resort houses, even though the great majority are empty most of the year. For all their gregariousness, Trinidadians also relish the peace and quiet of a remote beach, even though they will undoubtedly enliven their sur-roundings with music and "old talk" late into the tropical nights.

Driving along the coast road from Matelot through the little villages of Grand Riviere, Sans Souci and Cumana to Toco provides a never ending delight of rocky coastal scenery. Coconut plantations flourish on some grassy promontories; but for the most part the winding road ducks under the shade of tall forest trees and along the edge of cocoa plantations, many now in a state of decay because labour is hard to find at a price which would be viable. Many rivers flow off the lush mountains into the sea causing the road to hairpin into each valley across a rickety bridge. Breakers thunder against the rocky shore line. Nearly every little beach is isolated, except at weekends when a family may be picnicking on an excur-sion.

By comparison Toco is a busy town and the crescent-shaped beach reached from it on the road to Galera lighthouse is jammed with excursion buses on Sundays. This beach is justifiably one of the more popular in the island even though there is a current which runs across it from east to west. From the eastern end Tobago can always be seen, as this is the nearest point to the sister island. Driving to the Galera Point provides the best view, being at a higher elevation. The lighthouse is now reduced to a vandalised mess. Graffiti blemish the broken walls and the outbuildings are filled with refuse and worse. Despite the number of visitors who have taken the trouble to ruin it, the authorities consider it too remote to warrant proper upkeep.

## *The North East*

The road back from Toco to Arima gives occasional glimpses of the sea coast past the broad and popular bays of Salibia and Matura. Most advanced in its development is Balandra Bay where an eighteen hole golf course has been laid out, and retirement homes are planned for construction. At the time of its promotion, the lots were avidly sought in anticipation of a boom in building alongside a golf course similar to that which accompanied a comparable project at Mount Irvine in Tobago. Most of the investors seem to have been in for a quick turnover at a profit, rather than to build. For this reason the scheme has stagnated, but will no doubt succeed in the course of time.

After Matura the road strikes inland through cocoa and citrus estates crossing limpid pebbled streams. At one stretch, Trinidad's only rubber plantation can be seen to the west. Although the tall trees, planted during the Second World War to provide an emergency supply when Malaya's rubber was lost, come close to the road, there is no natural undergrowth so that the avenues of trees in a delightful semi-gloom can be seen receding into the distance. Mora forest takes its place as one nears the Valencia Road. These imposing trees are cut both for their hardy timber, difficult though it is to work, and also to make charcoal in the age-old natural hearth process. Sacks of mora charcoal, or "coal" as it's called, there being none of the mined coal in use, are the best for barbecue pits or the "coal pots" still tucked in a cupboard in all homes even though propane gas and electricity is now used. Just at the Valencia Road, is a plantation of pine trees, incongruous in their tropical setting, but flourishing nevertheless. The Valencia

Road is the quickest way back to Port of Spain, passing through unspoiled forest. Only in the last few years have a few board houses been set up by the roadside by tenant or squatting farmers wresting a living from the soil around them. Close to the village of Valencia, the Matura River is crossed on a wooden planked bridge. There is bound to be a crowd of river bathers below, and a car or two being washed by the river's edge.

Before Valencia there are several roads leading into hidden valleys to the north being developed into horse and cattle ranches. Grass pasture is well sustained by the streams flowing south from the mountains. One such road leads up to Cumaca, a pocket of Spanish-speaking peasantry who work in an exemplary fashion on co-operative projects. Their curbs are always well maintained, their parish church spanking clean and its grounds well tended. Above their village rise the inaccessible Heights of Aripo for which a local guide must be used by the very few who ever try to climb Trinidad's highest peak. Much better known and visited are the Aripo caves occupied by the renowned oil birds whose squeaks provide a sophisticated sonar system for guiding them in the dark recesses of their caves. They fly out at night to eat the oily nuts of trees in the neighbouring forest which gives them their name. Their flesh is so filled with nut oil that it can be pressed to extrude an oil for burning a lamp.

Leading from the limestone caverns of Aripo is the pure water of the North Oropouche River which leads into a classic water catchment resevoir with all its tributary streams. Plans were laid to exploit this godsend which could have provided the residents of greater Port of Spain with potable water of the highest quality at minimal price back in 1968. A small coffer dam had proved that a constant supply, never less than 15 million gallons a day, would fill the natural reservoir of the surrounding hills which closed to a narrow neck at the optimum point. All that was required was a small catchment wall, a pumping station to gain a 50ft head and filtration system to prevent possible contamination of the pure water for a gravity flow to Port of Spain for eleven cents per 1,000 gallons. A large reservoir could later enhance the scheme into providing 65 million gallons a day. It was only in 1982, after a generation of families had survived constant water distribution inadequacies, that Government resuscitated the North Oropouche scheme and that of the Caroni Arena. By that time, of course, costs had soared tenfold.

The workers monitoring the project had made themselves at home in the bush in a manner which had not changed since Columbus landed. A large open ajoupa had been built from local saplings of timite thatched with carat fronds, proof against the many downpours. Rope was woven into a crisscross frame and covered with cocoa bags to make beds. A stove was built outside of mora ashes and blue clay. Three burners on top, two large for the cooking pots and the third smaller for the coffee pot, provided all the camp's cooking needs. Coffee was available locally and was roasted in a pitch oil tin. Pigeon peas and other provisions were planted around the ajoupa to make the work force more self sufficient.

The forests of Valencia are known for the vampire bats that live in the fruit bearing tall trees. Notices appear in the press warning of cattle being attacked by these bats, but it is only in the local mythology of the soucouyant, the old witch who can stay alive only by drinking fresh blood, that the sucking of human blood is known. The main worry from vampire bats is that they can carry rabies. Trinidad maintains the strict six month quarantine of its colonial past to prevent any dogs entering the country with rabies. Vampire bats can fly from the mainland of Venezuela and contaminate the local bats. It is for this reason a constant guard is maintained. More often seen are the huge fruit bats with a 14" wingspan flitting in and out of mango trees when they are bearing or down the islands to the west, the equally large fish bats swooping back and forth across the water, dipping down in the seemingly impossible task of catching fish. The casual visitor to Trinidad is hardly likely to see a bat of any type, and need have no fears of vampires painlessly nipping his toes through mosquito netting, and the uncoagulating blood dripping down on the floor until he wakes, any more than he need fear the tales of the evil soucouyant. Such stories have deep-seated feelings in the local populace, however. This was particularly borne out when a young girl admitted to murdering an old lady because she was convinced she was a soucouyant - in 1982.

*A Baptist gathering*

*Montserrat Estate House*

# Chapter 19

## *Central Trinidad*

Bird lovers have a field day in Trinidad. It is known throughout the ornithological world for the diversity of its species and the ease with which most can be seen close to the comforts of an air conditioned hotel. Tobago shares in this wealth having varieties of birds that are unique. The one disappointment in Tobago is the myth of the ultra shy birds of paradise which have not been sighted since the 1962 hurricane passed through, but to which references are still made in the fond hope that by some miracle they will reappear. Short of a fresh supply from New Guinea there seems little chance.

### The Caroni Bird Sanctuary

The Asa Wright Nature Centre in the Blanchisseuse Valley is the ideal combination of a friendly guest house set in the middle of a bird preserve. Many of those staying in the former estate house have come to Trinidad specifically for that purpose and little more. By far a greater number of tourists and visitors are likely to pay a sunset visit to the Caroni Swamp ten minutes outside Port of Spain on the main arterial north-south highway to view the unbelievably brilliant scarlet ibis winging their way home to roost, after the long day many miles distant from the swamp foraging for the little pink crabs which give them their colour. Scarlet ibis can be seen in many of the world's zoos excluding the one behind the Savannah in Port of Spain. They are reduced to a lacklustre reddish pink when deprived of their pink crabs.

Two families, those of Oudit Nanan and David Ramsahai, have monopolised trips into the swamp since the Second World War. They are experts at their trade and have both accumulated accurate information to impart to their passengers. A couple or a small group can nearly always be accommodated on one of the long flat-bottomed boats built specifically for the shallow waters of the swamp. Despite this, it is safer to telephone ahead for a reservation. Only naturally they will never turn away the trade which is their livelihood, but there are times when the ibis are "on sabbatical" in Venezuela and a poor impression would be gained of Trinidad's renowned ornithological carnival. In the rainy season, too, there is a serious likelihood of a drenching. Trips into the swamp are recommended by common sense, to be taken in the dry season.

It is occasionally possible to hire a fishing boat to take one into the swamp from the South Quay jetty in Port of Spain. This is a longer ride that winds up the Blue River, across into the Caroni River into the area protected for the birds' nesting. According to the time, the deeper keel of the fishing pirogue may scrape ominously on the mangrove roots negotiating narrow channels, awakening fears of being stranded overnight in the gloomy tangle of what can easily be imagined to be alligator-infested mangrove swamp. It is for this reason that Messrs Nanan and Ramsahai have little outside competition. You will be told to arrive for 4 o'clock, but when you do, there will undoubtedly be a wait for latecomers up to 4.30. The main objective is to leave in time to reach the nesting area before the birds start coming in, so that they are not disturbed and diverted to other trees further away.

One member of the family will handle the outboard motor, while a cousin or brother will point out the birds seen along the straight and narrow canal along which the boat, seating as many as thirty on its classroom-like benches, putters its way. Once the end of the canal is reached, the boat branches off into the maze of channels to the left, and the real magic of the trip into the timeless tangle of mangrove starts. To most people a swamp is a morass of mud interspersed with clumps of rushes through which passage would be possible only in a hovercraft. The Caroni Swamp will come as a pleasant surprise with its clear waterways and banks of mangrove, starting in the lacework of roots at the water's edge, holding the trunk of the tree they support, a foot or two above the damp mud.

Mangrove grows in the brackish water where fresh water draining from the hills inland mixes with the salt tidal water. There are several types of mangrove tree; in fact it is more accurate to say that "mangrove" is the style in which such trees grow in adapting to the tidal conditions. It is on their roots, exposed between high tides to the air, that the tiny but succulent tree oysters grow. Sir Walter Raleigh's reports of these oysters which grew on trees were one of the main reasons for the credibility gap he created in reporting his efforts to find the wealth of El Dorado. Oysters are harvested daily, not only in the Caroni Swamp, but in all accessible mangrove areas for the insatiable appetites of those attending the vendors around the southern perimeter of the Grand Savannah, the Croisee in San Juan and the junction in Curepe. Vendors set up their collapsible stands each evening, lit by a hurricane lamp or "flambeau" of kerosined wick stuck into a soft drink bottle. They deftly open hundreds of the gnarled oysters, popping the tiny occupant, no bigger than a gob of chewing gum, into the jar of highly peppered sauce. A small tumbler will hold two or three dozen. They can be drunk from the glass in their own fiery sauce, or for the more fastidious, eaten individually with a fork or spoon. Oysters are known for their therapeutic powers on the male sexual system, and in a country with a keen concern to maintain sexual adequacy to judge from the proliferation of tonics, stouts and other concoctions claimed to prevent such humiliation, these tree oysters would be consumed as avidly even if they were not a true gourmet delicacy.

After zigzagging through the channels for half an hour, seeing the occasional snowy egret on a mangrove branch, a blue heron flying away from the intrusion, the boat turns a corner and is abruptly in the open lake marked out with slender stakes set down into the shallow water by the handful of game wardens to whom Trinidad's bounty of living natural resources is entrusted. Already in place are half a dozen other boats, tethered to a stake, their bows pointing towards islands covered with mangrove and tall trees. The last boat quietly gets into position and turns off its outboard engine. The boatloads of visitors sit expectantly facing the lush islands, a brilliant golden green in the light of the setting sun, their cameras and telescopic lenses at the ready. Already a number of snowy egrets are in the trees, and among them the first signs of the vivid scarlet, which were at first taken for blossoms of an African tulip tree.

The first groups of ibis start to head into the islands three hundred yards away, their outline at first black in silhouette against the sky's unblemished blue, then scarlet as they pass overhead. Cameras start clicking away. Heads crane in every direction as more and more flocks zero in on the nesting islands. "Look there, quick," the tourists cry in urgent whispers to each other. The branches grow heavy with the new red blossoms. In each tree there may be forty or fifty birds. When the final arrow of late-coming ibis has arrived, the sun has set and the light grown too faint for further pictures. A breeze starts up and is chilly after the tropical afternoon. The broad boats untie, turn back into the mangrove channels and leave all their occupants content with rare and unforgettable memories. There are estimated to be around three thousand ibis which nest at the sanctuary. Young are being hatched all the time, recognised by their more dowdy buff-pink plumage. Feeding conditions dictate how large a flock can be sustained. No doubt many birds make the easy journey across to the Venezuelan mainland when food is more plentiful there. In the meantime Trinidad's Caroni Swamp can still boast the scarlet ibis in abundance.

There are fears, however, that the days of the ibis are numbered. Tilapia, a fresh water fish grown inland in ponds for its flesh have escaped into the swamp during floods. Their favourite food is the same pink crab on which the ibis depends. It is this which causes the ibis to search so far afield for its daily food. The coastal swamps get more polluted as the population moves closer and the ecology is disturbed. Local conservationists protested long and loud when an oil company's barge, the *Pelican* was allowed to stir up the muddy waters and otherwise wreak havoc on the delicate ecostructure of the swamp - but to little avail. The decision to use other means of supplying liquified petroleum gas to the area was based on economic motives, not conservational sympathy. It is much to be hoped that Trinidad will conserve the swamp so that these bright and beautiful birds which grace the national emblem, can be seen in their native habitat by generations to come.

Princess Margaret, then at the height of her popularity in the West Indies as the one member of the Royal Family who let her hair down, opened the new main road to the South. Until 1984 it was named the Princess Margaret Highway in her honour. A much-needed extension from the Churchill-Roosevelt Highway to the Eastern Main Road was added in 1984. It was named after Uriah "Buzz" Butler, an incendiary labour leader in the oil fields during the 1930s, originally from Grenada. Perhaps because it is now a republic, the opportunity was taken to drop Princess Margaret's name from her road at the time it was widened to four lanes. The whole highway is accordingly now named after Mr Butler, a respectability he would never have dared expect from his inflammatory background.

### Sugar Lands

Across from the edge of the Caroni swamp where tourists gather for their trip to the scarlet ibis, stretches the expanse of the Caroni Plain, pancake flat almost to the horizon. In the middle lies Piarco International Airport. The Northern Range marches along the northern edge. To the south the rolling

Montserrat Hills seem to merge with the distant knoll of Mount Tamana. These plains are devoted almost entirely to sugar cane production, now all handled by the government-owned, Caroni Ltd. This company also owns extensive lands further south all the way to San Fernando. The sugar lands beyond that belong to individual cane farmers who are obliged to take their cane to the Caroni Ltd sugar mill at Usine, Sainte Madeleine. This is done in trucks, the gigantic "taskers", or by rubber tyred carts drawn by ponderously powerful water buffalo. The French word *usine* signifies "factory". Ste Madeleine was the second largest in the world when it was established in 1872, and remained the largest in the British Commonwealth for many years thereafter. Caroni Ltd operates a second sugar mill at Brechin Castle close to the industrial estate at Point Lisas. Before the sugar industry was in effect nationalised, there were many other sugar factories. Gradually they were closed as the owners saw the futility of trying to produce sugar at a profit. By 1983 Caroni Ltd was operating three factories, but was able to convince Government that two would suffice. The company's hands are tied on most managerial decisions by the politicians because of the sensitive issues involved. The thousands of workers employed in these rural areas are mostly of Indian stock and each one has a vote.

Sugar is a lazy crop to farm compared to most others. The ground, which has to be well drained against the torrential downpours of the wet season, is first ploughed. Stumps of cane cut from a preceding crop are planted in rows. They readily catch. It takes fifteen months to reach its full height of eight feet formed in a clump of four or five woody stems. The rows will have been weeded once or twice during the growing year, and sprayed against pests such as the froghopper. Just before it is cut, the field is set on fire to burn off the trash of the loose dried leaves and weeds. It also drives out any scorpions which would make the work of the labourers hazardous. Sixty per cent of the cutting of the cane on Caroni Ltd's lands is still done by hand, the balance by mechanical harvesters. These require flat or at most, gently sloping terrain to operate efficiently. In the deep South where the cane farmers own their own lands, the terrain is even more hilly, making it impossible to use mechanical harvesters on more than twenty per cent of the land.

Stumps of the cut cane are left in the soil, from which grows next year's crop. This is the first "rattoon." These stools of cane can be cut without replanting for five or six subsequent rattoons. By that time the cane has usually deteriorated in quality. The stools are ploughed up and new stock planted.

The burning of the cane is a colourful sight at night even from the distance of Port of Spain. To those who live nearer it is a source of pollution. Cane should be cut and delivered to the factory for grinding within thirty-six hours of being burnt, otherwise the sucrose content of the stems drops rapidly. Malicious fires make this hard to achieve and a political blind eye is turned towards the "stale cane" brought in by the cane farmers three or four days after it was burnt. For this reason the conversion ratio between the numbers of tons of cane needed to produce a ton of sugar is invariably disappointing. Climatic factors also play a part, as do the types of cane grown. There are many varieties, and an experimental station at Carapichaima has worked hard to develop the best strains for the Trinidad soil and moisture conditions. Some experts feel, however, that a hardy variety with relatively low sucrose content is used because there are fewer administrative problems in getting it cut at the critical time.

For the hard working management team of Caroni Ltd it is a no-win situation. Even with ideal conditions, no cane fires, no stale cane, no industrial disputes - they could not produce sugar at less than double the price at which it can be bought on the world market. Were it not for the political issue of the thousands of voters who would be out of work, the country could save the hundred and fifty million dollars applied each year in subsidies to offset the operating losses of the sugar industry if it were to close down sugar operations. To make the best of a hopeless situation, Trinidad's sugar crop is exported to Europe's Common Market under artificially favourable prices of the Lomé Convention; or to the United States where it has a quota at well above the world price. Because it exports all its sugar, domestic needs are purchased on the open world market at much lower prices. Inevitably there are delays and other unforeseen screw-ups which have at times caused the ironical situation of a lack of sugar on the shelves. Housewives and industry alike have to wait for the imported sugar to reach them even as mountains of local sugar in local warehouses await shipment abroad. Trinidad could readily produce enough to meet not only its export requirements, but also domestic consumption. It deliberately restricts production to 75,000 tons so that domestic needs are met from the cheaper imports. The more sugar grown, the more the company loses, and the more it costs the taxpayer in subsidies.

The Uriah Butler Highway merges into the Sir Solomon Hochoy Highway at Chaguanas. Perhaps even Sir Solomon's name will yield to that of "Buzz" Butler, even though "Sollo" as he was endearingly called, was the nation's first Governor General when independence was attained. At this stage the monotony of the Caroni Plain is left behind and the drive south becomes a pleasure not only for the fast well-paved four lanes, but also for the delightful rolling green countryside which is passed. This continues all the way to San Fernando. Being a new road taking the optimum route through the countryside and with limited access roads, there is only sparse development at its fringe. One must turn off to see the flourishing urban centres of Chaguanas and Couva with nearby huge Point Lisas Industrial Estate.

*Couva and Chaguanas*

Government had intended that Couva and Point Lisas would be the major growth areas. Nevertheless it was the backward rural town of Chaguanas with its preponderance of Indians which experienced the most dramatic growth of any town in the country. This was entirely self-generated. There is no Government-financed factory or industrial estate nearby. The single main street of indiscriminate shops burst at the seams with increased economic activity, reflecting the general prosperity of the nation from 1974 to 1983. By the time the tide of prosperity had turned, three shopping malls had opened on the periphery of the main street, with plans for a fourth. Housing development nearby plays a part in making

Chaguanas the boom town of the 80s.

Couva is reached from the Hochoy Highway along a road which winds through canefields. It also stretches along one main street, the old Southern Main Road, which is crammed with traffic throughout the day. On the southern outskirts of Couva the vast conglomeration of the Point Lisas housing estate starts. Ten thousand housing units were targeted by Government, farmed out to a variety of contractors, each with his own style - some town houses, some bungalows, some two storey. The units were completed long before Government could get the infrastructural facilities finished, facing them with the embarrassment of completed units, unoccupied and rapidly falling into disrepair. Not that this was new. There had been similar lapses in planning at Malick, Curepe, Trincity and most other Government housing projects.

Those in the area ascribed political motives rather than managerial ineptitude, to the delay in handing over the houses. It was felt that Government was carefully controlling who were to be allocated the houses. The fact that of the first thirty, nearly all were negro in a dominantly Indian area, added fuel to the belief that deliberate steps were being made to bring negroes from the crowded East-West corridor into the new industrial heartland. They could be relied on to bring their PNM votes with them. The trouble was that fewer negroes were prepared to move into the Indian-dominated Couva area even with the enticement of housing, than Government had figured. Hence the empty housing units.

*Sugar Production*

Cheek by jowl with this vast housing development, is the sugar factory of Brechin Castle. When the crop starts at the end of January, by which time the clay of the fields has dried out enough for equipment to get in and out, the trailer wagons of wire mesh designed for the carriage of cane, and called "taskers" (for the day's task of cut cane the massive containers hold) start rolling up to the sugar mill. After the cane has been cut, whether by hand or the mechanical harvesters, it is gathered into piles on the ground. Tractors with claw-like grabs pick up the cane and load it into the trucks, which then pass through a weigh station to record the load. At the mill the cane is dumped into a vast concreted pit equipped with conveyor belts that drag the cane into the factory building for the first grinding. Several grindings are required to extract the full amount of juice from the cane which is by then shredded into a damp straw called bagasse. This refuse is dried for use as a bedding by poultry farmers. Attempts to make a cheap building board were given up after a vain but extended effort, even after they had overcome the deadly effects of a fungal disease called "bagasosis" carried into the lungs in its dust. Another by-product of the first screenings of the cane juice is collected and forms a black manure suitable for garden use. It is peddled round the houses of San Fernando from the back of vans after being bought at minimal cost from the factory

The extracted cane juice starts on its complex passage through the machinery of the factory, being filtered and cleaned before passing into the first of a series of cooking chambers. Molasses results from the first of several pressured crystallizations of the sugar syrup, when excess moisture is spun off in the centrifugal baskets. The raw sugar is subjected to further pressurized cooking, dilution and crystallization until the washed grey sugar, commonly sold in the supermarkets, rather than the highly refined white sugar, results. Trinidadians are lucky that the unrefined brown, amber and grey sugars which have better nutritive qualities than white sugar, make up their diet.

By any standards Trinidadians have a sweet tooth and consume heavily the crop which employs more than any other, and was the mainstay of the economy before oil took over.But it is not for their sugar or their sweet tooth that in praise of their island Trinidadians so often sing out in that ascending drawn out note, like a bird call, "Trinidad sweeeeet". It is for the love of life, the gaiety, music and devotion of their boundless vitality to the whole sweetness of life.

*Cocoa*

Often competing with sugar in importance, and surpassing it when the fluctuating prices were higher, was the magic crop of cocoa, brought to Trinidad in the earliest colonial days. From its mauvish brown beans, the highly prized drink of chocolate is made. In Mexico where the invading Spaniards first encountered the rich and tasty drink, the Aztecs considered it to have aphrodisiac properties. It was the unique appeal of cocoa's taste to Europeans who had only recently been introduced to tea and coffee, that immediately provided a strong demand for it. Before that ale, beer and mead provided the mainstay for the thirsty.

Cocoa is grown in the cool, well-watered valleys of the Northern Range and on the slopes where the rivers drain off through Valencia and Sangre Grande. It is in the Montserrat Hills, however, that the soil has just the right properties to provide a distinctive flavour to far greater proportions of lower grade cocoa. These "chocolate soils" provide the "flavour cocoa" which puts Trinidad cocoa at a premium of double that of the filler grades obtained in much greater volume from Ghana and Brazil. Across the Gulf of Paria, the Venezuelan cocoa estates also provide flavour cocoa, but their methods of drying and polishing differ. The London cocoa buyers prefer the gleaming polished beans with Trinidad marks on the jute sacks.

Generations of schoolboys have been mystified by the contradictory spelling involved with cocoa. All older texts spell it "cacao." How and why did the vowels get juxtaposed? Both spellings are correct, and the final "a" in cocoa is, of course silent, making it sound identical to the coconut, to which it has no relation. The same schoolboys also have only a hazy idea of the relationship of cocoa to chocolate. Both are hot drinks but the latter more often a foil-wrapped bar. The cosmetic industry has further complicated matters by publicising the virtues of cocoa butter in face creams and body lotions.

The cocoa tree takes five years to start bearing the fleshy pods shaped like a miniature rugger ball, nine inches long and three inches in diameter. The trees reach a height of twelve to eighteen feet and continue bearing, if they are properly tended, for as long as fifty years. In healthy cocoa trees, the majority of the pods grow directly from the stem of the trunk and the thicker branches, with a lesser number on the outer branches. If canker fungus attacks the xylen layer under the bark, the pods on the trunk are reduced in number, giving a lower yield to the estate. To avoid this and the dreaded witch broom disease which affects the pods themselves, the trees are sprayed with a copper-based fungicide. Cocoa trees like some shade and protection from the wind. For this reason they are grown under the magnificent coral blossomed immortelle.

The cocoa pods start off green, turning to yellow, red or a dark mauve when they are ripe. It is easy to lop them off with the sharp cutlass and pile them under the rows of trees for opening. The fleshy pods are deftly sliced open along their length, exposing the 25 to 36 large seeds covered in a whitish, sticky membrane. These are scooped out and dumped into the sweat boxes where they are kept for 36 to 48 hours. The gummy membrane ferments and dries. The beans are taken from the sweat boxes for further drying on large shallow racks in the top of the cocoa sheds. The galvanised iron roof above them rests on rails which are rolled back, weather permitting, to expose the beans to the sunshine. They are turned with wooden shovels and traditionally "danced" by the workers who shuffle through the drying beans in their bare feet, often to a folk tune they sing while they work. This process, entrenched in popular lore, is now rarely seen. More modern estates use electrical or gas drying to speed up the process. Nevertheless the glossy result on the reddish mauve beans gives them a market appeal supposedly only achieved with the rubbing of the bare calloused foot.

Broken beans and imperfect ones are carefully removed before the cocoa is sacked for shipment to the Cocoa Planters Association which acts on behalf of all the estates, expertly blending to meet the exacting demands of the buyers. To make the end product, the beans are carefully roasted to enhance their intrinsic aroma. They are then ground into a fine powder which is subjected to intense pressure to extract the rich oil from the beans. This oil coagulates into large round slabs of a milky translucency and is the "cocoa butter" advertised in cosmetic products. The remaining ground beans still have a certain amount of the oil in them. If all the oil is removed, the powder resulting is what we know as the drink of cocoa. Vanilla and other spices will be added by the manufacturer to make it more palatable. It is the powder from which not all the oil has been removed, making it far richer in flavour, that gives us chocolate, again with the expert addition of vanilla and spices, and of course sugar. The difference between cocoa and chocolate is accordingly only in the presence of the rich oil.

No tastier, richer or more fattening drink can exist than the "country cocoa" made into thick turd-like sticks by the country people who grind the beans they have roasted themselves, adding their own formula of spices. Grate a chunk in boiling water and watch it dissolve, the cocoa butter rising to the top to prove its richness. Once thoroughly dissolved into a thick "tea," milk and sugar are added in the normal way. Aphrodisiac qualities notwithstanding, aficionados of cocoa extoll its virtues in loving terms.

*The Montserrat Hills*

Turning east off the Hochoy Highway at the sign to Gran Couva, the road is hedged in on both sides by sugar cane, until abruptly the cane ceases and towering trees indicate the start of the cocoa plantations. They can be seen in their cool shaded tranquility to best advantage by turning off to the right before reaching the clapboard police station with the national flag flying proudly outside. Even for those not used to a tropical climate, a walk through the shady trails of a cocoa estate is a refreshing pleasure. The estate houses encountered will be set on an open knoll for the benefit of the breeze. The ornately carved wooden bargeboards will be surmounted with steeply sloping roofs of rusting galvanised iron. Facing the front steps will be a saint's statue or the Virgin Mary on a plinth. Nearby will be the cocoa sheds, roofs open to expose the beans to the sun; further off are the old workers' housing; rather mean little rooms scarcely bigger than stables. In a temperate climate such conditions could never be tolerated. In the open air life of the tropics where shelter from the cold is never necessary, only shelter from the rain, they do not seem quite so bad. Few of them are still used. Even in the private world of these estates the workers generally now have adequate houses, albeit without the colour television and automatic washers of the civil servants of the East-West Corridor.

For those persons keen to explore the lesser known side of Trinidad, it will pay to press on past the Gran Couva police station, past Pepper Village, eventually coming out on the road from Longdenville to Tabaquite. Turning to the north, first one reaches the deserted Caparo Road, and further on the Todds Station Road, both of which lead through remote countryside to the village of Talparo with an imposing Catholic church school and a handful of country stores. From there it is a short drive through citrus estates to San Rafael which is the centre of an unusual cooperative.

A type of reed grows in the area called "tirit." After being cut tirit is split down its length into three sections, the pith being cleaned off from the inside. Whole families sit together in a communal shed weaving the tirit into laundry baskets, wastebaskets, lamp shades and a variety of smaller shapes. The appeal of these baskets which are light and strong, comes from the designs made with the black and straw colours in which tirit comes. Like so many other such craft industries, the days of the tirit baskets may be numbered. Stocks of wild tirit are dwindling, but one can still see the baskets on sale at the Maraval corner of the Savannah in Port of Spain each weekend. Thousands of homes depend on their tirit laundry baskets, which with reasonable care will last more than ten years.

The Brasso-Tabaquite Road leads south to the comparative metropolis of Rio Claro through the largest teak forest in the Western Hemisphere. This was a thoughtful legacy of the colonial forestry service which has taken fifty years to come to fruition. At present, teak is available for fence posts and small size boards, but as the forests mature, a thriving teak industry is ready for development. The teak trees at present thirty feet tall, have large round floppy leaves, and clusters of flowers like bunches of miniature grapes. The bark is smooth, and the trunks of the trees still no more than a foot in diameter.

Rio Claro owes its activity to the large catchment area of country people that it serves. It is on the main road leading from San Fernando to the oil rich east coast, where Amoco has its base of operations for the off-shore wells. Most of the drilling equipment is taken to the rigs by marine barge rather than by truck across the island, which is just as well, as the road is subject to subsidence. Many people taking the road are on their way to the ten mile long beach of Mayaro with beach houses nestling under the shade of coconut palms for its entire length. Off-shore drilling has caused marine tar to pollute the beach, and for this reason it is no longer so popular with weekenders from Port of Spain, who thought nothing of the long drive for two days of fish broth and scotch and coconut water in the constant breeze off the Atlantic.

Pierreville and Plaisance are the two names shown on the map, but it is Mayaro to all those who visit it. Two small hotels have struggled to survive over the years under changing ownership. They are too remote to attract the normal tourist for a Caribbean holiday, providing nothing but the bare amenities of hotel life. They are ideal for those who, for whatever private reasons, may wish to slip away for a hidden sojourn. And the fish is fresh from the sea each evening, sold for much less than the high city price. The former inadequacies of the transport and marketing system have been remedied. The days are gone when piles of fish rotted on the beach after a large catch because there was no adequate refrigerated storage.

### The Cocal

One major reason why the drive never put off visitors to Mayaro was the stretch along the Manzanilla Beach known simply as The Cocal. Before the road was built, one drove along the straight flat beach for twelve miles, apart from a little wooden ferry across the Nariva River draining the extensive Nariva swamp. The road now used runs parallel to the beach fifty metres inland under a continuous canopy of graceful coconut trunks and fronds, the beach always in sight. To drive mile after mile under the arching silver and rusty red trunks curving above has a mesmerising effect, like a strange dream of a never-ending monastery arcade. The brilliant blue and white of the nearby breakers contrasts with the dappled shade of the road. Even if the canopy of coconuts lasted a mile it would be impressive. For it to last for over ten miles has a dramatic effect on all visitors seeing it for the first time. Copra estates are passed where the nuts, harvested by expert tree climbers who shinny up the forty-foot trunks aided by a leather or canvas strap, are split open for their oil-rich contents.

It is not uncommon to see mistaken illustrations of desert islands with the same hairy little coconuts one sees in fair grounds shown at the top of a coconut tree. The coconut has a thick husk around this nut, so that a coconut is slightly larger than an adult's head, and weighs about fifteen pounds. Falling from the top of a tree it can, and does, readily break the windscreen of a car. There have even been one or two tragic cases of babies being killed by falling nuts when placed in their shade. It takes some skill to remove this thick outer husk of coir, which when separated makes a dependable if uncomfortable mattress stuffing.

It is also woven into coconut matting and rope. If harvested when "green" the nuts contain an almost clear water which is highly nutritious and good for the kidneys. Coconut vendors around the Port of Spain savannah and on Independence Square sell these nuts from the back of jitneys. Cutlasses, worn thin from constant sharpening, flash expertly. With three cuts the end of the husk is cut off, exposing the soft nut. A quick scoop with the point and a hole is exposed from which to drink, leaning forward to avoid dribbling down your front. When the water is finished, the nut is handed back to the vendor standing up on his jitney. Deftly he cuts the nut in half, laying it on the palm of his hand for the purpose. One final flourish cuts off, apart from a small retaining strand, a small outer slice. Pulled loose, the sharp edges of this are used to scrape and scoop out the translucent jelly of the inside of the nut. For those liking to chew sweet coconut meat, a more mature nut can be requested instead of the water nut. The water inside will be less but sweeter. The solid white meat will provide enough chewing to make your jaws ache.

The coconuts harvested at Manzanilla and Mayaro are allowed to mature. There is little or no water inside. It has all been absorbed into the meat which is no longer white, but a yellowish grey. Using a special stand to hold them, the nuts are split in half and the dense copra inside scooped out onto a pile, where it is left to dry in the sun. Later it will be shipped to the Coconut Growers' Association, the cooperative which extracts the oil for cooking oil, soap or other manufacture. The shredded copra from which the oil has been squeezed is excellent animal fodder. Driving past the CGA factory in Laventille the air is redolent of toasted coconut, but with an oiliness not associated with confectionery.

From the northern end of The Cocal it is a short drive through coffee and cocoa estates to the busy market town of Sangre Grande, rivalling in the north east, Rio Claro's control over the south - east of the island. If you happen to drive through a coffee plantation while the coffee is in blossom, the air will be as strongly scented as a perfumery. It is a surprise to find that the flower of a coffee bush smells as strongly as a gardenia. No perfume is sold under the coffee label as yet. The coffee cherries which the perfumed flower will later produce, will have an aroma of their own, when the coffee beans are roasted and ground.

## Sangre Grande

Sangre Grande, the Great Bloodbath, is reputed to recall a massive battle against the Caribs during colonial days. The little hamlet of Sangre Chiquito, is the little bloodletting that preceded the larger battle. There is nothing bloody about Sangre Grande these days, especially on a Saturday morning when the country people from the remotest villages of the whole north east of Trinidad gather for market day. They bring their produce to sell, and buy the housewares and goods they will need until next week. Apart from the occasional peddlar, now selling from the back of a van instead of a peddlar's pack, this is their only chance for shopping. Access to Port of Spain is easy by bus or the shared taxis, but to the country people Sangre Grande is the heart of their commercial world.

Sangre Grande was the furthest point of the eastern railway from Port of Spain. The extension from Arima was opened in 1886. Planters or friends visiting them took the train to Sangre Grande where they could overnight in the respectable Railway Hotel. The following morning they would set off by carriage to the estates of Manzanilla, Toco and Mayaro.

Stick fighting has its home in Sangre Grande. Fighting with staffs is an ancient practice found in varying forms in all ancient cultures where all those who travelled lonely paths had to be adept at defending themselves against brigands along the way. There is no written history whether the formalised contest between two opponents wielding slender four-foot long sticks came from Spain or elsewhere. Poui wood is preferred for its resilient strength. Only rarely can true stick fighting be seen these days in remote country locales.

It is frowned on by the authorities for the "bus' head" caused to losers necessitating stitches to scalp wounds. The mass of Trinidadians today know of stick fighting only as a historical ritual, half dance, half sport. Drums and chanting accompany it, lighted by the flicking of flambeaux. There is much posturing, flexing of limbs and nimble footwork, braggadocio and machismo as each assailant dares the other to make the first blow.

It is included as by-play in many "Best Village" competitions and stage presentations about country life. Most Trinidadians have seen it in no other form than on a stage. Often the real competition is over in a flurry as rapid as that of a cock fight. There is a rat-tat-tat as the "bois" strike and one man reels back, clutching his pate, seeking solace and medication from his backers. The winner will strut and pose boastfully.

Trinidadians are not by nature vicious people. They love to quarrel noisily, faces inches apart, shouting "Touch me!" implying to bystanders that retribution will be swift and final. But in the great majority of cases the quarrels never degenerate into blows for all the noisy froth. Stick fighting is, in a similar typically Trinidadian way, 90% "style" and theatre and only 10% action. It is an enjoyable and exciting spectacle for all that.

The road from Sangre Grande to Port of Spain is fast, and one is soon back on the busy East-West Corridor, passing factories and housing estates. It provides a marked contrast to the forgotten lanes of the Montserrat Hills, cool and shaded by the towering immortelles, and to the mesmerising monotony of the silvered arches of the Cocal's coconut palms. Central Trinidad holds great appeal for the nostalgically inclined who are not so much interested by modern development as they are in seeing vignettes of the past when carriages rolled up the lanes to elegant wooden estate houses and the countrymen caroused each Saturday night at the village rumshop. This part of the island has resisted change or been passed by it, more than any other. This situation is unlikely to differ in the foreseeable future.

*Pointe-a-Pierre Refinery and San Fernando Hill*

## Chapter 20

# *San Fernando and the South*

The distinctive outline of San Fernando Hill can be seen across the Gulf of Paria from any high vantage point in Port of Spain. When driving south, the hill is hidden until leaving the giant industrial complex of Point Lisas. Suddenly a rise on the rolling Southern Main Road shows the flattened profile of the hill across the cane fields. Only the right end retains the original rounded rocky outline. The left half has been flattened into a plateau by unauthorised quarrying. Quarrying had previously been done under licence. Licences were not renewed when the authorities realised that the scenic virtues of the hill outweighed its merits as a handy quarry. Quarrying continued, however, and no firm measures were taken to stop it until considerable further damage had been done.

In the foreground of the distant view of San Fernando Hill are several industrial undertakings that pre-date the Point Lisas development. The fertilizer plant of Federation Chemicals shows its age from its association with the defunct

Federation of the West Indies. Not far beyond is a plume of fine limestone dust from the cement factory. The limestone still comes from the quarry at Mayo in the Montserrat Hills, but the cable railway is abandoned. Instead, the quarry material is pumped in a pipeline in a liquid slurry. When the residents complained about the fine white dust that shrouded houses and plant life, a senior official quashed objections by saying the dust was in fact beneficial, and mixed a spoonful in with a dish of ice cream that he then lapped up to prove it.

Before the main Hochoy Highway was opened, the Southern Main Road was the only route south. Cement trucks lumbering up the steep Pointe-a-Pierre Hill always created a traffic delay as they rounded past the little Catholic church perched on the hilltop on one side, the spacious tree-filled grounds of Texaco's hospital on the other. From the top of the hill San Fernando Hill looms up again, but this time with what was until 1984, the Texaco refinery in the foreground. In that year Government bought the refinery after extended negotiations. Massive capital investment will be required to modify the plant which was designed mainly to produce heating oil for the North American market, a market which is no longer there. Ironically the refinery cannot handle in its present form, the type of crude oil pumped by Amoco from the off-shore wells of the East Coast. This oil is pumped directly into Amoco's tankers for delivery to Port Arthur, Texas.

Government's wisdom in acquiring the refinery is open to question. Is the impressive tank farm still needed? The hospital and office block will be put to good use, but will the manicured golf course and grounds be properly maintained? Politicians are rumoured to have selected the house of their choice, formerly occupied by refinery employees. Camp life with its high wire fence and guarded entrances provides security for one's family in a time of rising crime, but will this be maintained? The school to which residents of the camp could send their children had already closed down prior to Texaco's departure.

Many fear that in taking over Pointe-a-Pierre government will be taking on one more white elephant. It will be hard to avoid operating at a substantial loss, however much it may salve the nation's ego to own the refinery. For a generation, Texaco's oil revenue was of pre-eminent importance to the Treasury. Of all the reviled multi-nationals, Texaco seemed the most impregnable. The left-wing Oilfield Workers' Trade Union led the campaign to buy out Texaco in the same way that the assets of British Petroleum and Shell had been when the lower price of oil made operations only marginally profitable. It never seemed to have occurred to the union or the powers that be that the country might be better off without the responsibilities of a refinery which would require major capital investment to refine its own East Coast crude, now that imported crude no longer came to Trinidad.

Further south, the complexity of the country's oil problems become more apparent. For the time being we see only the allure of Texaco's establishment. From the north-south highway the plumes of burnt off gas (a safety precaution, not a squandering of raw material) and the thousand lights of the catalytic cracker are mirrored in one of the camp's lakes. These are not just scenic. They represent the blood bank of the refinery, providing the means to cool the hot effluent streams from the process units. This cooling medium, supplemented by separate salt water from the nearby Gulf of Paria, is critical to the control and safety of the complex refinery process, some of which uses very high oil processing temperatures. Utmost vigilance is required to ensure that overheating followed by devastating explosions do not occur. All those who live on the lush green camp have one ear cocked for the warning siren. Those responsible for maintenance carry bleepers which can summon them without notice from a critical putt on the fourteenth green. In the bar of the elegant country club are scarred arms and faces to evidence the constant chance of one more crisis with the volatile equipment these men nurse for their living.

Across a river so polluted by the refinery that it has caught fire on more than one occasion when dry season bush fires came to its edge, lies the thriving building material centre of Marabella. Despite the proximity to Texaco's refinery there is scarcely an oil equipment firm to be seen. Yet half a dozen of the nation's largest suppliers of imported lumber, locks and laminate flourish in close proximity. Marabella heralds the more dynamic pioneering spirit which characterises the South. They are not branches of the Port of Spain creole establishment, but enterprises owned by hardworking Indians who have taken full advantage of the steady population growth and the ten years of building boom which accompanied the oil wealth.

Before metalled roads were built, the only ready means of travel was around the island by boat. San Fernando shows this more than any other town, being nestled against its hill in such a way that it creates an immoveable obstruction to all vehicular traffic in and out of the town. The port which gave the town its start back in the Spanish colonial days, is now dead. The railway which used to steam along the water front from Pointe-a-Pierre is gone, and the fretwork station building is now used by the bus depot employees. The gulf front which should be the centre of the town, and originally was, is a mess of derelict sheds and buses wheezing their way up the steep streets which comprise San Fernando. This is the metropolis of the South. Buses to the furthest points start and end their journey at this congested point, as do the route taxis.

The heart of San Fernando is at the top of High Street. From the street's start down by the bus depot, it is one-way past commercial banks, furniture shops, multi-purpose arcades steeply up to the foot of San Fernando Hill, meeting the perimeter road which circumscribes the lower boundaries of the hill. High Street is so steep that in several sections there are steps to the side walk. Walking is made even less easy by the number of pavement vendors hawking their wares from makeshift stands. Indians predominate in the pedestrian traffic. From far and wide, tubby Indian matrons clad in the traditional white ohrnis around their head and shoulders above normal dresses will lead their exotic-eyed young daughters in blue jeans, clutching their purses in one hand. Jewellery shops are frequent and well-patronised by a people who have never given up their love for gold ornamentation. As in Port of Spain, young men will squat on the iron railing or lean against a shop wall, one foot propped behind, watching for the next unescorted girl to "soot" and heckle with suggestive flattery.

"Sooting" is the sibilant hissing between the teeth which can be done unobtrusively yet carries clearly. "Limers" have perfected this art from years of practice, just as every Trinidadian becomes a master of the "steups." This is the inward sucking between clenched teeth, the lips in a slight sardonic sneer, which can drive teachers and employers wild with irritation when employed by a disdainful subordinate expressing disgust, disagreement and contempt with the person to whom it is directed. There are a thousand subtle varieties of meaning and degree from the loudest which can be heard across the street, to the scarcely audible intaking of breath which it is impossible to deal with by normal rules of discipline. It is a phenomenon of a common undermining of authority which has existed in Trinidad since the first British governor arrived to govern a majority of French planters.

Running roughly parallel with High Street up the steep side streets is Harris Promenade, running along the crest of a ridge, ending in a fine view of the Gulf. Harris Promenade has a parked area running between its two sides in which stand a statue of Mahatma Gandhi, a band stand and a railway locomotive. It is not the famed "last train to San Fernando" of Kitchener's calypso, merely one of the last steam engines in use on the tracks of a sugar estate. Two churches and the neo-classical town hall on the northern side, look across at squat granite school buildings and the police headquarters. At the top of High Street, Harris Promenade converges with it at the Carnegie Library, recently redecorated over a long period. Library operations were conducted in another building while renovations continued on their leisurely way. "Library Corner" as it is known, is the hub of route taxi operations supplied with an excess of chicken-and-chips fast food outlets. Off Library Corner, forming part of the perimeter road around the hill, runs Coffee Street, known familiarly as "The Coffee."

All the streets in San Fernando seem short and steep. There appears to be no more sense of planning in the buildings than in the layout. Decaying mansions stand next to modern cantilevered medical centres, wooden shacks to oil field equipment stores. To those who live in the South, this disorder has an endearing quality lost to Trinidadians of the north who get turned around by the ubiquitous hill and panic on the steep streets with deep open culverts at their edge. For an island as small as Trinidad, this is only one indication of the gulf in attitudes and outlook between the people of the South and those of the North. Southerners of European background come from two basic groups, the oil camps or the sugar estates. Today's parents may be in business for themselves, but they very likely grew up on an oil camp or sugar estate, and have passed on to their children their more domestic outlook.

Trinidadians are by nature hospitable, glad for company and a reason to carouse, preferably with music involved. Yet people from Port of Spain have a firm impression that the Southerners are much more hospitable to visitors. For lack of North's cocktail party circuit and cultural distractions, the people of South Trinidad are pictured giving lavish parties at their homes like something out of "Gone with the Wind."

This is a fallacy. Southerners are warm, genuine and family oriented, but they rely on their circle of close friends and family for socialising. While they will welcome relations and close acquaintances from other areas to their table, they generally stick to their own clique leaving newcomers to the South alone. When they entertain it will be on a lavish scale with plenty of champagne. Brought up and working in and around the oil industry has made Houston the cultural capital to many. Texan ostentation in entertaining as well as executive office decor is often the result.

A high proportion are white, with Indian doctors and businessmen living next door in the upper income residential areas of Bel Air, Gulf View, St Joseph Village and Vistabella. Negro families in this income group are rare compared to the North. Prosperous Indians will invite visiting businessmen and their bank manager to their home for a ceremonial feast of many courses, but as a rule their own large families keep them occupied, and they keep to themselves.

San Fernando secondary schools reflect the full gamut of ethnic origins, but with a higher number of Chinese faces than in Port of Spain. Very likely one of these Chinese will carry away the highest national academic honours. Around San Fernando middle class areas predominate over lower income groups. The union workers of the oil fields have enjoyed a high standard of living from good wages for many years. While there are ghettos only a block away from the air conditioned stores of High Street, poor housing is the exception rather than the rule.

The South businessman is known for his initiative and spirit of enterprise, ready to start up a new business when one fails. Unlike Port of Spain, there are no Government ministries and few civil servants. The Southerner will prosper only on his own ability. The independent attitude this engenders is feared by the powers-that-be in Port of Spain. They know the South Chamber of Commerce will never kowtow servilely to Government policies, but will speak out forthrightly with its own views. For this reason San Fernando is left to its own devices and receives little allocation of development projects. Believing him to be a survivor, the South businessman has been left to fend for himself. You will be told in Port of Spain, "The South is where the money is," assuming that oil means wealth. But it is the south which bears the brunt of recession while northern firms still flourish from Government expenditure.

*The Oil Industry*

The oil industry is a complex one of which the bulk of the people in the North know little, even though the country has depended on it for a generation for the bulk of the nation's external earnings. Trinidad can with justification, lay claim to one of the longest histories in the oil business. Hunters on the Lee Lum estate in Guayaguayare brought back samples of oil seepings in 1819. These were sent to England for analysis, but "were reported to be of such fine quality that the chemists regarded them as artificial." Nothing further was done. In 1857 the Merrimac Company started a search for oil, finding it at 160 feet. Cheap oil in the United States and financial problems prevented further efforts until 1867 when two companies made fresh efforts around La Brea and San Fernando. Again these were under-capitalised and the ventures were abandoned. It was in 1893 when most of the oil-producing areas of the world were still unknown, that Trinidad's oil production really started. The same Mr Lee Lum remembered the samples taken by the hunters and took fresh ones to a Briton, Randolph Rust in Port of Spain. Through Rust's continuing efforts for twenty-five years, Trinidad's oil resources were uncovered, becoming a significant producer from 1910 onwards. One historic result of this was that it caused Winston Churchill, then First Lord of the Admiralty, to switch the Royal Navy from coal to oil-powered vessels.

Drilling for oil is now a sophisticated science catered to by seismic analysis, geological surveys, logging technicians and "mud engineers." Logging is done by lowering a device into the drill hole on an electric cable often miles below the surface using electric, electronic and nuclear techniques. The results are read off calibrated tape many yards long. Mud engineers monitor the correct density for the heavy mineral additives, such as barytes, which must be added to the slurry of the drilling lubricant to hold down the upward pressure of escaping gas, water and, hopefully, oil. As drilling proceeds, steel casing is lowered into the drilled hole to prevent the rock from collapsing. Smaller diameters are used as the well gets deeper, in a reducing telescope. To add a smaller diameter casing, the whole drillpipe string must be removed ("making a round trip") and stored temporarily in a dense hanging cluster of short sections at the top of the drilling rig. If the rig is not properly balanced, the weight of the hanging pipe can tip it over, letting scores of heavy steel pipe each 40 ft long, go crashing to the ground, imperilling the rig workers.

Drilling is done 40 ft at a time, the length of a section of pipe. When the top of the pipe is down to the level of the drilling platform, an additional section is lifted above it and screwed onto the threaded top. Drilling resumes until the added section has sunk to the drilling platform again, at which time the process is repeated until the intended depth is reached. Casing is lowered into the drilled hole, and is set in place within the space so that there is an even space around it. A special concrete is then pumped down to the bottom of the hole under intense pressure. Like toothpaste it squirts its way up the outer sides of the casing and the rock. Poured incorrectly the cement can set too fast, ruining the hole which will have to be abandoned if the cement cannot be drilled out. With the casing cemented firmly into place, explosive charges are lowered to the level of the oil bearing strata. These perforate the sides of the casing and cement. A string of production pipe is lowered into the casing to allow the drilling mud to be displaced by water or oil. This reduces the pressure on the formation and allows the crude oil to flush through the sand in which it lies, into the casing, displacing the oil or water up to the surface. At the top end of the production string is fitted "a Christmas tree", a concoction of pipe, valves, restriction orifices and pressure gauges which controls the flow of oil and dissolved gas into the collection pipeline leading to a separator, separating the gas from the liquid crude oil, which flows into the storage tank.

In its initial life, the well will probably flow freely, without assistance due to the high pressure in the oil reservoir; but in later months or years flow may cease and "artificial lift" may be required in the form of injected gas under pressure ("gas lift") or by the lowering of a mechanical reciprocating pump on a long string of steel "sucker rods" down into the casing where the oil lies. The pump operates by raising and lowering the sucker rod string at the surface, usually by means of a pumping jack, the familiar "rocking horse" of the older oilfields, powered by an electric or gasoline engine. Production rates are limited in the first instance by the pump size and operating speed; but ultimately it is the flow rate into the wellbore that determines the well's productivity. A decline in flow may initially be due to plugging of the casing perforations by mud or fine sand. This can be remedied by "washing the perforations", or perhaps by a gravel packing operation to filter out the sand before it reaches the perforations.

In a reservoir's old age when maybe 20% of the oil-in-place has been produced, flow from the formation into the wellbore declines to an uneconomic rate. If the price of oil justifies the expense, secondary or even tertiary recovery methods can be applied to the reservoir as a whole (not to an individual well). Such techniques may increase recovery to perhaps 40 or 50%

of the oil-in-place. This can take the form of gas injection into the top of the oil reservoir which restores the pressure on the remaining oil, helping it to the various wellbores. Alternatively waterflooding may be effective. Water is pumped down selected dead wells into the oil-bearing strata, displacing the oil into the producing wells. In Trinidad's heavy viscous oil wells heat is introduced into the reservoir usually in the form of steam. The combined effect of the pressure, heat and flushing of the water condensed from the stream makes the oil more runny which assists flow to the producing wells.

Well production rates may vary from thousands of barrels a day in a good well's early days' (In Trinidad this only occurs in the offshore marine fields) down to only a few barrels a day at the end of the life of a well. At that time the cost of producing the oil may not be justified by the price gained, and it will be closed down.

An oil field may start with wells drilled in a 400-yard grid. Additional wells will be drilled within the grid until, like a pincushion, the substrata is pierced with wells only fifty feet apart. At this stage, after secondary recovery methods, the reservoir is considered to be sucked as dry as is economically feasible. Some wells will keep on producing at a steady rate for decades; others may quickly run dry.

The oil company concerned may own the oil rights to the land drilled, or may have a lease and pay royalties to the owner according to the amount produced. Apart from that, and the geological research, the oil company contracts all aspects of production from the initial drilling to various workover services to separate companies. Fifteen or sixteen companies may have staff at a wellhead at one time. However, the capital outlay for secondary recovery techniques is more than a service company could manage, so the oil company undertakes this aspect for itself.

### The Deep South

San Fernando is called "The Industrial Capital of the South." It would be more correct to rephrase this into "The Capital of the Industrial South." If one drives to the end of any of the roads leading steeply up the sides of San Fernando Hill from its perimeter road, it is a brief clamber up the slopes of broken stone and gravel to the lofty plateau of quarried rock which makes up the mutilated eastern two thirds of the hill. The higher western end is a tougher climb, tree-lined much of the way, but well worth the magnificent panorama from the summit. Laid out like a carpet far below, is the southern countryside. Where is the industry? To the north is the refinery of Pointe-a-Pierre, the kilns of Trinidad Cement Ltd at Claxton Bay, then the spires and domes of Fedchem, and in the haze the leviathan of Iscott's huge shed. Inland is rolling sugar land. Apart from a single garment factory, San Fernando has no industries or factories, merely a proliferation of machine shops and supply yards.

Driving south from San Fernando along the by-pass to Mosquito Creek the signs confirm that oil country is at hand. "Dowell Schlumberger," "Halliburton," "Baroid" - names familiar throughout the oil world, line the edge of the highway with the other local companies. Idle rigs can be seen in yards, mammoth cementing trucks and trailers loaded with drilling pipe thunder down the road. At Mosquito Creek the highway is at long last being rebuilt at a higher level to prevent the high-tide flooding which has plagued motorists for sixty years. A swamp lies inland and the only other road winds far inland through Debe and Penal. Traffic, always heavy, is slowed to a crawl when the frequent Hindu cremations are held by the bridge at the mouth of the Mosquito River. The park-like new cremation site provides adequate parking. Formerly the funeral pyre was at the water's edge, and cars parked by the road. The cremation site and that on the banks of the Caroni River outside Port of Spain were the only two in the country. Hindus must not only be cremated, but also in a suitable holy spot at the river's edge. Any Christian wishing to be cremated had to use the same spot, as a bank manager found out when his visiting father died. Christian attitudes have stuck with a good old-fashioned burial, and until the 1980s no modern cremation facilities were provided or permitted. Wrangles continued for years as to where one should be sited, taking mythical pollution and health hazards into consideration. It was Dr. William's own death, and his express wish for cremation that got some action. A portable crematorium was flown down from Florida for the ceremony on the tarmac of the flying boat terminal at Chaguaramas. Afterwards it was not used again. But a crematorium has been built adjacent to Long Circular Mall in Port of Spain, and after various other bureaucratic precautions are taken, non-Hindus may be able to be turned to ashes other than on the blazing bonfires by the banks of a muddy river.

The Southern Main Road follows the rolling hills along the edge of the Gulf often revealing fine views back to the Bocas and the mountains of Venezuela. Indiscriminate villages all have roadside clubs to welcome the thirsty truckers. The first pumping jacks can be seen in clearings at the side of the road, sometimes nodding away slowly, sometimes idle, waiting for the oil to seep back into the well hole. Private gravelled roads of the oil companies lead off into the bush guarded by signs admonishing the public not to trespass.

The "Trintoc" name is common on these signs and at the gate of a large pipe farm. This is Trinidad and Tobago Oil Co. Ltd., Government-owned successor to the legacy and assets of Royal Dutch Shell. The countryside, part grazing land for cattle and buffalo, part swamp, gives way to stretches of forest.

### The Pitch Lake

All of a sudden houses appear and the land is cleared. La Brea has been reached, and with it Trinidad's claim to the Eighth Wonder of the World - the Pitch Lake. Every Trinidad schoolchild knows of its discovery in 1595 by Sir Walter Raleigh during his search for El Dorado. More likely it was discovered by Robert Dudley who had landed as Raleigh's advance guard, and had explored the area before Raleigh arrived. But it was Raleigh who wrote to his Queen of the limitless material for caulking the planks of his little galleons. The seaside town of Brighton is so close to La Brea that they are referred to in one breath - Brighton/La Brea in the same way as Minneapolis/St. Paul. Brighton has a jetty and customs house for the few vessels calling to load asphalt or steel drums from Van Leer's factory. The asphalt, purified of grosser impurities, is dangled in wooden barrels or steel drums along a cable railway that runs from the factory to the dockside a mile away .

To most foreign visitors a trip to Trinidad would be incomplete without including the Pitch Lake on their itinerary. Many will have read disparaging comments by Noel Coward that it resembles a dozen hard tennis courts badly in need of repair, or others who compare the dark grey surface to the wrinkled skin of an elephant. Curiosity is a powerful force and few will be put off. How could they face their friends when asked, "And what was the Pitch Lake like?" The main road passes close to the lake which can be seen through the fringe of trees below the road to the right. Tourists know they must be near when several lean rastas raise themselves from recumbent lethargy and bound out to stop the car in its tracks. They will spiritedly press their guide services until one is chosen for an agreed fee. If one has done some research on the lake, no guide is necessary, but as this is probably their sole means of income they are outspokenly hostile to those who insist on going without them.

Such organisations as the American Women's Club can arrange matters best. They may fix up a tour of the factory with the plant manager before being escorted out onto the pitted, rain-flooded and in parts, reed-covered surface of the 100-acre lake. The high point of the factory tour is to see a nimble workman hopping along the edges of the open barrels as he fills them with molten pitch before deftly hammering home the lids. A slip into the boiling pitch would be his last.

Geologists have shown that the deepest part of the roughly circular lake is 232 feet below sea level with the top of the lake surface now 110 feet above sea level, a total depth of 342 feet in the centre. In 1893 the lake surface was 27 feet higher and the area 120 acres. It lies in the bowl of an ancient volcano crater into which asphaltic oil seeped and was thoroughly mixed with volcanic ash by hot gas bubbling up deep below. There is a constant influx of new material, all of which is of unvarying consistency. Even on the hottest day the surface is solid enough not only to walk on, but also for the ditching machinery to quarry out the asphalt from trenches and load

5-ton trucks. The trenches fill in after a few days from upward pressure far below. Stories of abandoned bulldozers being swallowed up are almost certainly apocryphal. Theoretically it might happen, but it never has. Bulldozers are far too valuable.

A narrow railway track at the edge of the lake takes dumper loads of quarried asphalt, looking like pieces of unglossy broken coal, up a ramp into the factory where the water and gas are refined off by a simple hydration process in stills. Two products can be made; refined asphalt for road surfaces which is packed in light wooden barrels, or ready-fluxed asphalt to seal roofs, packed into small cylindrical steel drums. These materials, so little changed from their raw state, provide a harder wearing road surface and weather proofing than can be manufactured from the heavy sludge of crude oil, to which in the case of road surfaces aggregate is added.

It is hard to understand why such a unique gift from the gods should not be a thriving commercial success. Legend has it that the Great Spirit was angered when a Carib tribe celebrated a tribal victory by killing and eating the sacred humming bird, and engulfed the punished Caribs in the crater of pitch. But it must be for better reasons that the lake asphalt company failed financially, forcing Goverment acquisition to protect hundreds of jobs. With an endless supply of good quality raw material readily accessible to ocean transport and a limitless market, how could it fail?

Quarrying and refining are straightforward, but a major injection of capital for gargantuan machinery has been recommended to boost productivity and offset labour costs. International marketing is another problem requiring expertise not currently available. In its wisdom Goverment did not allocate, when it had the chance, any of its petrodollar millions to revive this unique industry and put it on an economic footing.

Amazingly, too, only a fraction of Trinidad's roads are surfaced with its own natural asphalt. Only the villagers of Brighton/La Brea take full advantage of the phenomenon, covering  the banks of their front gardens with the freely available pitch to keep down the weeds. Motorists must not assume that the proximity to the finest road surface material means fine road surfaces. Oblivious to the potential international publicity, the authorities permit them to heave and swell in the broiling midday sun, making La Brea's roads some of the worst in the island. Photographers will find the asphalted front gardens a subject they can capture better than the lake itself. Only from the air can the extent of the lake and its proximity to the sea be fully appreciated and captured on film. It would save visitors a tiring drive and likely disappointment if all planes landing at Piarco could take a slight detour and pass over the Pitch Lake. Trinidad's World Wonder could be seen to best advantage.

*Point Fortin*

The road from the Pitch Lake to Point Fortin runs inland through pleasant rolling countryside, partly forested. The sign for Point Fortin waterworks is misleadingly far outside the town, and it is only after passing oil storage tanks, pumping jacks and miles of distribution pipes from the fields to the tank farms, that the tyre factory, formerly Dunlop's, is passed and the dynamic but scruffy town centre is reached. At the far end to the right are the refinery and office buildings built for Shell, now occupied by Trintoc. Beyond them stretches a tank farm appearing as extensive as that at Pointe-a-Pierre.

Appearances are deceiving. The Trintoc refinery is much smaller in capacity than that of Texaco and less sophisticated in the products it can make from crude oil. Before the acquisition of Texaco, Government had planned a $600,000,000 upgrading of the Point Fortin refinery so that the country's needs would not be dependent on a multi-national corporation controlled from Coral Gables, Florida and New York.

Implementation of the upgrading was so slow that the boom which Point Fortin could have expected never took place. Trintoc's refinery idled along at just enough to keep the equipment in working condition. One reason causing this was that 35,000 barrels of crude oil a day was diverted on Government's orders to Texaco's refinery to make up the shortfall in the 65,000 barrels a day the larger and more valuable refinery required to operate. In the drawn-out in-fighting Texaco claimed that the bench-mark price set by Government on which taxes and duty were assessed made it uneconomical to increase crude oil production from their own wells. They would not import oil, and if they did not receive 35,000 barrels a day from another source, the refinery with its 2,000 jobs would close down. Calling Texaco's bluff, Goverment gave its own company, Trintoc, the short end of the stick by diverting 60% of Trintoc's normal crude oil throughput to Pointe-a-Pierre. Meantime Trintoc's staff marked time, improving their golf and tennis, hoping that perhaps one day they would be needed to run Texaco's refinery.

As is normal in multi-national oil camps, Shell had built attractive houses on its compound to keep its staff content. Clifton Hill has the best residential site in Point Fortin overlooking the Gulf to the hazy mountains of the Northern Range forty miles north. Executives of other companies were permitted to buy Shell's houses when they sold out. Inflation had not at that time hit housing, and they acquired the houses for a fraction of their present value.

The club is still operating for residents of the camp, an attractive legacy of Shell's heritage, and the social centre for those permitted to use its exclusive facilities. In creating a private world for their staff in the camps of Pointe-a-Pierre, Clifton Hill, Palo Seco and Guayaguayare complete with schools, golf courses, swimming pools, tennis courts and supermarkets, the oil companies were providing an inducement to tolerate the otherwise primitive local conditions. With a wholly expatriate staff of executives this made sense, but as the expatriates declined in number and their place was taken by qualified locals, the irony of the two-tier structure became apparent. Local staff yearned to enjoy the facilities created for expatriates, which had doubtless played a part in their motives for working for an oil company. To remove these amenities now that they were within their grasp seemed unfair. With government acquisition of the oil companies, the greater expenses of camp facilities can no longer be justified and are being steadily eroded, to the disenchantment of the local staff now deprived of what they had foreseen as traditional perquisites.

To reach the extreme end of the Cedros peninsular one leaves Point Fortin on the Cap-de-Ville road, soon rejoining the Southern Main Road. There is surprisingly little to see but rolling countryside as the road runs along the watershed with views of the sea to north and south. In a country concerned about its population growth, it seems surprising that Chatham and Granville have not yet attracted more development; conditions are ideal.

Nearing Bonasse, the highway goes through the Blanquizales Lagoon, dense swamp in which one fully expects to see alligators slumbering. They are there, but unlikely to be seen from the road. Bonasse and Cedros appear one and the same like Brighton/La Brea. There is a sea-side air about the village with the beach at the road's edge and gaily painted pirogues hauled above high tide. Only children with buckets and spades are missing. Despite the sea-side atmosphere, the heart of Cedros is its shrimping industry, aided it is said by smuggling across the Boca del Sierpe, the Serpent's Mouth, with nearby Venezuela.

The shrimp themselves are probably contraband as they are largely seined from waters falling under Venezuelan control. For a number of years the shrimping industry flourished, with refrigerated trucks daily taking the catch to Port of Spain for packaging and export. Seeing fortunes being made at their expense, the Venezuelans changed their formerly *laissez faire* attitude and began arresting the shrimp trawlers and pirogues. The crews were thrown into the Pedernales jail and their boats and catch confiscated. This caused a furore as the Venezuelan pirogues fished openly in the bays of the North Coast. Ministers from each country consulted time and again over the problem, drawing up "accords" which still work imperfectly. Shrimping continues but it is not the prosperous trade of the 70s.

At the far end of Cedros Bay is Fullerton with its police station perched on a knoll overlooking the Gulf. It is here the road to Columbus Bay and Icacos Point turns left into luxuriant coconut estates which continue until either popular beach is reached. Icacos Point is the nearest point of Trinidad's main island to the South American continent eight miles away across the Serpent's Mouth. The Boca Grande is narrower, being only five and a half sea miles across, but this does not take into consideration Trinidad's small islands of Chacachacare, Huevos and Monos before the mainland is reached.

Columbus has the credit for discovering Trinidad and for making his landfall at the south-western promontory of Icacos in 1496. Whether he ever went ashore is in doubt. In making his usual overtures from his galleons to the Indians who lined the beach, their bows and arrows at the ready, Columbus had his men play music and dance on deck. Thinking this must be a preparation for invasion, the islanders unleashed a flight of arrows, and Columbus retaliated with crossbow fire. This must be one of the few recorded occasions when Trinidadians did not jump at the chance to have a fete! Finding no signs of gold or even the golden hospitality for which the island is now justly famous, Columbus proceded on his way, having claimed the island for the Spanish monarchy.

*Raleigh and El Dorado*

A far more significant visit was paid to Icacos a hundred years later by Sir Walter Raleigh, but there is no bay or point named after him to recall his stay. Raleigh used Icacos as his base camp first to take control of Trinidad and then as his base of operations for his two expeditions up the Orinoco River in search of El Dorado, the Gilded One, where the fleeing Incas were rumoured to have set up a new kingdom on an inland lake, bringing their treasure with them.

It is well known that Raleigh had been banished by Queen Elizabeth from the court and her favour for marrying one of her maids of honour without her consent. In a desperate effort to get back into his queen's favour with all the financial advantages this had previously provided, Raleigh offered her the prospect of El Dorado's golden bounty. He researched the project thoroughly beforehand, reading all available accounts including those in Spanish. His research was assisted by a stroke of luck. An English privateer looted a Spanish ship in 1594 among whose papers were details of the latest efforts to locate El Dorado, and the prospects of finding it. Most experienced of all the Spaniards in the search was Don Antonio de Berrio, at that time Governor of Trinidad.

Raleigh had previously sent a vessel captained by Joseph Whiddon to spy out the lay of the land. A landing party had gone ashore at Mucurapo to hunt for fresh meat. They had been captured by the Spanish and after being tied up, had their throats cut in cold blood. If this was intended to frighten off further interests it had the opposite effect. It confirmed in Raleigh's mind that de Berrio must be on the threshold of fresh discovery. Whiddon returned to England with two Arawaks who were to return with Raleigh as guides and interpreters.

Raleigh managed to put together a small flotilla of four boats for his expedition two of which landed at Icacos in 1595. Far to the north of the island Governor Don Antonio de Berrio had no idea that the English had returned until Raleigh's punitive expedition marched inland from Port of Spain to San Josef de Oruña, overcame the eighty Spaniards, sacked and burnt the thatched huts of the mean capital and took Don Antonio back to Icacos as his hostage.

Don Antonio was by then an elderly officer of 75 who had spent the last 15 years in the quest for El Dorado. An inheritance had brought him to the New World, only to learn that the terms of the legacy stipulated that part should be spent to continue the search for El Dorado. This Don Antonio did conscientiously. On his first expedition he stayed in the hostile jungle for seventeen months, on the second, three years. Two thirds of his force died off from poisoned darts, fevers and general hardship on the third. He was planning a fourth trip, having narrowed down the area south and east of the Orinoco to where all legends focused. Because of his efforts and his commitment to staying in the area he had been made governor of Trinidad, ideally placed at the mouth of the Orinoco for further forays inland.

In capturing de Berrio, 48-year-old Raleigh was knowingly acquiring the most expert of the seekers for El Dorado. The older man put all arguments in Raleigh's way, but to no avail. The trip 300 miles up the Orinoco was successfully made, assisted by friendly Indians, getting as far as the Caroni rapids and the 5,000 foot barrier of the Sierra de Imataca. When the expedition turned back it was the stockaded fort they had built at Icacos which served as base camp, and where they readied themselves for the journey back to England.

Don Antonio de Berrio was put ashore in Trinidad un- harmed where he continued to live until his death, still dreaming of a further quest of his own for El Dorado. During the months of the expedition no retaliation had been made from the small force at Margarita, and Trinidad had remained under English control. By leaving the island and returning to England, Raleigh handed back Trinidad to the Spaniards without a shot, with even its governor intact. Twenty two years later Raleigh was to return to Trinidad for his final and disastrous attempt to find El Dorado, during which his beloved but spoiled son, Wat, was killed in an unnecessary skirmish with the Spanish. Sir Walter Raleigh was by then an old man and could not make the trip up the Orinoco himself. He remained in his ship anchored off Icacos, no doubt obtaining water and provisions ashore, awaiting the tragic fate of the expedition on which he had gambled everything he had.

*The Rest of the South*

The only way out of the Cedros Peninsular is back along the main road to the Erin cross road. Turning south to Erin Bay the road passes through dense forest to San Francique. In the days when a coastal steamer made regular trips around the island, San Francique was one of its ports of call. When the steamer stopped, San Francique's importance died. What development there has been in recent years has taken place at nearby Palo Seco. This is the oil camp set up by British Petroleum and its antecedents. Government acquired BP's assets for a negligible sum in the 60s when prospects for profitable operations seemed nil. When the price of oil quad- rupled, government sold a half interest to Tesoro Inc, a small American oil company. Secondary recovery methods made the venture highly profitable. Bribery scandals arose which resulted in protracted bargaining with Government over the acquisition of Tesoro's shareholding. Government was set on having the whole hog of the land-based oil industry even when there was little bacon left.

From Palo Seco the San Fernando-Siparia-Erin Road leads quickly over a good surface to the old town of Siparia. Founded as a Dominican mission in the 17th century, it became the market town of the deep south, just as Sangre Grande did in the North East. Two weeks after Easter, devout Catholics from all over the island congregate in Siparia for the pilgrimage of La Divina Pastora. The small leather covered effigy of the patroness of the Capuchin missions was brought from Venezuela around 1750. It is paraded through the crowded streets on a luggage rack on top of a car. Hindu women of the South also adopted the Black Virgin as their own Supare-Ke-Mai, and crowds of them take over Siparia on Good Friday making offerings of rice in thanks for the harvest. Many votive gifts have been made over the years and the jewelled finery festooning the diminutive figurine makes a fine occasion.

Apart from cricket matches or athletics at Guaracara Park, La Divina Pastora is the only event that brings Trinidadians from the north into the deep south.

Fyzabad, four miles from Siparia sounds like a transplant from the Ganges Delta, but it is predominantly occupied by people of African descent. Like Point Fortin, Fyzabad was a magnet for Grenadians and Vincentians wishing to leave their backward agricultural islands for the oil fields of Trinidad. This migration, now illegal, continues because so many of the "small islanders" have family to whom they can go for a new start in life.

A few miles south-east of Siparia is a small village which has received a renown out of all proportion to its size. This is the village of Morne Diablo, Devil's Mount, lying in the shadow of the hill by that name. Dr. Williams sponsored a cultural scheme to give his new nation a greater sense of identity. Each village throughout the islands of Trinidad and Tobago would be asked to put on a stage performance using dance, song, drama, stick-fighting etcetera as best they could. The best village performances went to the grandstand on the Port of Spain Savannah for final judging. Most consistent in the high quality of their performances and several times outright winner has been this remote village deep in the bush. How did they manage it? Perhaps it was because there was nothing else to do. If by chance one happened to drive down the road passing through the village on a weekend, the gay dresses for their show would be hung up on many galleries, being worked on by seamstresses. Children in leotards would be scurrying off to a dance class. Sounds of drums could be heard from the makeshift community hall. Morne Diablo was already hard at work practising for next year's Best Village competition.

A map of Trinidad will give the impression that south of the Montserrat Hills the land is fairly flat. What the map does not do is to convey the deep gullies that characterise the rolling land of the South that is only two hundred feet above sea level. The geology of Trinidad is as mixed up as its ethnic roots. The geological map of the island is so complex one would think someone were playing a prank. If there is one generalisation one can make, it is that there is clay somewhere under the surface in nearly all the south. This clay has serious implications to the building industry. Piles must be bored or driven through the clay layer if the sub soil is not to heave and slump as the clay gets filled with water during the wet season, only to shrink during the dry months. The piles and raft construction for the foundation of homes places a substantial extra cost to Southerners building block homes. It also accounts for the large number of homes still being constructed of timber. They can bend with the movement of the soil without falling down.

For some reason, lost in the mist of time, there are two rivers in Trinidad named the Oropouche. The Northern Oropouche flows out of the limestone caverns of the Northern Range onto Matura Beach on the East Coast. The South Oropouche flows westerly getting bogged down before it reaches the Gulf of Paria, to form the Oropouche Lagoon. The vale drained by the South Oropouche is the largest piece of flat land in the South readily flooding because the run-off is so gradual. It is Indian agricultural land, largely in sugar cane, with water buffalos wading happily through the oozing mud. Barrackpore is the suitably Indian name for the village which serves the needs of the area, before getting to the always bustling town of Princes Town.

Princes Town, like so many others in the South, runs along a ridge from which deep ravines drop off each side. This forces the main road to be too narrow, and the shops which front the road to have large basements to the rear to fill up the drop in the land. The centre of activity and the perennial traffic jam is the tiny triangle in the junction of the road leading north to the Montserrat Hills. Route taxis and mini-buses clog the street waiting for a full load before they leave. Shoppers shout happily to each other in the bedlam of hooting vehicles and vendors touting their wares. There is nowhere to park, but with their customery belief in their luck, motorists will stop their cars anywhere, hoping the harassed policeman will make out a traffic ticket to another offender. For a visitor it is a good place to steer clear of, if only there were a way out. This is the main route from San Fernando to Rio Claro and the east coast, and one is trapped by the topography. Make an attempt to find a way around the congestion and after driving up hill and down dale through the residential side streets, and you will still come back to another part of the traffic jam that is Princes Town.

Until 1880 Princes Town was referred to as "Mission" after the Franciscan mission established there in the earliest Spanish colonial days. The Spanish called it Savannah Grande, but the name faded into disuse over the centuries. Queen Victoria's grandsons, Princes Albert and George, later to become George V, visited Trinidad in 1880 where they were wined and dined in lavish style. A trip to Mission was included for a banquet at Francis Brash's Lothian's Estate. This would be the only time the little town was graced with royal visitors, and the opportunity was taken to perpetuate the honour by the name change. The princes made the journey on horseback. If they had come six years later they could have taken the newly opened railway line extended via San Fernando from Port of Spain.

One reason the unsuspecting tourist may have come to Princes Town is to see the Devil's Woodyard, a natural eruption of sulphuric mud, whose name conjures up greater mystery than a pitch lake or swamp. Getting to the Devil's

Woodyard takes the visitor through the villages named after the "companies." Loyal soldiers who fought for the British in the American War of 1812 were rewarded with the grant of lands in wide open Trinidad. New Grant is one such village. The soldiers kept together in the strange island by retaining the names of the companies in which they had previously served. These people were followers of the Baptist faith, as they are to this day, retaining much of their sense of community. Fate dealt them an unlucky blow with regard to the legal allocation of the land on which they have lived for over 159 years. No records were made of which family owned what, no title deeds given out. To this day the problem remains unsolved. Nobody disputes rightful title, but no insurance company or bank can grant a mortgage secured by the land not registered in their names. Because they are a hard-working Christian community this has not stopped them from prospering.

Devil's Woodyard is reached down Hindustan Road now well marked by the Tourist Board's yellow sign. A narrow grassy track leads into a circle of gloomy trees, open in the centre into a glen bare of any vegetation. No mud spouts up into the air, yet one feels a sense of menace in the cracked and broken surface as if it could without notice open up and engulf all intruders. This is particularly true late in the evening when the light is dying, a time when many who have underestimated the time taken to reach it will have arrived. Once there, most people are content to turn back after taking a photograph in evidence, and wend their way back to a more hospitable environment. This is best done by avoiding the traffic still congesting Princes Town and passing through the far from busy hamlet of Busy Corner behind the cocoa estates of the Montserrat Hills.

*The New Team*

# Chapter 21

## Why No Tobago?

The island republic of Trinidad and Tobago comprises two islands totally different in character and history. They were lumped together out of administrative convenience by a British Order in Council as late as 1889. They have stayed together mainly because there has been no compelling reason for Tobago to go its own way, nor did there appear an economic viability for doing so until recently.

Tobago is certainly large enough to be independent. With 116 square miles, it is larger than independent Antigua and Montserrat. Its predominantly Negro Anglican rural population has stayed small at 41,000 in the 1980 census despite the large families that Tobagonians raise. No doubt the population reflects a steady flow to the larger sister island where job opportunities beckon. Many Tobagonians have risen high in the civil service to the extent that Trinidadians occasionally murmur about a "Tobago mafia" running the country - and this was before Tobagonian "ANR" Robinson became prime minister.

Being essentially an island of people of African descent with none of the ethnic admixtures of Trinidad, the Tobagonian is an entirely different character to a "Trini". Slavery was much more deeply entrenched in Tobago from the 17th century. The island was fought over by French, Dutch and British, changing hands repeatedly. In 1778 an American squadron of six vessels even tried to capture the island. The Tobagonian's roots in Africa remain clearly defined, particularly with the practice of obeah. His music, his dance, his whole attitude to life differs from his Trinidad counterpart. Stepping off the plane at Crown Point Airport one sees immediately that the nervous hustle of Trinidad gives way to a lazier pace of life. In some ways Tobagonians differ more from Trinidadians than the people of Grenada.

Poor communication between the two islands has contributed to these differences. It is a rough six-hour passage into the wind against the Venezuelan current along the North Coast. All goods have to be transhipped from Port of Spain to Scarborough as there is no suitable port on Trinidad's exposed east coast. The two aging ferries, the *Scarlet Ibis* and the *Bird of Paradise* provided a deteriorating service. A third was purchased second hand from Venezuela, but proved defective and caused a major political scandal. Instead, the *M.V. Gelting* was leased from a Dutch company, and this eased the situation, until the *M.V. Panorama* was bought which became the cause of an even greater financial scandal.

In 1987 construction of a deep-water harbour was put out to tender to allow freighters to ship goods directly without the costly and delaying transhipment in Port of Spain.

Even for air transport, Tobago was denied an international airport with its own customs and immigration. Tourists could not fly in direct, but invariably had to overnight in Trinidad. However, Government did keep the flights subsidised at well below actual cost, a policy which caused the failure of Caribbean United Airways, and forced state-owned BWIA to take over.

Costs of building in Tobago also reflect its orphan status from geographical isolation. Architects are forced to calculate construction costs for mansions on the rolling fairways of Mt

Irvine's championship golf course at 50 per cent to 100 per cent more than Trinidad. Tobago building suppliers are accused of adding to the problem by taking advantage of near monopoly status. Building contractors claim it is cheaper to send a man over by plane with a package of nails and screws than to buy them in Scarborough.

The PNM government counted on Tobago's two parliamentary seats in every election, and rewarded the island for its loyalty by generous allocations from the budget. Tobago's roads were in noticeably better condition than Trinidad's. Historically Tobago had been a major producer of agricultural produce whose surplus went to Port of Spain. The side effects of making two films, "Heaven Knows Mr Allison" and "Swiss Family Robinson", combined with the ravages of 1962 hurricane Flora, are blamed for a radical change in Tobagonian attitude. The former work ethic was replaced by a conviction that life was easy. Agricultural production plummeted to the extent that the island could not feed itself, let alone export.

PNM's "main man" in Tobago was Tobagonian lawyer, Arthur Napoleon Raymond Robinson. He had been one of the early members of the People's National Movement, becoming minister of finance and deputy prime minister. "ANR", like many other able ministers, ran foul of Dr Eric Williams who was jealous of any potential rival. When asked along with other cabinet members to provide his leader with an undated letter of resignation, Robinson refused and quit the government. Tobago grew disenchanted with Government and stood behind the Democratic Action Congress which "ANR" formed. Without Tobago's votes, PNM turned against Tobago and cut its budget.

For the first time there was talk that Tobago might wish to secede. Marine petroleum surveys suggested that Tobago might well be self-sufficient economically. In an effort to nip such sentiments in the bud, Tobago was granted its own House of Assembly, placing it on a completely different status to the other counties of the republic. "ANR" became head of Tobago's assembly, but was not closely associated with Trinidad's politics where his DAC had little success. Besides the DAC, the opposition to PNM was divided between the sugar workers of the United Labour Front led by unionist lawyer, Basdeo Panday; the Organisation for National Reconstruction led by former attorney general, Karl Hudson-Phillips and the afro-marxist National Joint Action Committee.

Although the ONR received substantial voter suport, they won no seats in the 1981 election. There was a feeling that calypsonian Mighty Chalkdust was right and that the people were indeed "fraid Karl." Out of this came the formation of an initially uneasy coalition called the National Alliance for Reconstruction with A.N.R. Robinson at its head. In the 1986 election the PNM was overthrown after thirty years of uninterrupted rule, winning a meagre three seats. Instead of a Port of Spain dominated government under the PNM, the prime minster was from Tobago and the main Trinidadian support was rural. Talk of secession by Tobago was forgotten. The twin island republic was re-united.

Despite this restored unity, Tobago is still too different to treat in the same book as Trinidad. It has its own cultural fascinations and merits a book of its own. But it must be written by someone who knows it intimately over an extended period. Scenically it is considered the pearl to the Trinidad oyster. Tourism will probably always be Tobago's main industry, if one discounts mixed agriculture. Tobago boasts over 500 hotel rooms, all of them taking advantage of the idyllic beaches and bathing. Nevertheless the existing hotels are only a fraction of what international tourism could sustain if the central government took tourism more seriously. Hopefully Tobago will remain unspoiled even if tourism is expanded.

*Sea Serpent Weather Vane - Red House Rotunda*

# Postscript To The Second Edition

An author is always gratified when his book is successful enough to warrant a second edition. It enables him to correct errors, typographical and factual, that crept into the first edition, and also to update any significant changes that have taken place.

In a vibrant society such as Trinidad's one rightly expects changes to be constant; fortunately most of them have not affected this text, which is largely retrospective. Nevertheless this is a good opportunity to mention the most notable.

*Getting There*
There has been an improvement in the facilities and attitude of Immigration at Piarco airport now that foreigners and their investment are actively encouraged.

*The Red House*
Mention must be made as to how the Red House lost its proud weather vane, a precious example of 19th Century cast iron craftsmanship, in the aftermath of the 1991 election won by the PNM. It is the kind of footnote to history which seems too unlikely to be more than a figment

268

of legend. During the electioneering, word was put around by PNM supporters that the sea serpent or dragon which was the main feature of the ornate vane atop the rotunda, was being used for nefarious and magical purposes by their political opponents. Voters were promised that if the PNM were elected, they would replace the obeah dragon with a less spooky decoration- a dove of peace. Sure enough when they were returned to power one of the first campaign promises PNM honoured was to employ a crane to remove the offending weather vane. In its place now rotates with the winds a locally crafted replacement which an eminent science professor criticised in the local press as having little ornithological resemblance to a dove, and more to a "defecating duck."

## *Queens Park Hotel*
This historic architectural landmark designed by George Brown as the home for the famed Warner family has sadly been demolished. It is being replaced with a modern office complex to house Amoco Oil Company, and is an indication of the inevitable commercialisation of the Grand Savannah.

## *French Creoles*
A paragraph regarding Trinidad's good fortune in having the French Creoles as the backbone to its social heritage mysteriously disappeared from the First Edition. Alone among islands of the Caribbean which so often attracted the flotsam of Europe, the French who sought refuge in Trinidad from the French Revolution were to a signficant extent genteel "cadet" aristocracy, younger sons of good family if not petty nobility, seeking fortune as planters. For this reason Trinidad's local society was from 1783 a cut above other Caribbean islands. This remains reflected in its taste and social patterns.

## *Carnival*
The schedule of events may vary slightly each season as better formulae are sought to please the paying public. The masquerade bands are more populous than ever. If they are

less varied and splendid than in the past, they are still a fantastic spectacle for visitors.

*Birds*

I am delighted that the Tranquillity Square flock of Amazon parrots has flourished and that many trees of Port of Spain resound morning and evening with their far from tranquil raucous screech as they search for fruit and palm nuts.

*Cricket*

Fortunately Brian Lara was mentioned in the First Edition, but since then he has broken Sir Gary Sobers' world record test innings and reigns as a cricketing superstar. The grateful nation gave him among many things a house at the foot of Lady Chancellor Road and named the western stretch of Independence Square in his honour.

*Cuisine*

Restaurants come and go more rapidly than any book can keep up with, but had Woodford Cafe, conveniently sited in a tastefully preserved dwelling on Tragarete Road, been around at the time of the First Edition it would, with its modestly priced and varied local cuisine, have earned honorable mention.

*Politics*

The uniquely Trinidadian version of revolution was again represented by "Imam" Abu Bakr's armed insurrection in 1990. The parliamentary chamber was stormed, the prime minister brutalised and other officials murdered. Far from being immediately shot for terrorism, there was a lengthy trial in which Bakr got off on an amnesty technicality. With true Trini panache he turned round and sued Government for damage done to his group's mosque in Mucurapo, and there was talk that he might be made a senator. This had all the deja vu earmarks of the 1970 Uprising when ringleader Raffique Shah was exonerated at court martial due to a slip-up by the prosecution, and later became a respected political commentator.

The NAR coalition led by Prime Minister Ray Robinson actively tackled the disrepair of the infrastructure that had been left by the PNM; but NAR proved unpopular with an electorate pampered for fifteen years. The PNM led by Patrick Manning regained control in the next election but could achieve only lacklustre results. By then the NAR party and Robinson, who had never fully recovered from his ordeal during Abu Bakr's insurrection, were spent forces. It was the Indians of the UNC led by leftist lawyer Basdeo Panday which won the election.

For the first time in Trinidad's history there would be not only an Indian but a non-Christian (Hindu) prime minister. There were predictions of disaster from "curry-politics" but in a delightfully Trinidadian way, the country soon came to realise that Panday and his fellow politicians were true "Trinis." They have not upset the applecart with radical changes, but have won grudging respect for doing a much better job than feared. Panday's latest move was to appoint his former ally A.N.R. Robinson as the nation's new president.

*ISCOTT*
The huge plant was sold to Indian steel interests and renamed ISPATT. (an acronym whose letters have no specific significance). It now has more effective overseas marketing and appears to have good prospects. Similarly the urea, methane and ammonia plants at Point Lisas are contributing an increasing share to the nation's economy as the petroleum sector continues its natural decline. In its 1997 report the Caribbean Development Bank said that Trinidad and Tobago's economic prospects were good with a 3% growth rate reflected in 1996.

*Independence Square*
Perhaps the most visible change that has taken place is the demolition of the "Drag Brothers" area and the old

Legion Hall building. A tree-lined promenade named after cricketing star Brian Lara now stretches from the docks at Wrightson Road past the statue of Andrew Cipriani at the foot of Frederick Street, all the way to the Catholic cathedral. The broken concrete and bolts for Carnival stands facing Salvatori Building have given way to benches and neat brick paving.

*Down the Islands*

The Gasparee Caves are now regrettably closed once again, the stairs, gates and lighting in need of repair. Omitted in the First Edition was mention of Hart's Cut. This was a canal dug by convict labour under the control of the Supervisor of Prisons, Daniel Hart in 1856. It stretched across the narrow neck of Pointe Gourde from Chaguaramas Bay to what is today the Yachting Association bay. This provided an invaluable shortcut to returning fishermen and mariners enabling them to avoid the headwind and currents between Pointe Gourde and Carrera Island. It was filled in by the U.S. Seabees in 1942 to prevent German submarines from sneaking among the troop ships, despite the fact it was only seven feet deep and fifteen feet wide.

*East to Arima*

When describing the Carib Queen's bathchair I knew nothing of the Arima Cannon which was donated to the Caribs by Governor Harris around 1850. The Blomefield six-pounder had probably been part of the British ordnance in the 1797 invasion, and was given to the Caribs to replace the conch shell they had traditionally used to mark the start of the Santa Rosa Festival. In 1995 the cannon was replaced in its original position on Calvary Hill.

There are certainly other changes which could be mentioned, but I believe I have covered the main ones relating to the original text. It is good to be able to say that the hills of the Northern Range are still greenly wooded despite an increase in illegal lumber cutting. It scarcely needs to be said that the indomitable Trinidadian joie de vivre remains as irrepressible as ever.

# Index

# Select Bibliography

Anthony, M. & Carr, A. *David Introduces Trinidad & Tobago* London 1975

Brereton, B. *A History of Modern Trinidad 1783-1962* London, Heinemann '81

Bridges, Y. *Child of the Tropics* London 1980

Brierley, J.N. *Trinidad Then and Now* Port of Spain 1912

Bryan, R. *Trinidad & Tobago - Isles of the Immortelles* London, Faber 1967

Carmichael, G. *The History of the West Indian Islands of Trinidad and Tobago* London, Redman 1961

Carmichael, G. *Calendar of the Flowering Trees and Plants of Trinidad and Tobago, Port of Spain 1959*

Central Statistical Office - *Annual Statistical Digest*

Cosier, A. *West Indian Cricket*

De Verteuil, A. *Sir Louis de Verteuil, His Life and Times*

ffrench, R. *A Guide to the Birds of Trinidad & Tobago* Valley Forge '66

Fermor, P.L. *Traveller's Tree*

Fodor, E. *Guide to the Caribbean* New York, McKay 1984

Gomes, A. *Through a Maze of Colour* Port of Spain, Inprint 1974

Herklots, G.A.C. *The Birds of Trinidad & Tobago* London, Collins 1961

Heskovits, M.J. & F.S. *Trinidad Village* N.Y. Knopf 1947

Hintzen, Percy *The Costs of Regime Survival* Cambridge Univ. Press 1989

Hill, Errol *Trinidad Carnival*

La Guerre, J. *Calcutta to Caroni - The East Indians of Trinidad* Bristol, Longman 1974

Lewis, J.N. *Ajoupa* Port of Spain, Inprint 1983

Mahabir, Dr. W. *In and Out of Politics* Port of Spain, Inprint 1978

Mavrogordato, O.J. *Voices in the Street* Port of Spain, Inprint 1979

Naipaul, Shiva, *Beyond the Dragon's Mouth* London, Andre Deutsch 1984

Naipaul, V.S. *The Loss of El Dorado* London, Andre Deutsch 1969

Naipaul, V.S. *The Middle Passage* London, Andre Deutsch 1962

O'Connor, P.E.T. *Some Trinidad Yesterdays* Port of Spain, Inprint 1975

# Bibliography

Ottley, C.R. *The Story of Port of Spain* Port of Spain 1962
Paton, W.A. *Down the Islands* London 1888
Rodman, Selden *The Caribbean* New York, Hawthorn 1968
Ross, G. *History of West Indian Cricket*
Retout, Sr. M.T. *Parish Beat* Port of Spain, Inprint
Severin, T. *The Golden Antilles* London, Hamish Hamilton 1970
Waugh, A. *Hot Countries* New York Literary Guild 1930
Williams, Dr. E.E. *History of the People of Trinidad and Tobago*
    London, Andre Deutsch 1964
*Trinidad Guardian, Sunday Guardian, Trinidad Express*
    newspapers

## ABOUT THE AUTHOR

Adrian Bird adopted Trinidad as his home in 1961. He was born in 1934, the son of a regular R.A.F. officer, and moved to the U.S.A. in 1952 after his father died as British Air Attaché in Moscow.

He graduated in three years with honours in Literature from Duke University, N.C. having worked as a journalist, sign painter and carpenter to pay his expenses. Upon graduating he worked as an international grain trader before going to Wall Street with Morgan Guaranty Trust.

In Trinidad he worked as managerial odd-job-man for Barclays Bank, later Republic Bank before becoming a branch manager. He acquired his intimate knowledge of Trinidad from scouting the countryside to research where banking offices might be established, and from excursions with the Field Naturalists Club.

For many years he was on the Central Committee of Little Carib, Family Planning Association, SCAPE, and the Advertising Standards Authority. He was also an active member of Port of Spain Rotary Club for twelve years. His articles are well known to readers of the *Daily Express*.

Adrian is now based in Barbados. "I would be at a loose end retired in Trinidad " he explains. He frequently returns to Trinidad with his Trini wife and two sons.

*August '91*